AN INTRODUCTION TO MODERN SOCIAL
AND POLITICAL THOUGHT

AN INTRODUCTION TO MODERN SOCIAL AND POLITICAL THOUGHT

ANDREW GAMBLE

St. Martin's Press New York

All rights reserved. For information, write:
St. Martin's Press, Inc., 175 Fifth Avenue, New York, NY 10010
Printed in Hong Kong
First published in the United States of America in 1981

ISBN 0–312–43102–3

Library of Congress Cataloging in Publication Data

Gamble, Andrew.
   An introduction to modern social and political thought.

   Bibliography: p.
   1. Political science—History. 2. Economics—History.
3. Sociology—History. 4. Civilization, Occidental—History. I Title.
JA83.G27 1981 320.5'09182'1   80–54686
ISBN 0–312–43102–3

Contents

Preface

This book is intended as an introduction to Western social and political thought in the modern period, and particularly since the French Revolution. The material that could be included in such a survey is vast, the need for selection great, and I am conscious that much that is important has had to be omitted, and that it has scarcely been possible to deal adequately with the thinkers and the theories that appear in the text. The aim of the book is to encourage all who read it to read further, both the works of some of the writers discussed in these pages and the ever-multiplying literature about them. I have provided a short bibliography which I hope will be useful for this purpose. Biographical material has mostly been left out of the text and placed in a separate section at the end. I have also included a short glossary of some of the more important terms and concepts used in the book, not in an attempt to provide final definitions but for reference.

I do not think it possible to stand outside the Western tradition and pronounce upon its character and its value from the standpoint of eternity. I have not tried to do so. I have tried to be objective and accurate in my exposition of different theories, but the evaluation of them and the selection of what is important is naturally shaped by the overall approach I have adopted.

I have enjoyed writing this book and hope it will be rewarding to read. Many people, teachers, colleagues, and students of mine have contributed to it, most of them unwittingly. I give thanks to them all, but especially to Chris and Tom and Corinna for not complaining too much or too loudly.

1

The world and the West

1 The meaning of the West and the Western tradition

The terms West and Western carry many associations, historical, political, cultural, and geographical. They are often freely used as though they denoted particular entities, whose reality is undisputed. But only a little probing is necessary to discover what ambiguities and complexities lurk inside them. To name only the most obvious, the geographical boundaries of this 'West' are far from clear. Is it Europe that is intended? In which case should Russia and Poland be included? Or only Western Europe? Does Western Europe include Germany, and Spain, and Greece? And what of Europe overseas, the lands of predominantly European settlement, particularly the United States? To limit the term to Europe seems arbitrary when today the West also denotes a series of military and political alliances that stretch from North America throughout Europe and the Middle East to Japan and Australia.

Since the geographical definitions can be so confusing, cultural and ideological definitions are often preferred. Here the problem is deciding whether there exists a common 'Western' civilisation which can be distinguished from other civilisations, and whose characteristic features can be observed in many countries. The problem is complicated for us because we still live in the Western era, the period in which Western techniques, Western ideas and Western states have dominated the world as no other civilisation has ever done. This has encouraged many historians to construct a history of the West that sees a steady unfolding of Western civilisation over three thousand years from its dual origin in the Greek and Roman civilisations of classical times and in the religions of the Jews (Judaism and Christianity).

It is an extremely influential history and one that pervades most accounts of the tradition of Western social and political thought. One of its most common features is to divide Western history into three parts — Ancient, Medieval, and Modern. Ancient history is the classical era up to the fall of the (western) Roman Empire in the fifth century A.D. Medieval history is the period that embraces the 'Dark Ages' after the fall of Rome, when 'barbarians' overran and settled the former Roman colonies, as well as the history of the feudal states of Europe up to the end of the fifteenth century. Modern history covers the period that commences with the *Renaissance* and the *Reformation* in the fifteenth and sixteenth centuries, then moves through the *Scientific Revolution* of the seventeenth century and the *Enlightenment* of the eighteenth century, to culminate in the *French Revolution* of 1789 and the English *Industrial Revolution* which began in the 1780s. These major events prepare the ground for the 'European Century', 1815 to 1914, the century of liberty and progress, during which Western ideas, techniques, and political rule were spread around the world. In the twentieth century after two great wars caused a sharp decline in the status and power and relative wealth of Europe, the spirit of the West migrates, and the *Western ideology* and Western world interests discover a new champion in the United States of America, a nation built upon European migration, and the first 'new nation' of the modern world.

The unique path of development taken by the West, which these histories celebrate, has long been a favourite object of enquiry for Western thinkers, and there has been no shortage of attempts to show that the technological and material superiority of Western states in modern times reflects the cultural and moral superiority of Western civilisation over all others. According to some of these epic accounts, Western civilisation is a unique historical organism which like the acorn has gradually unfolded all the potentialities contained within it from the beginning. As many critics have pointed out, however, such histories assume that the most lasting values and most important traditions of civilisation have a special and exclusive connection with Western Europe. They have to assert that the values and ideas of classical and Christian civilisations are preserved and enhanced in modern industrial civilisation, and indeed that they made this civilisation possible.

Whilst the profound influence of classical and Christian culture on that of the modern West cannot be ignored, it is a highly misleading way of looking at the development of the West and at modern Western thought. It places greater emphasis on abstract ideas and values, the products of reflection and contemplation, than on the ideas and purposes which are embodied in social relationships, the practical ways in which human beings relate to one another and to their natural environment. Because intellectual history of the first type has been so dominant, far too much continuity has often been ascribed to Western history, so that the important gaps and breaks are not noticed, and it becomes impossible to conceive of the process of world development in terms which are not Western-centred. What also slips from view in these cultural histories is that the 'West' has no monopoly even of its own roots. Islam and Russia, both non-Western civilisations, drew heavily upon classical and Judaic traditions. A Western-centred view of world history too easily forgets that the fall of the Roman Empire in the fifth century, hailed so often as one of the most important events in the history of the world, only involved the loss of the western Empire, which included some of its most backward provinces. The Roman Empire lived on in the east with its capital at Byzantium (Istanbul) for another thousand years.

The civilisation and the system of states that were established in Western Europe in the early modern period (1500–1800) were undoubtedly distinctive, but its superiority over all other civilisations was not clear cut. Again, it is easy to forget what a recent thing Western superiority is, and therefore to forget in what this superiority consists. In the early modern period when Europe was beginning to expand overseas and to colonise other parts of the world, European civilisation was in many respects inferior to other civilisations, and those civilisations that were protected by organised state power were able without difficulty to repel Western intruders. China and Japan, for example, expelled all foreigners at this time and closed their borders. Western expansion proceeded fastest in those areas which were either sparsely populated or lacked a strong central authority to organise resistance. The strange coincidence that Europe and China both began voyages of exploration at roughly the same time (in the sixteenth century) has often been remarked. China's voyages abruptly ceased, Europe's multiplied, but there was no inevitability about the world-wide triumph of European civilisation even as late as the eighteenth century. Before 1800 civilisations tended to be isolated, self-sufficient, and more or less equivalent in material terms. Their states experienced periods of prosperity and periods of decline. They were also mostly ignorant of one another because contacts were so restricted. It was not difficult for the thinkers of each civilisation to imagine that their own civilisation and leading state were the most important, the most advanced, and the most powerful in the world.

This is one major change that has occurred in the last two hundred years. The traditional societies of China and Japan which were strong enough to resist Western ideas and Western penetration in the seventeenth and eighteenth centuries were powerless to do so in the nineteenth. But the real meaning of this major change in the history of the world, the opening of a period that has seen the foundation laid for a common civilisation based on a new economic and political interdependence, is not always seen. The sudden change in the balance between civilisations which led to the unprecedented world dominance of a few West European states was not so much due to a triumphant flowering and climax of Western civilisation, as to a decisive break with it. The reason why the West has towered over the modern world and has undermined the traditional culture of other civilisations is because it first of all undermined and steadily rejected its own. In the process of transforming the rest of the world the West has also devoured itself.

This is the central paradox of the modern age. The revolution that shook Europe and has come to shake the whole world, initially gave unprecedented wealth and power to a few Western states, and by opening up such a great technological and material gap between the West and other states, compelled all other states to modernise themselves. Such modernisation is often called Westernisation, but it never

meant that these states had to accept the traditional civilisation of the West — the civilisation they had for centuries
rejected. What they accepted were the ideas and techniques
which, though arising out of it, proved in practical terms to
be a radical denial of that traditional Western civilisation, and
indeed of all traditional civilisation.

2 The coming of world history

Of what did this revolution consist? Whilst many writers have
defined the 'West' in cultural terms — the spirit and ethos of
Western civilisation — those more directly at the receiving
end of Western expansion saw mainly the superior technology and organisation of the West. It was not the Christian
doctrine of brotherly love or the Roman conception of
justice that destroyed the Chinese fleet. The major alternative
to cultural definitions of the West and to idealist histories is
to define the uniqueness of the West in social terms. For
example, in place of the idea of the progressive unfolding of a
unique civilisation, history can be arranged into a number of
periods whose boundaries are fixed by technological changes.
On this view the history of the world is once more divided
into three parts (only this time it is the history of the world
and not just of one part of it). First comes the stage of
hunting and gathering, of interminable duration; next the
stage of agriculture and settled communities, which began
some 10,000 years ago; and finally the stage of industry,
which began only some 200 years ago. This conception
oversimplifies, and gives too predominant a role to techology,
but it has the merit of emphasising, in rather stark terms, the
dimensions of the change that has occurred. The traditional
civilisations of Asia, Africa, Europe, and the Americas were
based upon the economic surplus that could be generated
from stable communities working the land and increasing its
yield, and the opportunities for the building of cities and
support of states, priesthoods, and armies, that this provided.
The productivity of labour-intensive agricultural production
was necessarily limited. With the coming of industry, the
raising of the productivity of labour through the general
application of industrial techniques provided a new material
basis for civilisation for the first time in ten thousand years.
This has decisively altered the character of the relationship

between human societies and the natural world, and with it the way in which human societies are themselves organised.

If this change is viewed solely in technological terms, its origins and its essential character are obscured. Besides technology the revolution involved new forms of social, political, economic, and intellectual organisation, and these were not directly caused by the technological changes. Without them the technology could not have been developed, and could not continue to be applied. States that wished to adopt Western technology soon found that they were also forced to adopt Western organisation and Western science. Westernisation involved not just a technological but a social revolution, of the kind which was already wrenching Western societies from their traditional culture and traditional social organisation.

In the West this transformation is inseparable from the development of a capitalist economy. Capitalism itself has been given many meanings in Western thought, and its distinguishing features and the conditions that are necessary for it to function, have been much disputed. In this book the rise of capitalism will be related to the broader 'bourgeois revolution', which ultimately left no social relations in Western society, ideological, political, or economic, untouched. This social revolution occurred at different speeds and in different ways in different countries, but inexorably it transformed first Western Europe, and then the whole world. It is the indispensable context for understanding modern Western social and political thought, and forms the subject of the next chapter.

Three main aspects of it will be considered. All led to the creation of conditions on the basis of which capitalism was able to develop. There were, firstly, changes in economic relationships which included, most spectacularly, the gradual organisation of a world economy and a world market, following the voyages of exploration and conquest that began at the end of the fifteenth century. The opening up of the world to European trade gave a tremendous boost to the development of a commodity - exchange economy, in particular to the amassing of capital and the development of a financial system, and encouraged the application of new technologies. As important, however, as the growth of money capital and a class of merchants, was the internal transformation of the relationships between those who owned and those who worked the land. This released serfs both from their feudal dues and from the land itself. Huge areas were enclosed and farmed more intensively by landowners who, desperate to increase their revenue, oriented production away from self-sufficiency towards the market. An increased agricultural surplus and a 'free' labour force available for employment as wage labourers resulted.

The second major feature of the bourgeois revolution was the development of the modern state. This originated in the long conflict between the Church and royal power, and eventually led to the organisation of states whose authority was entirely secular, and which constituted public power that was supreme within a given territory and not identical with the personal authority of any single individual. This public power became organised through permanent agencies and institutions and was crucial in the establishment of conditions favourable to the rise of free markets in labour, in goods, and in land, and therefore to the organisation of a *'civil society'*. This civil society was conceived as a private realm where individuals were free to pursue private interests. It depended on the state, but increasingly asserted its independence of it.

The third feature was the rise of science, 'the new philosophy', which was at first of only limited practical significance, but which has since so enormously increased human powers that human experience of the natural world has been transformed beyond recognition. Modern science became possible theoretically because of a radical alteration in the way in which nature was conceived. Most strikingly this involved a different conception of the place of the earth in the universe, a new cosmology. This prepared the way for a radical change in the practical relationship between human societies and their natural environment and also unleashed intellectual energies and initiatives that influenced all social thought by assisting in the development of empirical, sceptical, and rationalist modes of thought, as well as the creation of international communities of scientific intellectuals. Their activities, though not always their beliefs, have proved corrosive of traditional values and patterns of behaviour.

3 Western social and political thought

This book is an introduction to some of the central ideas in
Western thought. It does not seek, however, to provide a
cultural history of the whole Western tradition conceived as
an unbroken chain stretching back to Plato and Aristotle,
important though many earlier thinkers are to a full understanding of modern thought. It is concerned instead with
intellectual responses to the major changes brought by the
bourgeois revolution and the subsequent development of
the doctrines and ideologies that this revolution created. For
this purpose it is the social organisation of the 'West' rather
than its cultural or geographical organisation that is most
relevant. Modern Western doctrines can be regarded as a
series of attempts to define and evaluate the character of the
new society and to pose the problems it presented for
theoretical analysis and practical action. If Western doctrines
have become dominant throughout the world in the last two
hundred years it is not primarily because of their roots in the
problems and preoccupations of either the Mediterranean
world of ancient times, or of medieval Europe, but because
of their roots in the problems and preoccupations of the new
developing capitalist world economy and its nation-states.

Nevertheless, it remains true that however great the discontinuity in Western thought and experience which the
advent of the modern world marks, the legacy of classical
and medieval thought still weighs, in Karl Marx's phrase like a
nightmare upon the brain of the living. This legacy is firstly
and perhaps most importantly the many fundamental conceptual distinctions that were made by Greek thinkers. Much
of ancient thought has been lost completely, and much of
what has survived was lost for a long period, or forgotten and
then rediscovered. Amongst the writings that did survive, the
impact of Plato and Aristotle on subsequent social and
political theorists has been by far the greatest. Many ideas
and distinctions of great importance in modern Western
thought are to be found in their writings. They include the
idea of contrasting the natural condition of human beings
with their social condition; the idea of theory — speculative,
abstract, timeless, and true — which is contrasted with the
idea of praxis — knowledge that is practical, concrete, time-
bound, and relative; the division of experience into what is

real and therefore essential, and what only appears and is therefore inessential; the idea of a utopia, a perfect state of affairs, contrasted with the actual state of affairs; the idea of cycles of development in human affairs and the history of states; the idea of a chain of being, a hierarchy of forms, each form of being, including man, possessing a purpose and a potential which it seeks to realise.

Many of the contrasts drawn by Greek thinkers recur again and again in the work of later Western thinkers — nature/ society, theory/practice, appearance/reality. They are the framework within which many of them have sought to understand the modern world. But also very important have been certain ideals and institutions deriving both from classical and medieval times. Foremost amongst the ideals are the Greek concept of the city state and the Christian concept of the individual. Both have exercised and continue to exercise enormous fascination within the Western tradition. The Greek city state, particularly in its Athenian form, was founded on the full participation of all its citizens, and on the idea that such participation was not just the duty of every individual citizen, but the essence of the good life itself. Private life, time spent in the family and time spent on economic activities earning and securing the necessities of life, was *deprived* existence. Freedom existed outside this sphere of necessity, in the realm of public thought and public action. The small-scale autonomous political communities of the Greek world, in which the public communal experience overshadowed the private household existence, was an ideal that influenced the thinking of, amongst many others, Machiavelli, Rousseau, Hegel, and Marx.

The second fundamental ideal for modern Western thought was the Christian ideal of the individual. Every individual was considered important because every individual was equal before God and possessed an immortal soul. By contrast, both Plato and Aristotle had accepted the idea of the natural inequality of man. This provided a justification of slavery and the basis of Plato's argument that justice was a state of affairs in which every individual performed the function to which he was best suited. Christianity helped introduce the notion that all individuals, whatever their race or creed, were equal and should be equally valued. The Christian ideal was the community based on fraternity and the holding of goods in common, in which all individuals were entitled to equal respect, and in which human relations would be governed by altruism (concern for others' needs and interests) rather than self-interest (concern for one's own).

Amongst the institutions, the most important that were bequeathed were the different legal traditions of Rome and the Germanic tribes; the organisational independence of the medieval Church, and the character of the feudal economy, with its varied organisation of the labour process, and its enclaves of merchant capital and commodity production. These were to influence greatly the rise of the bourgeois state and the capitalist economy.

Yet despite the importance of earlier influences and legacies the more striking fact about the Western tradition is its discontinuity rather than its continuity. There is still a strong tendency to view the history of the Western tradition in terms of the Greek distinction between theory and practice. At the level of abstract contemplation of the ideal forms of existence the Western tradition is indeed a seamless web of ideas, a series of attempts at answering the same constant problems of human existence. But at the level of practice where ideas arise and function within particular social contexts, the gaps in the tradition are much more apparent. So is the extent to which Western thinkers have been attempting to explain modern developments within frameworks of ideas that were developed in other contexts and for very different purposes.

The approach adopted here faces a number of pitfalls. The most serious is that what particular writers were intending to say may be misconstrued by understanding them in terms of ideas and events of which they could have had no knowledge. This arises partly because in thinking through the problems of the transition to the modern world Western thinkers naturally thought in terms of the distinctions, concepts, and models of past thinkers. It would have been remarkable if many of them had been able to anticipate the shape of the new society, and this is reflected in the major division that continues to exist in the writing of the history of Western thought. On one side are those historians who, conscious of what is to come, look for the first stirrings and formulations of later ideas in earlier thinkers. On the other there are those who have insisted that a sharp line be drawn between the significance of a particular writer for later generations and his significance for his own generation. Piecing together what a writer thought he was saying and could have said in the intellectual climate of his time often gives a very different impression of his work than assessing him primarily as a link in an intellectual chain that stretches up to the present. For example, to mention only one important recent controversy, the English political philosopher, John Locke, has been viewed both as an early theorist of liberalism and the free market economy, a seventeenth-century advocate of 'possessive individualism', and as a seventeenth-century thinker whose primary conceptions about property and society are derived not from any notion of capitalism, but from Christian ideas about the purposes of God and the nature of man.

Such contrasting evaluations are inevitable given the magnitude of the historical transformation that the world has undergone in the last two hundred years, and that has given Western thinkers such a powerful idea of *history*, a sense of constant change and therefore of the transient and relative nature of all ideas and human creations. When nothing is fixed for very long, truth and certainty lose their solid quality. This has inspired attempts to show how discontinuous and fragmented culture and history have become, and how little from one period can be used to understand another, but it has also encouraged others to try to detect the continuity that is felt to run through the diversity, in the belief that there is an overall coherence and meaning in human experience.

This book is not directly concerned with philosophies of history or methods of enquiry. But it is important to remember that many of the ideas that will be discussed and many of the most powerful doctrines that continue to rule the world, including liberalism and socialism, are firmly rooted in a pre-industrial (and sometimes a pre-capitalist) social context and intellectual tradition. It could not be otherwise. The rhythm of traditional agricultural societies was cyclical, based on the regularity of seasons and harvests, encouraging speculations that were timeless and universal. They could cross centuries and even cultures because of the common problems and the underlying similarity of experience in communities far apart in place and time. Industrial capitalism has destroyed that unity within different cultures, and modern thought is necessarily very different from ancient thought, however much it may be cast in the same mould, and use some of the same basic conceptual distinctions.

4 The Western ideology

Central to modern Western thought are the notions of ideology and history. Every history has always to be constructed through a constant reworking, reselection, and re-evaluation of facts and interpretations received from an earlier generation of historians. To be a historian is to be constantly revising the work of previous historians in the light of new knowledge and new perspectives. This sense of constant change in human affairs and the provisional and relative character of all truths is very marked in modern Western thought. It leads naturally to the idea that if no ideas can claim to be universally and permanently true, modern thought is made up of a number of doctrines or *ideologies* which have to be understood in relation to the circumstances in which they were developed as well as with the interests with which they are associated.

Ideology, a term which first originates in the French revolutionary era, has acquired many meanings. It can for instance be used to mean ideas that are false, or that express false consciousness of a group's real interests, but its more settled meaning came to be simply any systematic set of moral and factual beliefs held by a group, or members of a party, or a class. Such a definition implicitly recognises one aspect of modern Western experience − the impossibility of finding a single universal doctrine that can unify ends and means, and facts and values, in a way that commands general assent, and channels conflict away from principles. From this angle modern Western thought is best approached as a collection of doctrines and ideologies, most of which (even most recently natural science itself), have gradually abandoned their claim to be accepted as exclusively true. The pluralism of modern Western thought, the way in which it manages to maintain its diversity despite the fierce intolerance of the many doctrines that compose it, is one of the most striking facts about it. At the same time the diversity should not be exaggerated. There are enough unifying assumptions in modern Western doctrines for the whole of them to appear from one angle as a single ideology, a single system of thought.

To speak of modern Western thought as 'the Western ideology' is not therefore to deny the value of understanding the origin of its key terms in ideas and distinctions that go back a long way in the Western tradition. But it does mean that by itself this approach is not sufficient. In the period of transition to the modern world certain ideas began to be formulated which, when formalised into doctrines in the nineteenth century, became the universal ideologies that spread across the world, because they could be utilised by all societies that embraced and were embraced by the new world civilisation. That is not to say that liberalism and socialism were fully adequate for the task, or that they were not modified greatly in contact with other cultures, or that glaring weaknesses in both have not been exposed. Nevertheless, this new Western ideology, fashioned from diverse elements of the Western intellectual tradition, and shaped by the new practical experiences and problems of the modern world, became an essential weapon in the hands of all those groups that wished to modernise and industrialise their countries. This was true whether the initial desire was to accept capitalism and the world division of labour imposed by the European states, or to fight it. If Western ideas have a universal scope it is because they grapple with the new and unfamiliar problems of industrial civilisation. Liberalism and the counter to liberalism within the West itself, socialism, still provide the basic vocabulary and perspectives for responses to industrialism, and the challenge of economic and social development.

The formation of the Western ideology was the product of several centuries of ferment amongst small groups of Western intellectuals. A general tendency of thought which culminates in the national Enlightenments of the eighteenth century, can be seen developing in several centres and several fields from the sixteenth century onwards. Enlightenment is a useful term for the whole modern intellectual movement,

since the most obvious tendency of this movement was by
degrees to elevate rationalism and the new rational spirit of
enquiry into a guiding principle for all knowledge. This was
to have profound consequences in every branch of human
activity. Central to the concerns of the intellectual Enlightenment were reflections upon the emerging shape of the new
state, the new economy, and the new science. In France, the
monument of the Enlightenment was the publication of the
Encyclopédie between 1751 and 1772. The faith in reason, in
natural science, in progress, and in the individual, were
central themes running through the contributions, which
covered all branches of human knowledge. The fame of the
French Enlightenment, however, sometimes causes other
Enlightenments such as those in Scotland and Germany to be
neglected. The Enlightenment in France was part of a much
broader European Enlightenment which reflected a considerable international exchange of ideas. Voltaire, for
example, one of the leading figures in the French Enlightenment, was the individual most responsible for introducing
and popularising the scientific system of the British scientist
Isaac Newton in France.

Reflection on the new form of the state that was emerging
produced the great age of political theory, which includes the
work of the major thinkers from Machiavelli to Hegel.
Reflection on the principles appropriate for the regulation of
civil society produced important schools of political economy which included Adam Smith and David Hume in Britain,
and the Physiocrats in France. Reflection on the new natural
science stimulated the development of major philosophical
schools, including those of Descartes, Hume, and Kant.
Enlightenment thought was marked by an absence of rigid
subject boundaries. Its intellectuals were interested in everything, dabbled in everything, and wrote on everything.
The speculative and the practical were often pursued side by
side. In the nineteenth century disciplines began to become
specialised and consolidated; the range of knowledge across
all the sciences became too great for any single mind to
encompass, and the speculative and the practical tended to
become separated. Discussion of facts and of means was
divorced from discussion of values and of ends. This increased the technical precision of Western thought but

weakened it as a discourse concerned with questions of fundamental human concern, such as the nature of right conduct, of justice, and of the good society.

Out of the Enlightenment and the revolutionary era at the end of the eighteenth century emerged the two central doctrines of the Western ideology — liberalism and socialism (discussed in chapters 3 and 4). They did not enjoy undivided sway, since they were challenged from the outset by conservative doctrines that were anchored in the traditional institutions, practices, and beliefs that still survived so strongly in many societies. This Reaction, the anti-Enlightenment, reached throughout the continent, but proved particularly strong in countries such as Germany, which in terms of European development were initially behind both politically and economically. This great conservative Reaction to Enlightenment ideas (explored in chapter 5), and still more to the new popular forms of state and economy, was inspired by both traditional and new romantic currents of thought. Though it was unsuccessful in its principal objective of reversing liberalism and rationalism, it did succeed in heavily influencing liberal thought, particularly after the emergence of the increasingly strong intellectual and political challenge mounted by socialism. Socialism shared the same rationalist assumptions and values as its liberal adversary, and one response of many liberal intellectuals was to bid for leadership of the new social forces that socialists claimed to represent. Many liberals took an active part in the organisation of social democracy. Another response, however, was to abandon the beliefs in progress and perfectibility, and turn instead to the dangers besetting the liberal order, rather than emphasising the fresh fields liberalism had to conquer. The great wars of the twentieth century, the cult of the irrational that culminated in fascism, the Bolshevik revolution in Russia, and anxiety about the 'decline of the West', have deepened liberal pessimism. For many liberals history seems no longer to be the story of emerging and expanding liberty, but the defence of liberty against totalitarianism. The development of the various strands of liberal doctrine are discussed in chapter 6.

5 Conclusion

Many attempts have been made to capture the essence of modern Western thought. One fashionable ploy is to distinguish two traditions, most often within liberalism. A virtuous and by implication 'true' liberalism is contrasted with one that is vicious and false. The first leads to liberal democracy, the open society, the freedom of the individual, whilst the other leads to totalitarian democracy, the closed society and the subordination of the individual. Western thinkers can then be assigned to either tradition, depending on how their contribution is assessed. Such approaches generally yield more insight into the minds of their authors than into the nature of modern thought. They founder because they are based on the notion that there is a continuing struggle between good and evil in the world, which is essentially a contest between ideas expressed in the writings of individual thinkers, and later in political movements and states. This is a conception with deep roots and wide consequences. In intellectual history it involves promoting certain thinkers for their fidelity to the fundamental ideas of the Western tradition and condemning others as renegades and heretics. This means assuming that the fundamental ideas of the Western tradition can be described without ambiguity and in isolation from the broader Western impact on the world. In this way certain Western liberal values, such as the doctrine of individual rights, and the 'experimental sceptical tradition' of modern science are proclaimed as the key elements of the Western experience and the Western message.

It is a wholly Western-centred view of the matter. The civilisation and ideology of the West have been both liberating and repressive in the way they have affected the rest of the world, and the liberating and repressive aspects of Western practice cannot neatly be assigned to separate intellectual traditions. In particular, Western ideas cannot be abstracted from the central role that force and conflict have played in Western history. Nobility of sentiment is no security against oppression, as subject colonial peoples so frequently discovered. Western civilisation has to be examined as a whole, and the enormous role which force played in establishing and propagating it not forgotten.

Overcoming backwardness and catching up the leading

industrial states provided the spur for nationalist movements
first in Europe itself, then throughout the world. What has
been significant about such movements outside Europe has
been their strong hostility to dominant liberal ideas combined with a thorough embrace of Western technology,
-industrial, organisational, and military. Sometimes this has
been accompanied by a nationalism that has drawn on the
symbols and values of the traditional culture; elsewhere it has
been joined to the internal critique that originated within the
Western ideology itself — socialism (discussed in chapter 7).
Almost nowhere has there been a total rejection of the West.
This is because the 'West' has come to stand for that industrial civilisation which, it is recognised, must to some extent
be accepted by all societies. In this sense the coming of
industrialism appears to mark a progress rather than a cycle
in human affairs, an advance to a stage from which there is
no going back, no return to older forms of experience.
Whether this progess has been beneficial or detrimental to the
human race is a separate question.

Western thought is immensely intricate and all its strands
are densely interwoven. No one doctrine or concept can
stand by itself as the heart of the tradition, but there are
clearly some ideas that have assumed a greater importance.
They include the freedom of the individual, equality, rationality, and sovereignty. A great deal of modern Western
thought is concerned with the meaning to be assigned to
these terms and the ideas associated with them. In part the
different meanings arise out of still more fundamental ideas
about justice and human nature — what constitutes security,
human fulfilment, and human happiness, in short, what is the
nature of the good society. And in part they arise from the
emerging structure of industrial civilisation in the West and
the different political and social movements to which that
has led.

This book is an introduction to some of the different
meanings that have been assigned to these ideas and explores
some of the ambiguities that have become inseparable from
them. Freedom of the individual, for example, has been
presented in terms of individual rights, the rights of the
individual against the state and collective authority, but it has
also been defined as the extent to which the potential of

every individual for creative and satisfying work and for acting as an independent, rational subject is realised. The one enjoins a minimum of government action to safeguard liberty, the other regards government action as indispensable for it. Equality too has been advocated as an equality of conditions, which means equal treatment by the state, for example equality before the law or equality of votes; as an equality of means or opportunities, the state ensuring that every individual has an equal start in terms of the provision of such essentials as health and education; and as equality of outcomes, which means distributing income and resources in order to ensure not that all are alike, but that those with the greatest needs do in fact receive the greatest consideration.

The ideas of reason and rationality have been used in several different and important ways. Understanding the world as rational meant first of all believing that it could be analysed and changed by human action. The natural world and the social world could be controlled and shaped in accordance with human purposes and both were rational to the extent that human beings had the knowledge and the will to exercise such control. Obstacles to such control were irrational and needed to be swept aside. In this manner rationalism became associated with the idea that individuals should be free to act as rational, independent beings; that all social arrangements should be justified by the standards of reason and should contribute to the liberation and all-round development of the capacities of each individual; that the natural world should be mastered and subordinated to human purposes.

Rationalism was also understood not simply as a set of moral values but also as a set of technical means. Purposive rational action meant action governed by the search for the most effective means of reaching a specified goal. This was technical rationality. The search itself was conducted in accordance with rational and scientific methods—for instance through rigorous logical deduction from certain axiomatic principles or general rules; or through the method of observation, classification, and experiment. The continual adaptation of means to ends is often seen as the most striking characteristic of modern Western culture in comparison with all traditional cultures (including that of the West). But although technical rationality and the rationalist ideal of human liberation were once closely allied, they have become increasingly separated. The pursuit of technical rationality within all social and political organisations in industrial society has come to involve the increasing subordination of wider ends to its imperatives. Technology and material progress have become idols and radical alternatives eliminated.

Finally sovereignty, the question of legitimate power, is one that has received many contrasting answers. Ultimate authority has been held to lie in the nation, in the masses, and in classes. Debate has centred on how the particular interests and decisions of those who actually govern the state can be reconciled with the general interests and general will of the sovereign body. What kind of institutions most surely allow the general will and general interest of the nation or class to predominate? Should individuals be represented through parliaments or through the corporate bodies to which they belong? Does a professional bureaucracy or a nationally elected President more securely embody the national interest? Do classes speak through parties, or workers' councils, or trade unions?

All these questions are related to the greatest of all the dualisms in modern Western thought — that between state and society. The distinction between a public and a private realm was made in Greek thought, then disappeared during the Middle Ages. It reappears with new insistence in the modern era, only this time the private realm — civil society, the new economic order of capitalism — is given much greater importance. How these two realms are to be distinguished, what are their crucial relationships, which should predominate, what conflicts and benefits they give rise to; such questions contain much of the substance of modern political thought and will be returned to again and again in these pages.

If there is a basic theme running through this book, it is this. The Western ideology can be examined as a set of moral discourses and practices, concerned with the question of the good society and of right conduct, of social justice and the full development of human potential. But it is also a set of rational discourses and practices that are concerned with the question of truth and knowledge and with discovering the most effective and most efficient means for realising given ends. The images of the good society that arise in the moral discourse are images strongly influenced by classical and Christian values — particularly the Greek idea of the polis, the community of citizens; the Christian idea of the individual, the community based on altruism and fraternity; and the medieval conception of natural law.

Tension arises in modern Western thought between these images and the practical consequences of scientific rationalism as it has unfolded in the social and political relationships of industrial capitalism. The new scientific conceptions of the universe and society did not produce capitalism but they aided its rapid advance. They helped to systemise and universalise the techniques, values and procedures, appropriate to a capitalist order, throughout society. The most dramatic expression of this has been the growing practical and technological power of human communities to shape their societies and physical environments. Capitalism as a process of accumulation and rationalisation has created a world for which the moral discourse of the Western tradition is increasingly unsuited. Its images and utopias have been undermined but nothing has replaced them. Not just the religions but the ideologies of the West are short of believers today, and this may explain the pessimism and scepticism that abound in all the major schools of Western thought. Some have held that the moral and rational discourse and the practices within which they are embedded and which they express are logically separate and do not need mutual support. The various doctrines of the Western ideology, however, have always been a complex unity of the two. So have the greatest analytical works of modern Western thought, such as Hobbes' *Leviathan*, or Marx's *Capital*. That capitalism should have transformed the world in such a way as to undermine the moral force of the ideologies that guided, assisted, and interpreted it, is one of the great facts and the great paradoxes of the modern world.

There can be no definitive survey of the Western tradition. Its internal links are too complex and it is still evolving. But a start can be made in understanding some of its central themes and ideas. As for the elusive term 'West', it is perhaps most usefully used to denote those states which have fully embraced the trinity of capitalist economy, democratic polity, and scientific rationalism, the three pillars of the bourgeois revolution and the modern world, a world still dominated to a considerable extent by such states. It is to a closer examination of these three that we now turn.

2

The state and civil society

1 The idea of revolution

Revolution, like so many words in the political vocabulary, has undergone a major change of meaning in the last two hundred years. For Greek and Roman thinkers, revolution meant a political change in which one form of government, one set of rulers, succeeded another in a predetermined sequence. Political life was conceived as a wheel of fortune which as it revolved brought authority and rule to some, and ruin to others. These changes were thought to be as inevitable, as fixed, and as unalterable as the positions and movements of the heavenly bodies were conceived to be by the astronomers.

Plato, in the *Republic*, described the decline of political regimes from the ideal republic ruled by his aristocracy of Guardians, through timocracy (the rule of those with property but who retained some commitment to the public good), to oligarchy (the rule of the few in their own interests), then democracy (the rule of the many), and finally to tyranny (the rule of a despot). This account reflected a widely held classical belief in a political cycle which derived from the nature of political arrangements rather than being the product of human will and action. Classical writers, like the Roman Stoics, thought of change in human affairs as repeating a basic pattern. Nothing new could ever occur. Everything instead recurred. The bounds and destinies of human life were already fixed by fate, and though human beings might learn their fate they could not alter it, so that the proper attitude was resignation and acceptance of whatever life brought. As the Roman emperor, Marcus Aurelius, expressed it in the second century A.D.:

> The rational soul . . . wanders round the whole world
> and through the encompassing void, and gazes into
> infinite time, and considers the periodic destruction and
> rebirths of the universe, and reflects that our posterity
> will see nothing new, and that our ancestors saw nothing
> greater than we have seen. A man of forty years, posses-
> sing the most moderate intelligence, may be said to have
> seen all that is past and all that is to come; so uniform is
> the world.

Classical thinkers were pessimistic about the human prospect
because of their belief that no golden age awaited mankind in
the future. On the contrary, the only golden age human
beings would ever know already lay in the past. Human
societies were caught in a long, slow decline. They could not
avoid social and political change, and such change would
always be for the worse, a move still further away from lost
perfection.

Such a low estimate of human abilities and such an adverse
judgement on human pretensions, directed attention away
from the future towards the past and encouraged a renunciation of the world and the possibilities of improvement.
The Christian tradition, particularly that deriving from Saint
Augustine, further strengthened this attitude, for although
Christian thinkers did believe in a future golden age, it was a
golden age beyond the grave, in another world, and one that
would be announced by the destruction of the existing
world. Christians rejected the pessimism and fatalism of the
classical conception. History had a meaning, and a beginning
and an end, and was the story of progress towards that end,
but the meaning with which human life was endowed was
only a meaning that related to human aspirations for an
eternal existence after death. The idea that human societies
might be radically improved, and that human energies should
be directed to securing such improvements, was not widely
entertained by Christians in classical times or in medieval
Europe.

All the great world civilisations that arose on the foundations of agrarian economies, on modes of production that

were therefore pre-capitalist, developed sets of beliefs that encouraged the diversion of human concern from the immediate world of practical and sensual experience to other worlds. Traditional cultures tended to be other-worldly, ascetic, and pessimistic about human affairs and human capabilities. All stressed the limited scope for human improvement and human advance, and tended to draw a sharp distinction between the mind and the senses. Abstract thought and rational contemplation of the universe or of God were regarded as the true reality and the expression of man's higher self, whilst sensual experience was regarded as a shifting uncertain world of appearances, which had to be repressed and mastered. In the Christian tradition with its deeprooted conception of original sin, not only the senses but the mind also could be a source of temptation and had to be mastered.

The modern concept of revolution and the idea of progress that is so closely tied to it, break decisively with the pessimistic outlook of the two main strands in traditional Western culture. It is often argued that this new direction for Western thought originated in the two complex historical movements in the period 1400 to 1600 which have acquired the labels of Renaissance and Reformation. The Renaissance, which flourished particularly in Italy, involved the rediscovery of the intellectual legacy of classical writers, classical learning, and classical models, and a rejection of much medieval teaching and medieval authority. The Reformation challenged the supreme medieval authority, the right of the Pope, as Head of the Roman Church, to determine the fundamental questions of Christian belief and Church organisation.

Important as these developments were, however, neither led directly to the revolution that was to come. Where medieval and Christian conceptions were rejected, the most usual result was the rehabilitation of classical ideas. In early modern thought classical ideas abound: the notion of an impersonal, objective fate; the idea that a good constitution for a state needed to be drawn up by an omniscient Legislator; the belief in the ideal character of the political regimes of ancient Athens or Sparta; the cyclical pattern of political development. Similarly numerous scholars have demonstrated that nothing was further from the intention of Luther or

Calvin in rejecting papal authority than to diminish the other-worldly and ascetic outlook of Christian believers or change the low estimate of the human mind or the human body. In themselves the Renaissance and Reformation did not mark the beginning of the modern world. That beginning comes only with the transformation of the economy, the founding of the modern state and the rise of science and ideology, in other words with the outbreak of the great revolution of modern times, the bourgeois revolution.

What distinguished the modern conception of revolution from the classical is the disappearance of the notion of a political cycle that recurs endlessly. The wheel of fortune no longer spins round on a fixed course. Instead a revolution of the wheel means a leap on to a new plane, and an escape from its predetermined orbit. The wheel is transformed into a giant stone which once propelled to the summit of a hill, does not slip back, but rolls forward on the new level that has been attained. Suddenly history is perceived as discontinuous, permanent human progress and improvement as possible, and human energy and human will as potentially decisive. Revolution as a political term comes to overshadow in importance terms like rebellion and revolt, because a rebellion involves only a challenge to an individual ruler as an individual, whereas a revolution came to mean not just a challenge to personal authority, to who should be king, but a challenge to the institution of kingship itself. An act of rebellion can cast down a king, but an act of revolution can transform a social order, permanently. This is one reason why the English civil war of the seventeenth century was called by contemporaries 'the Great Rebellion', and is now described by historians as 'the English Revolution', and why the relatively minor events of 1688, when the English king, James II, was swiftly deposed and a new king installed in his place, were named by contemporaries 'the Glorious Revolution'. Classical conceptions of the cycle of political change were still dominant.

The new concept became widespread only after the experience of the French Revolution. The celebrated exchange between Louis XVI and the duke who brought him the news of the fall of the Bastille neatly sums up the change in meaning that was about to occur. 'It is a revolt,' exclaimed the king. 'No, sire,' replied the duke, 'it is a revolution'. The idea that a political act could introduce permanent fundamental change, transforming the basis of a social order, and having effects far beyond the political sphere itself, these were conceptions that became widespread after the French Revolution had dramatised so starkly the change that was taking place in many European states, and that had already occurred in England.

2 The bourgeois revolution

This profound upheaval was the bourgeois revolution. The term bourgeois, like the term revolution, is ambiguous and unsatisfactory, because it too had an earlier meaning, and like revolution was subsequently extended vastly in its range. Yet there is no real alternative. Bourgeois is a term that always had much greater acceptance in continental Europe than in either Britain or America, because in the former it was used to refer to a division within the ranks of the property owners. The bourgeoisie was a group both legally and socially separated from the aristocracy. No such legal barriers existed in early modern times in either Britain or the United States. There was an aristocracy of birth in Britain, but in both countries a 'democracy' of wealth. That is why the continental notion never seemed appropriate to describe those divisions among property owners that did exist, such as that between landowners and industrial manufacturers.

In speaking of the revolution that created the modern world as the bourgeois revolution, an image is easily conjured up of a militant, self-confident, expanding capitalist class which found its economic activities blocked by the political control exercised by a landowning aristocracy. This aristocracy and its state had therefore to be overthrown before capitalism could fully develop. Such a model is simple to grasp but only a little historical knowledge is necessary to see that there is hardly an instance where capitalism was established by such an independent bourgeoisie. Even in France the conflict between the bourgeoisie and the aristocracy cannot be reduced to a struggle between opposed economic interests, since the two groups held many such interests in common. The political regime in France, resting on royal absolutism and the privileges of the aristocracy and the clergy, and which became known after the Revolution as the 'ancien regime' was overthrown not because of a narrow economic conflict, but because of the political conflict within the property-owning classes and the subsequent involvement of the propertyless masses in their dispute. The result was certainly to create many of the fundamental conditions for the development of a capitalist economy, but the French bourgeoisie which is sometimes credited with this transformation was far from being a class of industrial entrepreneurs. The term was used to mean those who had given up all active employment in a profession or business and lived off interest. They were the solid, independent citizens whose sobriety and conservatism were the target for aristocratic ridicule, as in some of Molière's plays. They were certainly far removed from the daring, ambitious, world-storming captains of industry of later capitalist legend.

In many other European states the conditions for the development of modern industry were achieved without any overthrow of the existing state and its institutions. These states were transformed from within, and sometimes their governments actively promoted the formation of a bourgeoisie, instead of the bourgeoisie overturning and refashioning the state in its own image. The most important cases of all, however, were England and the United States, whose revolutions came before that of France and whose significance was only fully appreciated in the wake of the French events. In England the conflict in the seventeenth-century civil war between King and Parliament was little concerned ostensibly with opposing economic interests, but with the legitimate political rights and powers of the monarch, particularly over taxation and religious freedom. The main protagonists on both sides belonged necessarily to the class of landowners. Broader political pressures did begin to emerge with the radicalisation of the army, leading to novel demands for equality and democratic rights, but these were stamped out and the revolution retained its character as a dispute within the landed gentry, in which one section remained loyal to the king and one rebelled.

The consequences of this rebellion were nevertheless momentous. Superficially the change seemed small because, despite the fact that the rebel Parliament won the civil war, executed the king and proclaimed a republic, this victory could not be consolidated. Within eleven years of King Charles I's execution his son was restored to the throne and the social order seemed to be intact. But the underlying balance between the centralised state power and the property-owning classes had been permanently altered, as was swiftly shown when James II was so easily removed from the throne in 1688. The tendency towards royal absolutism in England had received a lasting check, and with it the possibility of the state acting as it did in so many other countries in Europe to consolidate, preserve, and extend the economic, political, and legal privileges of one section of property owners, the landed aristocracy. As Alexis de Tocqueville later argued, England was the one country in Europe in which feudalism did not end in the creation of castes.

Social privilege naturally remained in England, but many legal privileges and the opportunity for their reintroduction were swept away by the English Revolution. This was immensely important. It meant that English landowners, unlike their counterparts elsewhere, could no longer count on state support to increase their incomes by exploiting more fully their legal rights over peasants. This assisted the development of a capitalist agriculture in England — the abolition of feudal tenure, the unrestricted enclosure of common land, the consolidation of estates, and the increasing employment of the rural population as wage labourers, the introduction of new methods of farming to raise the productivity of the land, and a production oriented increasingly towards a market, rather than to local self-sufficiency. The reputation of the newly united Great Britain (England, Scotland, and Wales) as the most advanced European state in the eighteenth century rested not on its industry, but on its superior agriculture and the additional wealth which this gave its landowners. The development of agrarian capitalism in England was aided by the unique political regime which had emerged from the civil war. The breaking of royal power meant the supremacy of Parliament, an assembly dominated by the representatives of the landed interest, but in which that section which perceived its interests to lie in capitalist agriculture and commerce predominated.

What was absent from both Britain and the state emerging in North America at this time were rigid legal divisions between sections of the property-owning classes. The principle was even clearer in the United States than it was in Britain, since in the latter it was overlaid by all the debris of rank and title. But the practical effect, which contrasted strongly with the dominant European pattern, was the same. New avenues to the creation of wealth were not blocked. All forms of wealth however they arose had an equal title, or at least could buy whatever title was required. Wealth was proclaimed indivisible — in this way one of the most important conditions for the spread of a capitalist economy was established. Despite the thickets of social status that continued to infest England, there was a greater equality of civil rights there in practice than anywhere else in Europe. The formal inequalities of legal status had been set aside, and a major obstacle to the free development of capitalist property and capitalist economy removed.

The important point to grasp therefore is that a 'bourgeois revolution' does not imply a revolution made by a self-conscious and self-confident bourgeois class. In the great political revolutions that ushered in the bourgeois era the bourgeoisie as an identifiable class was more often noted for its absence than for its active participation. What the term bourgeois revolution came to signify, is not a straightforward duel between a landed aristocracy and an industrial bourgeoisie with clearly opposed economic interests, but a long-drawn-out conflict within the ranks of the property owners, a conflict in which the participation of other classes was often crucial. Its eventual outcome was to make the economic, social, and political conditions of existence of the bourgeoisie predominant in every social formation of the West. Wealth was enthroned, privilege cast down, and a new mobile, restless, aggressive, competitive, and individualistic economic system began to emerge. In the seventeenth and eighteenth centuries this new form of economic society became known as *civil society*, the sphere where private individuals were free to pursue their own interests, forming associations and making contracts as they chose, free from detailed regulation and restraint by government.

The conditions for the formation and reproduction of

civil society were economic (new ways of organising production and distribution), but also political (new rules and
agencies for maintaining a private sphere of free competition
and exchange) and ideological (new modes of thought and
evaluation). The first gave rise to capitalism, the second to
the modern state and ultimately liberal democracy, and the
third to science. These three are the pillars supporting the
arch of the bourgeois revolution, the gateway to the modern
world, and each will be considered in turn in this chapter. It
is the total character of the revolution of the last two
hundred years that so struck those who lived through it and
that has left such a deep imprint on modern Western social
and political thought.

Though it is right to emphasise the independence of
economic, political, and ideological factors from one another,
their inner connections and the total character of the revolution must also be understood. The emergence of the democractic nation-state, for instance, cannot be fully grasped
except in the context of the struggle to make the state
subordinate and responsive to the new economic relationships that were emerging. The systematic application of
rational techniques to find the best means for achieving ends
brought the gradual downgrading of other kinds of knowledge, such as customary and intuitive knowledge, because
the new sciences increasingly supplied both the practical
knowledge and information that a capitalist market economy
demanded, as well as the justifications for its social and
political arrangements. The corrosive effect of rationalist
methods of enquiry and argument on established social
institutions and traditional culture was rapidly perceived by
many conservatives who fought this aspect of the bourgeois
revolution as fiercely as any other. Many, like the Swiss
historian Jacob Burckhardt, believed that the social revolution, which had commenced in France, was destroying
European civilisation because it was undermining the social
order, the religion, the artistic inheritance and the critical
standards that had been built up laboriously in traditional
Western culture.

The bourgeois revolution was not a sudden event, but was
spread over a long period, and cannot be simply equated with
the dramatic political revolutions that marked its course. Yet

it is true that its scale was only fully appreciated when the French Revolution, the most famous of the political revolutions, broke out. The French Revolution marks such an important stage in modern European history because many events before it, such as the English civil war, came to be interpreted in a new light, and because it created the need for an entirely new set of political concepts and eventually a new political vocabulary. The world still lives in the era of the French Revolution and is dominated by the movements, ideologies, and concepts — liberalism and socialism, radicalism and reaction, Left and Right — that have developed out of it.

In the French Revolution the issues of modern politics were first clearly defined, and the Western ideology in the various forms in which it has come to dominate the world first took shape. So although no other national revolution followed precisely the French pattern, its universal significance remains. By highlighting and even exaggerating the scale of the change that was taking place in European societies, the French Revolution changed the direction and substance of Western thought, permanently.

3 The industrial revolution

The rise of capitalism lies at the heart of the social revolution which has transformed the whole world. No mere discovery of new techniques, no dissemination of new ideas, could by themselves have brought such sweeping changes. The world of work and the social relations that defined it had to be reorganised before new ideas and new techniques could make their major impact.

Political changes often appear sharp and discontinuous, while economic and social changes evolve gradually and at times imperceptibly. There is no single moment when capitalism suddenly arrives or is established. Yet in a longer perspective it is still the rapidity of the change and the magnitude of the watershed which has been crossed that stand out. Many historians dislike and dispute the notion of watersheds in history, but there are certain major events that cannot be ignored; the fundamental change in the organisation of human societies in the past two hundred years is one of them. There can be little disagreement about this, even if there remains wide dispute over the character, causes, and consequences of this transformation. These disputes are the core of modern social and political thought in the West, and in many instances can be traced back to the remarkable speculations on politics, philosophy, and political economy that flourished in Europe during the period of transition.

Terms like capitalism and industrial revolution are terms applied afterwards by writers looking back on the great changes that inaugurated modern development. It is hardly surprising that before the rise of modern industry, and before the dimensions and power of the new society became evident, contemporaries did not view their own times as a slow preparation for capitalism and the modern world. It is of course possible to look in the writings of the past for signs of awareness of trends that would afterwards be significant, and for early formulations of ideas that were later dominant. In this sense every writer can be looked on as a precursor, working towards an adequate conception of capitalism or industrial society. It is important to emphasise again that such was never the writers' own intention nor could it have been. No one writing in the seventeenth or eighteenth centuries could have glimpsed the twentieth century or even the nineteenth. The problems around which Western thought became organised in the nineteenth century were different from those in the preceding two centuries. The political vocabulary changed, political action changed, society and economy were transformed world wide.

Yet because writers before the nineteenth century did not use the term capitalism, it does not mean that capitalism did not exist or was not emerging, only that they did not and could not recognise it in the terms that have since become familiar. The changes they observed were analysed with different sets of concepts and traditions of thought. Many of these earlier concepts and theories, which include Hobbes' theory of sovereignty, Rousseau's theory of the social contract, and Adam Smith's theory of the causes of the wealth of nations, were profound innovations and greatly influenced later thought. It is not surprising that they have subsequently been reinterpreted to fit in still more closely with the preoccupations of later theories, and have figured in quite different kinds of discourse.

Whatever the assessment of particular theorists and theories, debate continues to rage over the interpretation of the social revolution itself, in particular over whether the change should be called 'the rise of capitalism' or 'the industrial revolution'. In the latter case, a picture is drawn of the passage from *traditional* to *modern* societies. This process of *modernisation* is regarded as marking the watershed between the two worlds, between 'the world we have lost' and the world of modern technology. Traditional and modern society are contrasted as two ideal types against which actual social forms are measured; the qualities of one are presented as the opposite of the other. Modern society is seen as both individualist and interdependent; individuals have many freedoms and a wide range of choice between jobs, goods, activities, and associations, and are therefore at the same time heavily dependent upon other individuals' services and products for the satisfaction of most of their needs. Secondly, in modern society, change is constant and increasingly rapid, due in part to the constant new technological discoveries, and in part to the restlessness and the desire for novelty engendered by the spread of individual choice and mobility. The contrast with the stability, conservatism, and inertia of traditional life is vivid. Finally in modern society individuals are encouraged to pursue their own interests and maximise their returns. This encourages individuals to specialise and to make the exchanges that are most advantageous to them. In this way the interdependence of needs and interests grows, and this makes the society increasingly impersonal. The exchange process grows more complex and bureaucratic, so does the basic organisation of the economy and of the government required to sustain the widening division of labour. Aided by the unprecedented explosion of population a mass society comes into being whose members are far more isolated than the members of traditional communities which tended to be organised in large family groups. These appeared self-sufficient, inward-looking, and patriarchal, the head of the family enjoying great authority and control over the lives of the members of his family and his dependants.

In this theory the basic agent of change from traditional to modern society is seen as technology and the new rationalist and individualist ethos associated with it. The major alternative standpoint, which sees the change as the rise of a capitalist economy, acknowledges the importance of both technology and ideology in shaping the modern world, but puts most emphasis upon the change in the *mode of production*; the social organisation of labour which supplies the goods and services that are the material foundation of every human society. The term 'traditional society', it is argued, covers a number of different pre-capitalist modes of production, and is far too vague for historical analysis. The crucial event of modern times is the transition from the feudal to the capitalist mode of production, because it made possible the change from a predominantly agricultural to a predominantly industrial society. Industrialism and urban concentration, and advanced technology, are arresting and highly visible characteristics of the modern world. But to focus entirely on these changes, and to contrast them in an exaggerated manner with pre-industrial traditional societies, is misleading, because it ignores how the development of industry required major prior changes in society and in the state. The fundamental revolution was not industrial but social and political, new principles of social organisation that have proved revolutionary in their consequences and that are still unfolding.

4 The origins of capitalism

In order for capitalism as a new mode of production to develop certain conditions had to be established, conditions which ultimately completed the disintegration and disappearance of older forms of economic organisation. They centred around the development of a market economy in which acts of production and acts of exchange became separated, production became oriented to exchange rather than to use, and goods therefore acquired in addition to their specific use value, a generalised exchange value. In other words they became commodities which could be bought and sold. A commodity is a good which can either be consumed by its owner in order to benefit from the use that it has or exchanged in order to realise the value that others are prepared to pay for it. A society of simple commodity production is one in which most goods are produced not to be consumed by their producers but to be exchanged and consumed by others. In pre-capitalist modes of production markets have sometimes been important but have generally remained peripheral, confined to certain areas and certain sectors.

A mode of production is a specific way of organising the labour process. Labour means the constant interaction between human beings and their natural environment that is necessary if basic human physical needs for food, shelter, and clothing are to be satisfied. The way in which human societies collectively organise their labour is one of the most important features marking off one society from another, as is the level of the productivity of labour. If a community can only produce enough to meet its own subsistence needs then all available labour will be required for work on the land. But if natural conditions are favourable, if human skills increase, if new tools are invented, then communities can begin to produce a surplus above their basic requirements and to develop new needs. A surplus of goods reflects the creation of surplus labour. How this surplus is then distributed, whether it goes to support certain kinds of specialised workers or other groups who do not work is a key question in the history of economic development.

Every mode of production, therefore, comprises a specific way of organising the production of goods that the society needs to survive and a way of distributing what is produced, including any surplus labour. These social relationships that define how production and distribution are organised are class relationships if control over the labour process and its fruits is vested in the hands of one group in the society through this group acquiring the means of production as its property. The class that rules the labour process and whose position of privilege depends on the labour of other classes will only be secure if its privileged position which derives from its property is safeguarded through political, legal, and ideological organisation. Class modes of production generate states and laws and systems of beliefs whose effect is to protect the position of the dominant class.

In pre-capitalist modes of production that are also class societies, the class relationships are generally clear and unambiguous. The property, privileges, and power of Roman landowners and feudal barons rested explicitly on the forced labour of slaves and serfs. The gulf between such classes was immense and the refinements of civilisation belonged to the few privileged individuals who had some leisure and could avoid unremitting manual labour. The great inequality in the distribution of property, the compulsion to labour for the vast majority, the hierarchy of rank and power, all were openly acknowledged and openly justified in such societies. Aristotle, for example, a citizen of Athens which had enjoyed the most advanced democracy in the world, defended the institution of slavery on the ground that some men were slaves by nature. Inequality was a natural not a social institution.

Whereas the class character of some earlier modes of production is hard to dispute, capitalism is a different matter. This is because capitalism is the first mode of production which its advocates and defenders proclaim to be classless and capable of promoting freedom, happiness, and prosperity for all its members on a basis of equality. Its ideology is universal, not a particular defence of specific property rights or interests, but an appeal couched in terms of the rights and interests of all human beings. Whether capitalism is a class society similar to the class societies it succeeds is a question of major importance and continuing debate in Western social and political thought, and it forms the major dividing line between liberalism and socialism. Controversy focuses on the institution of the market and the nature of the exchange between labour and capital. The different views on this question are discussed in later chapters. But there is general agreement on the importance of markets in reproducing and expressing capitalist social relations. Under capitalism direct relations of dependence tend to disappear and all economic and social relations tend to be conducted through the market; they tend to become relations between individuals as owners of commodities. These commodities come to include not only direct products of labour, such as shoes and tables, but labour power itself. Workers' services are bought and sold in the market just like any other service or good for which there is a demand.

The existence of a market does not require, however, that labour should be sold in it. The term 'market' tends to disguise the fact that what exists (in the simplest as well as the most developed capitalist economy) is not one market but many markets for many different kinds of goods and services. These markets may be only loosely connected to one another. In order that capitalism should develop it is necessary, therefore, that two preconditions should be met: a system of market exchange should be established and guaranteed; and markets should develop for all major components of the production process — land, labour, and capital.

For markets to exist, private property must be secure, contracts must be enforceable and money stable. Because production and exchange do become so separated in time in a market economy, there is much greater need for security. All must know that the fruits of what they get from selling what they produce are protected, otherwise they will have no incentive to produce beyond their own immediate needs. Similarly, all must be confident that contracts entered into will be honoured otherwise stable accounting and forward planning become impossible. Finally, whatever commodity serves as money it must command general confidence. Money is the medium that connects all the separate individual labours in the community, because by acting as a universal equivalent in terms of which they can all be expressed, it makes possible the exchange of commodities in the market; it means that every producer can sell one day without having to buy again immediately. Exchange no longer has to depend on barter, on two producers wanting one another's product at the same moment and in the same proportion. Individuals can be paid in money and later use that money to purchase whatever they need. But such an economic system requires considerable trust if it is to work. The money must be reasonably stable in value, otherwise producers will feel cheated, and it must be acceptable as widely as possible, otherwise the chain of transactions will break down and the market will cease to function.

It should be obvious even from so brief an account as this that a market is a highly precarious and artifical thing, since a basic security for property, contracts and money must exist in order to guarantee a degree of certainty sufficient to make individual production and exchange flourish; yet at the same time such security does not flow spontaneously from the interaction of the producers, nor can any individual producer ensure it. Only a centralised power which enjoys legitimacy and can enforce obedience can do that. The existence of a market in which exchange is free and equal, in which contracts are honoured, in which the fruits of economic activity are secure, in which money is universally acceptable as a store of value and as a means of payment, requires a strong and active state pledged to maintain all three. But it must be a state that is separated from the producers themselves and so not tied to any particular sectional interest, but concerned only with the general interest of maintaining the fundamental conditions under which market exchange can take place. Such a state has to aim at the removal of restrictions on trade and production in the interests of widening and deepening the market, so that the widest possible range of economic activities are encompassed and the greatest number of goods and services come to be traded within it. In this way unified regional, national and international markets can emerge. A new market could be opened up by ambitious traders, but the consolidation of the trade into a permanent economic link always involved the intervention of a state or an agreement between states.

A further precondition for the emergence of capitalism is that all elements of the labour process become commodities and be traded. Here lay and still lie the most persistent obstacles to the establishment of a capitalist mode of production. Such obstacles were maintained by the social and political forces that were rooted in pre-capitalist modes of production and could count on state power to maintain their position and interests. These barriers are mostly restrictions on alienability; on the right of individuals to dispose freely of their property. For such a right to exist, property must be owned individually, the claim of each individual owner over a particular property must be undisputed, and no legal obstacles to the free disposal of the assets must be present.

For capitalism to develop, the alienability of all three main elements of production — land, labour, and capital — had first to be established. In many previous societies alienability was achieved in one or two of these and flourishing markets were established. On the basis of the system of exchange established by the Romans a legal code grew up which, when it was revived and revised during the Renaissance, provided the major legal concepts that the new capitalism required. But the similarity of legal forms and concepts developed by the Roman lawyers with those of modern market economies should not hide the crucial difference — the sale of labour power itself remained severely restricted in Roman times. The institution of slavery meant that labour itself in the form of the physical bodies of the slaves could be sold, but the slave himself had no right to dispose of his own labour freely. This set internal barriers to the development of the slave mode of production, by making unnecessary the most rational (that is, least wasteful) use of labour and the constant search for new technology, which are obligatory under capitalist conditions so that labour costs can be reduced as much as possible.

Making capital, land, and labour alienable, meant freeing them from any monopoly control, and from any conflicting legal claims as to their disposal. It meant setting individual producers free as individuals to sell whatever property they possessed or could acquire with a minimum of legal restrictions. A free market in land meant, for example, that estates were not entailed, that is, did not legally have to pass to the family heir, but could be sold by the existing owner; a free market in capital meant that prohibitions on the extension of credit and the earning of interest on loans were removed; whilst a free market in labour meant that a labour force emerged whose members were free in a double sense — free *to* sell their labour power to the highest bidder in the market, and free *from* any ownership of means of production, whether land or capital. If they did own property they would be independent producers, not proletarians, no longer obliged to sell their services to capital. The economy would be a market economy but not a capitalist economy or a class-divided society. Wage labour is an indispensable requirement for capitalism to exist.

It is relatively easy to specify those features that distinguish capitalism from previous modes of economic society, but a major problem still remains over how the change was ever accomplished, how the obstacles were overcome, and the tremendous power and authority of traditional relationships loosened. The difficulty lies in accounting for a process whose consequences in the shape of the organisation of the modern world are clearly apparent now, but which was not intended or consciously initiated by any social group. The strange paradox arises that, looked at through the eyes of its contemporaries, the change is often imperceptible; looked at through our eyes, the difference between pre-industrial and industrial society is enormous.

The debate on the transition from feudalism to capitalism or from traditional to modern societies is important because it involves so many of the characteristic positions that have dominated modern Western social and political thought — the significance to be attached to production, to exchange, to technology, and to social and political values. To take just one illustration: Marxist historians have been engaged over a long period in discussion of whether capitalism succeeded feudalism because of an internal breakdown in feudalism, or because of the development of a world market. In the first case attention is focussed upon the need of the feudal land-owning class to increase the surplus they acquired from their serfs, and their inability to do so. In the second case the emphasis is placed upon the ever expanding sphere of market relationships, which received tremendous impetus from the Western overseas expansion after 1500. Is the crucial trigger in accounting for the rise of capitalism the transformation of social relationships on the land, or is it the steady encroachment of the market? The issue has not been settled because of the different ways in which capitalism is being defined. One approach puts the emphasis on the labour process and contrasts the way in which an economic surplus is extracted from serfs and slaves on the one hand, and from wage workers on the other. (This is discussed further in chapter 4.) The other approach puts the emphasis on the market and contrasts production for use in families and small face-to-face communities with production for exchange and an ever widening division of labour. Whether capitalism is to be understood as a class mode of production or as a market order of exchange is one of the great dividing lines in modern Western thought and, as in this case, the line sometimes runs within particular schools of thought as well as between them.

5 The state of nature

Modern Western thought is preoccupied with its grand
typologies, such as the transition from feudalism to capitalism, and the modernisation of traditional society. But during
the centuries of transition (1500-1800) the concept that
comes to occupy a central place in discussion of the economy
is civil society. It was the character of the new exchange
economy, in particular its separation from the state, and the
consequences of this for social, political, and moral organisation that fascinated so many observers. If there is one theme
that unites the disparate strands in the various national
'Enlightenments' of the eighteenth century, it is reflection on
the new freedom of human beings in civil society. It is, for
example, the simplicity, and at the same time the power, of
social relationships when they are stripped down to relationships of exchange between individuals that inspired the
creation of the most forceful work of English political
philosophy, Thomas Hobbes' *Leviathan*.

In the various early theories of civil society conceptions of
human nature and of physical nature played a major role.
The idea of a *state of nature* that existed before societies
were created was used by countless writers less as an historical argument, more as an analytical device for bringing out
what was distinctive about individuals and about society. To
propose the existence of a state of nature was to contrast the
natural order with the social order, man as he really was (his
human *nature*) with man as he had become in society, and to
interpret the nature of human societies independently of
criteria supplied by the workings of the societies themselves.
This natural order was often regarded as the order created by
God, and therefore possessed of much greater legitimacy than
the contrivances of men. Societies were conceived as made up
of individuals, each of whom possessed certain natural, and
therefore pre-social, needs and drives. This being the bedrock
on which societies were built, it formed a standard against
which all human social contrivances, whether in the field of
politics or of morals, could be measured, and it provided a
means of answering the question how societies had come into
existence and how states were formed.

Since the state of nature was an analytical device (the
anthropological study of early societies was still rudimentary)

it is not surprising that many different kinds of nature were imagined, depending on the image of human nature that was adopted. Some like Hobbes emphasised the never ending struggle for power and gain between individuals, which made the state of nature a war of all against all:

> In such condition, there is no place for industry; because the fruit thereof is uncertain: and consequently no Culture of the Earth; no Navigation, nor use of the commodities that may be imported by Sea; no commodious Building; no instruments of moving and removing such things as require much force; no Knowledge of the face of the Earth; no account of Time; no Arts; no Letters, no Society; and which is worst of all, continuall feare, and danger of violent death; And the life of man, solitary, poore, nasty, brutish, and short.

Others treated the state of nature as a lost Paradise, a Garden of Eden, the realm of the 'noble savage', uncorrupted by civilisation. This assumed that human nature was essentially and spontaneously benevolent and co-operative, and that it was social arrangements that caused human misery. What many of these theories which took the notion of a *natural* law as their starting point had in common was a belief in the fundamental *natural* equality of all human beings. This notion was at the heart of the conception of civil society, and was to become the foundation for liberal doctrines of all kinds. If all individuals shared the same human nature, in the sense that all had the same human attributes, all confronted the same natural physical environment, all had the same capacity to labour, the same instinct to preserve themselves, and the same drive to better their condition, then society had a natural basis also, and its arrangements could and should be brought into conformity with the underlying natural law ordained by God.

Apart from the great tradition of political theory which included the masterpieces of Rousseau and Hobbes, the most important theories of the new civil society and its implications for social and political organisation were the attempts to trace systematically the relations individuals spontaneously formed amongst themselves as they attempted to satisfy their material needs. One powerful and influential image of the individual in the state of nature was in Daniel Defoe's novel, *Robinson Crusoe*, which draws a picture of the civilised, eighteenth-century man who is shipwrecked, thrown back on to his own resources and forced to learn again how to survive independently of society. Robinson Crusoe was presented as the modern human being forced to work out, in an environment stripped of all the complexity, distractions, and evils of modern society, how to fend for himself and satisfy his most basic needs. What was rational for Robinson Crusoe, how he divided his time between work and rest, how he calculated the costs and benefits of different activities, how he made plans and took precautions, was taken to reveal the essence of rationality itself, the constant search for the most efficient means of accomplishing what were demonstrably the natural and therefore essential and proper ends of human action. Society could be imagined as being made up of a multitude of individual Robinson Crusoes, and all potentially as rational, as foresighted, as industrious, and as self-reliant.

In one approach, therefore, civil society came to be conceived more and more in economic terms; the sphere of economic individualism where individuals would rationally pursue their self-interest by seeking in their bargains and their choices always to maximise their advantages and benefits, while minimising their disadvantages and costs. Such a conception of human interaction is only possible where a market exists or one can be imagined. It is the spread of exchange relationships — of commodities and money — that gives rise to such notions. Societies are conceived simultaneously as both very simple, because they are based upon the natural propensities of individuals, and at the same time as exceedingly complex, because individuals become more and more dependent on one another for the satisfaction of their needs as the division of labour spreads and their own work becomes more specialised. Markets extend over wider and wider areas, and the production process is subdivided and subdivided, leading to steady increases in productivity and in the scale of production. A vast pool of services and goods grows up, all of which are commodities because they are produced for and traded on the market. All can therefore be expressed in terms of one another as definite amounts of money.

The results of the new civil societies were most spectacular in the economic sphere. The simple notion lying behind exchange was that everyone should treat others they encountered in the market not as ends in themselves but as means to an end. As Adam Smith expressed it:

> It is not from the benevolence of the butcher, the brewer, or the baker, that we expect our dinner, but from their regard to their own interest. We address ourselves, not to their humanity but to their self-love, and never talk to them of our own necessities, but of their advantages. No one but a beggar chooses to depend chiefly upon the benevolence of his fellow citizens.

This principle reflected the freeing of economic activity from earlier restrictions. The more goods and services became alienable, the greater was the impetus given to the competition between individuals and to the liberation of individual effort and initiative. Already contained in this conception of economic activity is a new political conception of the state, a state authority that has considerable powers but is restricted to a specific role — enforcing the general rules that govern civil society. It must be strong enough to discharge that role, but restrained enough not to interfere in detail in the events and arrangements and contracts of civil society. If the state regulates but does not interfere, then competition between individuals is not only a natural human propensity but also the means by which the general interest is realised. Individuals by pursuing their own interest within such a framework must also realise the general interest because they are adding to the pool of goods and services that are traded on the market at the least possible cost to society. As Adam Smith expressed it:

> Every individual is continually exerting himself to find out the most advantageous employment for whatever capital he can command . . . the study of his own advantage leads him necessarily to prefer that employment which is most advantageous to the society.

6 Political economy

The conception of society as a civil society, as a community of self-sufficient individuals propelled by their physical needs and psychological drives, emerges as one of the dominant ideas in Western social thought in the seventeenth and eighteenth centuries. It was gradually perceived that the system of market exchange, although still rudimentary and limited in extent, was fundamentally subversive of many existing social ties and conceptions, and offered a wholly new perspective on society. Civil society, the system of needs, became a separate area of intellectual enquiry, and a new discipline, political economy, arose, emancipating itself from moral philosophy.

The significance of this step was that it followed a very real social development. It was the apparent separation of society as a private sphere of needs and interests and the state as a public realm which individuals entered as citizens that made a distinction between economics and political science possible. Once civil society was seen as containing its own organising principle, and as constituting the inescapable material foundation of all politics and culture, then the way was opened for the study of it on its own terms without importing distracting considerations from either politics or philosophy.

This was a profound change in Western thought, although political economy has not always been accorded the importance it warrants. The change was partly concealed because of the continuing use of inappropriate terms. The concept of economy, from which political economy and economics both derive, comes from the Greek idea of the management of a household. It is therefore concerned with the balancing of income and expenditure, weighing what is received against what is spent. The idea of political economy was at first the idea of managing the 'public household' of the sovereign — bringing royal expenditures into line with royal income. Such household economy was typical of the economic relations of traditional pre-capitalist societies, where economic relationships and ties were not clearly separate from other relationships, but on the contrary were deeply embedded in them. Economic activity was organised through families, the heads of families having considerable control over the lives and activities of their members. Economic roles were not sharply distinguished from other roles and individuals' economic activities were part of a much wider social role within a family group. Society was not made up of 'individuals' enjoying a considerable degree of personal freedom, choice, and mobility, but of families, tribes, and clans — entities where the scope for *individual* freedom of action was much more restricted. The contrast should not be exaggerated. The freedom of the individual in civil society was often heavily qualified and the subordination of the individual in traditional society was not total. Yet it was the real social change that accompanied the rise of modern civil society that transformed Western understanding of the economy and of economic relationships.

Instead of the 'economic' being an aspect of the management of households it became the term assigned to the system of market exchanges that constituted the heart of the new society. The economy was no longer the household, or rather it was no longer the individual household. Instead it was now the system of relationships between all 'households', which were conceived as individual subjects who were rational to the extent they were pursuing their own interests and seeking the most effective means of doing so, and in the process maximising their satisfactions and minimising their costs.

Despite its name the 'economy' of modern Western thought is, therefore, no longer the economics of the household. It is the market order itself, the system of individual exchange in civil society which has gradually supplanted traditional economic and political relationships, that becomes the basis for study. This was possible because civil society was the result of a great mass of individual economic decisions and interactions, which created regular patterns and trends, such as price movements, that could be observed and measured like natural phenomena. Such regularities appeared at times to have a natural force beyond human agency, and to constitute a set of natural laws to which societies organised in such ways were necessarily subject. The unravelling of these laws and the principles that governed the development of civil society became a major concern of the schools of political economy that grew up in the eighteenth century in Britain and France, but their chief aim was to provide guidelines for advising statesmen how to manage the economy as though it were a public household. Only at a later stage of its development did political economy abandon its direct preoccupation with policy and (especially with David Rocardo) concentrate on analysing the general principles governing the economy.

7 The idea of the state

The modern Western conception of the state developed alongside the conception of civil society as a market order, a system of exchange of commodities between self-sufficient, rational, and independent individuals. It was inspired by reflection firstly upon the experience of the absolutist states that arose in Europe from the sixteenth century onwards, and secondly, upon the various challenges to the authority of these states. The successive struggles between the Church and the State and between the State and the People gave rise to a body of sustained writing about the state that has no equal in Western thought. In the line of writers from Machiavelli to Hegel the nature of the modern state is thoroughly explored and many of the fundamental positions taken up. My intention here is not to follow the course of this debate in detail, but only to indicate some of its main features.

The conception of the state that slowly emerges is of a public power that is both independent and secular. It is independent of other social powers and it is independent of any particular office holders — it does not belong to them, and it has a life beyond their tenure of office. Instead of the state being identified with the royal household and regarded as part of the king's own possessions and domain, the state is now seen to exist independently of the king. He is merely one of its agents. The state is secular in the sense that its authority and function are no longer seen to derive from God or from some higher moral purpose. This means that the actions of states are no longer assessed and justified in terms of religious principles. The state comes to be seen as a human creation, created and maintained for human purposes.

The ground is prepared for conceiving the state as an association between the members of a society rather than as the personal domain of a monarch, and furthermore as an association that is unique among all the associations in civil society because of the role it plays. Thinking of the state as an association between all members of a society means ascribing to it supreme authority to make and enforce laws — the general rules that regulate social arrangements and social relationships. If the state is accorded such a role, and if it is to be a genuine association between all members of the community, it follows that its claim to supreme authority cannot be based upon the hereditary title of a royal line, but must originate in the way in which rulers are related to the ruled.

So the modern state has come to be understood in terms of two central ideas. On the one hand it is a centralised power that attempts to overawe all other powers in a given territory. Its power is exercised through its familiar permanent institutions — the bureaucracy, the judiciary, and the military — which have varying degrees of prominence in different states, but all of which are indispensable if the state is to be governed centrally. The state as a centralised power is founded on the ability to deploy force, and the tendency of the governments of such states is to claim a monopoly of force and to disarm their people. But such a monopoly is never complete, and in many spheres of social relationships, particularly where property is concerned as in the organisation of the labour process, the state does not interfere with the exercise of force that is basic to relationships between classes, but underwrites it.

The state's existence as a centralised power organised through permanent agencies and based on force is only part of its reality, however. Its second major feature is that it is founded on consent, on a relationship between those who direct it and those who are subject to it. Its purpose and justification have become secular and social. The idea of the state as a civil association, and therefore of the government of the state as an instrument of society leads to the notion that if the state is a 'true moral community', then the laws that it establishes and enforces must be binding on all its members. Under certain conditions all must have an obligation to obey the laws that are passed. At the same time it follows that if those conditions are not met, individuals are released from their obligation to obey the commands of the agencies of the state. A dynamic and subversive principle is introduced into the discussion of political arrangements. The sovereignty of the modern state is proclaimed but this means not just that the state is recognised as a power, but as a power that must be made legitimate, so that it is transformed into authority. Controversy comes to centre firstly on which institutional arrangements make the exercise of the power of the state legitimate and secondly on the purposes to which the authority to make and enforce laws should be directed.

What also receives attention is the question of who belongs to the political community that comprises the state; which of the governed are entitled to choose the governors, and to have their interests and wishes consulted in the formulation of policy? Because the modern state is independent and secular, acknowledging no authority higher than itself in its own sphere of activity, its social basis has tended to widen constantly, and the legislative powers of the state have been used to create rights, extend freedoms and confer privileges on groups and individuals they did not previously possess. As a civil association the modern state has not been simply a negative guarantor of civil society and its interests, but an active creator and moulder of that civil society, and has come increasingly to be used to plan societies along certain preconceived lines, wrenching societies away from traditionalism towards modernisation and development. The idea that social change can be accomplished politically, and that the state is the crucial association to which all members of a society belong — these are notions that gradually emerge in modern political thought.

8 Sovereignty

The theory of the modern state can be tackled in terms of two central themes: sovereignty, concerned above all with the relationship of the individual to the state; and political economy, the problem of the relationship of state power to civil society. In the development of the concept of sovereignty can be seen the attempts to assert theoretically the character of the new secular public power against older views. Several writers, including Jean Bodin, in the sixteenth century, and Thomas Hobbes, in the seventeenth century, argued that the sovereignty of the state had no limits in principle, and no need for justification outside itself. The state was not confined to administering traditional laws but could create new laws. The claims of other associations, particularly the Churches, to share in this supreme authority were denied. There had to be established one single centre of authority charged with making and enforcing laws for the whole community. If the claims of other associations and groups, whether Churches, feudal landowners, or independent regions, were to be set aside in favour of consolidating a central administrative, legal, and military authority, early theories of sovereignty might seem to reflect no more than the need for the new absolute monarchs of Europe to justify the increase in their powers. But in what is often taken to be the most uncompromising statement of all in favour of untrammelled sovereignty — Hobbes' *Leviathan* — the argument already points beyond the identification of sovereignty with the institution of monarchy (although Hobbes himself was in favour of it). This is because Hobbes does not justify the sovereignty of the monarch and the obligation of all subjects to obey his commands either in terms of the conventional justifications for kingship, which stated that kings must be obeyed because they had been entrusted with their powers by God and were descended from the first Patriarchs, the sons of Noah, or because everyone had a natural duty to obey their prince. Hobbes instead locates the obligation to obey in the indispensable need that human beings have to surrender some of their natural rights to liberty in order to secure their lives against death and their property from plunder. In this way Hobbes based an understanding of politics and the state upon the basic needs and drives of all the individuals that make up the political community. He argued that human beings placed security above all other goals and that individually all were rapacious because the desire for power and gain was insatiable. He then attempted to show that unless security were guaranteed by a public power, so that human needs were held in check when their pursuit infringed the physical security of others, society would quickly revert to the state of nature, which he so vividly described.

The implications of Hobbes' doctrine were enormous because he conceived of the state as a civil association between members of a community to serve their interests; not as an association serving divine purposes. He argued that it was the establishment of sovereignty in the shape of an independent public power which was the crucial condition that made organised social life possible. The legitimacy of this public power was derived from the relationship that the state had to the basic needs of individuals that made up the community. Because there existed a fundamental equality between all individuals in terms of strength and abilities, no one individual was able to guarantee his own security. In the light of this analysis the institutional form taken by the public power was secondary to the question of its existence. A republic could do as well as a monarchy. So long as the state preserved their security, individuals had a moral obligation to obey its commands and laws. But a further principle followed inexorably. If the state, whether monarchy or republic, ceased to maintain the security of its subjects, those subjects were released from their obligation and had the right to resist the state — by force of arms if necessary.

Although occasionally he has been misunderstood on this point Hobbes does set clear limits to the operation of the principle of sovereignty. The state power is only sovereign when it is fulfilling the basic functions for which it was instituted, and even then there are many areas with which it should not be concerned. Hobbes does not deal in detail with them, nor does he offer clear criteria for determining what the state may legitimately do and what it may not; but he mentions several, including the freedom to buy and sell and to make contracts, without giving any very good reasons why these limits should be observed.

This question of the limits of the new sovereign power is taken up much more forcibly in a second, rather later, strand of political reflection on sovereignty, that associated with Locke, Montesquieu, Spinoza, and Kant, which greatly influenced the political ideas of the American Revolution. This line of thought does not question the status of the modern state as an independent public power or its claim to supreme authority. What is emphasised, however, is that the state is only one association amongst many to which individuals belong in a civil society and that it does not have an exclusive claim over them. To establish this point, Hobbes'

account of human nature had to be challenged or at least
supplemented, because it was hard to escape his logic if his
initial premise of the overriding importance of physical
security was accepted. Once again the idea of a state of
nature was freely used in order to derive a theory of the
political obligation individuals owe to the state. As already
emphasised, to assume a state of nature was to base political
arguments on the characteristics individuals were presumed
to have before they had any contact with society. The state
of nature was always a fiction and as a concept it was often
illogical and full of anomalies, but as a mode of political
argument it had important consequences. In particular it
implied that every individual had certain *natural* rights
which were pre-social in origin and could not be removed,
though they might be infringed, by the individual's contact
with society. Their importance was that they provided
criteria by which social and political arrangements could be
judged. The idea of the state of nature enthroned the individual as the ultimate foundation of political authority in
early liberal political thought.

This second strand in discussions of sovereignty was
chiefly concerned with what limits could be placed on the
exercise of state power and under what circumstances individuals had the right to resist and even overthrow their
government. The practical force behind such reflections lay
in the series of religious and civil wars of the sixteenth and
seventeenth centuries, and the fight of particular groups and
associations against specific kinds of oppression inflicted by
the governments of absolutist states on their subjects. The
struggle for freedom of religious belief, for freedom of speech
and publication, for freedom from excessive taxation and
interference in economic activities, all contributed to the
development of doctrines that furnished arguments for the
increasingly powerful and vigorous interests of civil society
and prescribed limits to state authority. Certain things came
to be held as so indispensable to individual autonomy,
freedom, and happiness, that no government would ever be
justified in infringing them. The idea of specific civil and
political rights which could guarantee a private sphere free
from government interference was born. The fanaticism with
which Protestants and Catholics insisted that each possessed

the only true Christian doctrine eventually reduced (at least for a time) the force of all claims that were total and exclusive in their scope, and paved the way for the idea of toleration of different beliefs, and the subordination of religion to politics. This was then strengthened further by arguments in favour of allowing free enquiry and public discussion and more freedom in economic affairs. The assertion by groups and individuals in practice of a right to be left alone by the government and to be free from oppression was justified in theory by the doctrine of natural rights and the idea of limited government — the notion that the sovereign power should be so constituted that its tendency towards a monopoly of power should be restrained by a system of checks and balances. The favoured means of achieving this, loosely reflecting the practice of the British constitution of the time, was to divide power between different agencies which could all check and monitor the activities of others. This idea received its most celebrated expression in the American constitution. The essential aim was to prevent the concentration of power and so safeguard the natural rights of all the individuals in the community from intrusion by arbitrary government. That government was necessary was not disputed; that it was likely to be arbitrary and despotic unless held in check was widely believed; and so ways were sought by which the government of the modern state could discharge its essential functions whilst respecting the liberties and wishes of the citizen body.

John Locke provided one of the most influential statements of this point of view, arguing that the state was the result of a contract between the citizens and the government they established to serve their interests. Every citizen had certain natural rights based on the natural capacity inherent in every human being for labour. The state of nature was, however, for Locke, not necessarily a state of war in which every man's hand was against every other man's. Civil society was highly organised and interdependent prior to the institution of civil government, and the function of government was to protect the natural rights that men enjoyed in the state of nature. Making secure 'every particular man's goods and person' was important, but it was not such a supreme good that men were obliged to give up their liberties to a despotic government. A government that failed to respect individual natural rights forfeited the claim to obedience and could be overthrown. The legitimacy of governments depended on how they exercised the power of the state, and what ends they promoted. These notions provided a rhetoric for resistance to oppression and a rallying cry for groups seeking to redefine the nature of the state as a civil association, and to subject government power and government policy to the test of how far they promoted individual liberty. The tremors occasioned by such doctrines are still being felt.

9 State and civil society

The second major theme in the theory of the modern state concerned political economy; how government should relate to the private, individualist world of civil society organised around commodity production, individual exchange and money; what policies and purposes it should pursue and how the general interest should be defined. Two principal lines of thought emerged. In the first the state came to be regarded as necessarily subordinate to civil society; in the second it was seen as a sphere which included but also transcended civil society and countered its harmful effects. These different conceptions were later to form one of the major dividing lines in modern liberalism.

In the first conception the proper organisation of the state ,was seen to depend on what best promoted the working of civil society. Since competition between individuals bred insecurity, there were important political conditions to be fulfilled by the state for civil society to flourish. Many of these appeared negative: prohibitions of certain kinds of state activity and involvement — because the practical struggle in the eighteenth century was to free economic activity from the intrusions and exactions of arbitrary government. In this process the great cry was for economic liberty and for the conditions that promoted it. The political stance of the British school of political economy from Locke to Adam Smith was not for policies that promoted 'capitalism' but economic liberty. The eighteenth century political economists, like their French counterparts, based their reflections for the most part on their experience of agriculture and the conditions for a successful agrarian economy, although Adam Smith was also able to observe the new industrial workshops that were developing in Glasgow. The political economists were writing about economies that were not industrial and in which only pockets of economic individualism existed. Their political concern was that these pockets should expand and that governments should assist the process by concentrating their energies on removing obstacles to competition and maintaining the framework for individual activity rather than controlling and restricting the economy.

The reason why Adam Smith can be read and is still so read by many admirers as an articulate advocate of free market capitalism is that he first grasped the inherent dynamism of an economy organised around market exchange. He did not envisage the process leading primarily to the accumulation of capital but to a widening and deepening of the division of labour as the market expanded. Nevertheless, the British school penetrated to the fundamentals of the new civil society by perceiving the wealth of a country to be dependent on the productivity of human labour. This was a marked advance over the conceptions of rival schools of political economy, which included mercantilists and physiocrats, the former arguing that wealth was best measured in terms of the quantity of money and precious metals, the latter arguing that all wealth derived from the productivity of land. To see labour instead as the ultimate source of all wealth was only fully vindicated once industrial capitalism had created wealth far beyond anything experienced in traditional agricultural societies. Adam Smith is thus one of the many Janus-faced thinkers in modern Western thought. He looks back to the agricultural economy, but his thought also looks ahead to the new industrial society that was beginning to emerge. His intention was to recommend changes in government policy that would enlarge the sphere of economic liberty, improve the public finances, and promote a prosperous agriculture; but in doing so he uncovered the principle embedded in the new kind of economic organisation which, once it began to develop fully, was to transform all economies and societies beyond any conception of economic development that the political economists could have imagined.

The British school of political economy with its emphasis on those conditions that would best promote economic liberty was closely associated with 'Whig' ideas about constitutional arrangements. The essence of the Whig notion of politics in eighteenth century Britain was that the essential function of government was to guarantee, and at the same time respect, a private sphere of individual liberties. This negative view of government and its functions closely reflected the British political experience and later the American. It was fundamentally challenged by practical and theoretical developments elsewhere in Europe which will be looked at in the next chapter. Despite the important differences between them, Hegel and Rousseau were the two major theorists of this rival tradition, which rested on the perception that the modern state was potentially far more than simply the guarantor of the conditions necessary for the successful functioning of civil society. Because the modern state was founded on the equality of all its citizens it was not simply a means for achieving certain collective ends such as guaranteeing a market order in which individuals could pursue their own ends. It was also an end in itself, the supreme end of social existence, a moral community in which all participated. Not private but public existence was the highest value in human life. Whilst recognising the reality and importance of civil society and the emancipation of the individual which it represented, both Hegel and Rousseau argued that it did not comprise all social relations, nor did it provide a basis for social harmony and social stability, and the fulfilment of the higher moral nature of human beings. The relationships that individuals contracted in civil society as individual property owners had to be supplemented and transcended by their relationships in political society. The life of the private bourgeois, the owner of commodities, only acquired meaning and purpose when the individual recognised himself as a citizen and accepted the claims of citizenship. The separation of economics and politics, the point of departure for all varieties of liberal thought, was not to be healed by subordinating the state to civil society, but subordinating civil society to the state.

10 The new technology

The third force at the centre of the bourgeois revolution was science. In both its theoretical and practical aspects science is inseparable from the modern world outlook and world impact of the West. The principal reason for this lies in the success of modern science as a practical project. The increase in knowledge about nature is less important than the increase in mastery over nature in accounting for its prestige and importance. Yet science as a theoretical project was at first only loosely and indirectly related to science as a practical project. It was only much later that theoretical research and practical applications became joined together much more closely in the vast economic and educational enterprises of industrial societies. At this stage science became closely integrated into the productive process itself as the source of the constant technological improvements that were required to maintain the pace of economic advance. When industrial production was only just beginning, however, the technological inventions that were utilised were often not only primitive, but were often developed independently of the existing body of theoretical knowledge.

It is sometimes argued, however, that it is the 'Scientific Revolution' of the seventeenth century in Europe that must be credited with the creation of the modern world. Once the new theoretical foundations had been laid down, the steady increase of knowledge made inevitable the gradual transformation of the human world through the continual discovery of new techniques. This view is mistaken in its emphasis. As a systematic system of rational knowledge science required a climate of practical rationality in social institutions if its methods and conclusions were to be widely accepted. Modern science did not create either modern civil society from which industrial capitalism arose, or the modern state which made civil society possible; but once these new social and political relationships became established, it certainly increased the range and power of both. The new military technology permitted the penetration by Western states of vast areas of the rest of the world and the consolidation of their power; the new industrial technology created such differences in economic development among states that it helped force many countries into economic dependence on the West. The modern history of first Europe and then the whole world has been transformed by the interaction between capitalism, the modern state, and science, but it is a total process that does not have a single cause, and can only be grasped as a whole.

The later undisputed status of science as the main source of knowledge and truth, objectivity, and rationality in Western societies, however, was initially prepared by the increasing success of science as a practical project concerned with improving techniques and tools. Many of the most famous early scientists, like Galileo and Newton, were not only interested in theoretical speculations about the universe and in the method of scientific enquiry; they were also active in developing and improving new scientific instruments. Galileo did not invent either the telescope or the microscope, as used to be said, but he did design greatly improved versions of both. The practical needs to which the scientists responded were, as in the case of the telescope, often concerned with navigation. Better compasses, more accurate calculation of distances and tides, the design of ships, were all improvements introduced in the seventeenth century, prompted by the great surge of overseas exploration. It was no accident that science flourished in urban and commercial centres that were not only closely involved in the emerging world market, but were also pockets of the new economic individualism of civil society. The greater restlessness and mobility, and the variety of stimulation of these centres encouraged open and critical enquiry; innovations were more likely to be applied in practical uses; bold speculations to receive sympathetic attention. When industries began to expand in Britain in the eighteenth century, much of the innovation that occurred at first was undertaken by people working directly in them.

11 The new cosmology
From the stimulus to invention and enquiry, which the new horizons opened up by European overseas expansion brought, there steadily emerged an increasing practical mastery over nature. Human powers seemed to be measurably increasing and this was seen to rest upon a more exact knowledge and description of how nature worked. It was accompanied by theoretical speculation that overthrew accepted notions of

the cosmos and the place of the human race and the earth within it, and led to a major new departure in Western thought and a new conception of nature, which both justified the growing practical mastery over nature, and enormously extended its potential scope.

The single most important step was taken by the Polish astronomer, Copernicus, when he challenged the notion that the sun moved around the earth with the idea that instead the earth revolved around the sun. The real importance of his work, however, was not because his theory displaced the earth as the centre of the universe, but because it introduced the idea that the universe had no centre at all. He challenged implicitly not just one aspect of Greek and Christian cosmology, but its whole basis. This basis was derived from Aristotle. The universe was conceived as a single living organism in which everything had its place and its purpose and was therefore intelligible, despite there being basic qualitative differences between the elements that composed it. These elements — earth, water, fire and air — were not composed of a single substance, matter.

This cosmology assumed and encouraged an attitude towards the natural world that was contemplative. It treated the human species as part of that natural world, allotted its own particular sphere and a relationship to the whole that was unchanging and unchangeable. The great novelty introduced by the new cosmology of Copernicus, Galileo, and Newton, was that it presented nature as outside man and outside God, indeed alien to any living intelligence, a realm of dead matter which could for that reason be observed, analysed, appropriated, and mastered by human intelligence. If the earth was no longer the centre of the universe and the universe had no centre, the universe came to be understood as a realm of matter, which was both everywhere, and only differentiated by the way it was spread out in space and time. This meant that knowledge of it came to depend on measurement, on the purely quantitative criteria that the concepts of space and time allow. To understand a natural phenomenon no longer depended on understanding its *final cause*, its purpose in the universe given to it by God, but understanding its *efficient cause*, the combination of circumstances and factors in the physical world that had given rise to it.

What the new cosmology achieved was an understanding of nature that encouraged detailed observation and constant experiment, and the rejection of all explanations coming from hypotheses that could not be derived either logically from first principles, or empirically from observation. The new cosmology was not a direct assault upon religion – none of the early scientists thought of challenging the existence of God. Rather what emerged was the conception of a lifeless material world that was outside both God and human beings and had to be understood in its own terms, rather than through knowledge of God's purposes. Conceived in this way as a vast machine, nature could still find a role for a Creator who was needed to set the processes of nature in motion and to correct their movements. Newton, for example, imagined the universe as a giant clock that God had constructed and periodically rewound as it ran down.

It was not necessary to accept the new cosmology to practise the new attitude towards nature – Francis Bacon for instance rejected the findings of Copernicus. But the elaboration of the Copernican system by Galileo and Newton provided the new conception with intellectual arguments of overwhelming force, arguments that were buttressed by the obvious practical results of the new empirical and logical methods for studying and analysing nature that were systematised by thinkers like Bacon and Descartes. Bacon helped pioneer empirical method, the collection and classification of facts, and ways of making valid generalisations from them. Descartes established new rules for analytical thought, for making logical deductions from first principles. Those who became acquainted with the new science became gripped by the vista of an indefinite expansion of knowledge to be brought about through the collective labours of generations of scientists, and the interplay between the techniques of observation, measurement, and experiment and the techniques of logical and mathematical reasoning, which were to prove crucial in the establishment of so many sciences.

12 The new philosophy

So important was this change that the new science often went under the name of 'the new philosophy'. Its wider social, political, and ideological implications for long seemed greater than its implications for technology, although it was in the shape of the latter that it was eventually to have its greatest impact. Science has come to be identified as a natural ally of liberalism and democracy and 'open' societies. This is true, although many of the early scientists themselves were stongly opposed to liberal ideas in other fields, and especially to any suggestion that science undermined the claims of religion. Nevertheless there was a connection between the rise of civil society and the exchange economy and the flourishing of scientific investigation. This was to become still more marked as capitalism developed. The reason is not hard to see. The constant revolutionising of the conditions of production and the constant search for new avenues of wealth that characterise a developed capitalist economy, require forms of knowledge that are experimental, rational, and which produce useful results. Whatever the intentions of individual scientists, once science was organised as a collective enterprise based on the new cosmology, and the new methods of observation and of logical analysis, it began to be allied with the social forces that were overturning social and political relationships, and acquired a momentum which proved irresistible.

Science appears today as the essence of modernism. National revolutions that overthrow traditional regimes and announce programmes of modernisation are almost invariably associated with attempts to foster scientific education and scientific research, and to encourage scientific approaches and scientific techniques. The basic demand of modern science as a form of knowledge is that its investigations should not be restricted by any taboos or prohibitions; there should be no privileged or reserved areas. Scientists should be free to follow their arguments wherever they lead. All ideas and scientific findings should be subject to scrutiny and testing by the scientific community, in order to provide a guarantee of the truth, the objectivity, and the universality of scientific work. There could be no 'national' sciences, no French physics or English chemistry, and no individual bias or error that would not be corrected, so long as all scientists subscribed to the same set of basic concepts for understanding the universe and the same criteria for making and recording measurements. The majority of disputes would then be solved by experiments.

The emphasis upon free discussion, upon testing of their own and other scientists' results, and upon measurement, made scientists as a group and science as a form of knowledge subversive of most other forms of knowledge in the society, particularly those based on traditional authority. In a number of cases this brought direct contests between organised religion and science, the most famous being the battles in which Galileo and Darwin were involved. Galileo was told by his ecclesiastical judges that the Copernican hypothesis about the movement of the planets and the sun was an 'opinion' which could 'in no wise be probable', for it had been declared and defined to be 'contrary to divine Scripture'. He had nevertheless 'dared to discuss and defend it and to argue its probability'. Galileo could agree that it was an opinion, and other scientists might argue that it was in no wise probable, but not on the grounds that the Church offered. Only new knowledge, new experiments, observations, and calculations could confirm or disprove Copernicus' original hypothesis, as far as followers of the new philosophy were concerned.

The attack launched on Darwin and his theory of evolution by certain sections of the Church illustrates the same point. By challenging the notion of the fixity of species — the idea that species had not altered since their creation by God in the year 4004 B.C. — Darwin attacked the last and most stoutly defended bastion of the old Christian cosmology by placing the human species in the natural world rather than outside it. The speech made by Thomas Huxley, one of Darwin's friends and close followers, in reply to Samuel Wilberforce, the Bishop of Oxford, is a powerful example of the modern scientific attitude. Wilberforce had attempted to ridicule Darwin's theories, and he ended his speech by asking Huxley whether he claimed descent from an ape on his grandmother's or grandfather's side. Huxley, after recalling the persecution of Galileo, and the long and patient scientific studies that had led Darwin to his conclusions, retorted, 'I would rather have an ape for a grandfather than a man who misused his gifts to obscure important scientific discussion by rhetoric and religious prejudice'.

The implication of the new philosophy was that no claim to truth or knowledge could be entertained unless it was presented in a way that could be accepted by the scientific community, so that other scientists could in principle reach the same conclusion. All forms of authority could be subjected to this sceptical, critical, questioning attitude. Nothing was to be treated as certain, fixed, or indisputable. Rational criticism, not censorship, was to be the cure for wrong ideas. Alongside this conception went the idea that the purpose of knowledge was practical. Against the lament of the Old Testament Prophet Ecclesiastes that 'Knowledge increaseth Suffering', was set Bacon's proclamation that 'Knowledge is Power'. The rise of modern science is closely associated with the rise of modern rationalism, the basing of claims to truth and knowledge upon human reason and one of its central ideas, the idea of progress — the possibility of continual human, social, and material improvement. Whatever may have been the personal inclinations of some of the early scientists, the whole thrust of modern science has been against asceticism, against the renunciation of pleasure and sensual enjoyment of nature and in favour of the full appropriation of the earth and its fruits for the benefit of its inhabitants. The idea of nature as a realm to be subjugated, mastered, and made to serve the needs of the human species, marks a sharp break with traditional conceptions of the relationship between human societies and their environment, but is the principle that underlies the unchecked exploitation of the natural environment by all modern industrial societies.

13 Science and the intellectuals

Newton conceived of the universe as a giant piece of clockwork designed and maintained by God, and in this way reconciled science and religious faith, but the significance of his theoretical system was that God had become superfluous in a scientific account of the material world. The French chemist, Laplace, told Napoleon who had asked how he fitted God into his account of the universe, 'Sire, I had no need of that hypothesis'. Religion and science were eventually to become quite separate, as it was recognised that the cosmology of modern science provided no support for religious faith and that religious faith did not need such support. But what it did do was to create a new kind of faith, a faith in human capacities and adaptability, by legitimising the limitless exploitation of nature by new technologies and the use of rational discourse as the criterion for social and political judgement and practical decisions.

This is why the new philosophy of science, so important a part of the modern Western outlook, is often regarded as Faustian. In the Faust legend which has exercised such fascination over so many Western thinkers, Doctor Faustus sells his soul to the devil in exchange for the powers to gratify all his desires. He realises his dream of total mastery but at the expense of his ultimate destruction. It is a parable that has often been applied to the modern West, whose rationalism (the search for the most efficient means available to realise desired ends) has always been linked to a Faustian will to dominate. This in turn is closely related to the idea of progress in human affairs, the notion that, as Gibbon wrote in his history of the decline and fall of the Roman Empire, 'Every age of the world has increased, and still increases, the real wealth, the happiness, the knowledge, and perhaps the virtue of the human race'. Because the Western ideology is inseparable from rationalism, it is also inseparable from the notion of progress, despite the strenuous attempts of certain thinkers to dispense with it. Belief in progress does not entail a belief either in a future utopia, or in the perfectibility of the human race, although at times it has included both. It does imply, however, a faith in reason and the conviction that rational enquiry and rational discussion in the Western sense are means which provide a better basis for the organisation of human societies than do religious beliefs.

The bearers of these notions are the intellectuals, and intellectuals as a distinct social group have assumed an importance in modern industrial societies that is greater than in any previous civilisation. This is because the importance of rational behaviour has become so great at all levels, and rational behaviour involves the systematic application of techniques of measurement, calculation, and reasoning. These techniques require the training of larger and larger numbers of intellectuals, whose specialisms and expert knowledge set them apart and lead to a growing divorce between intellectual and manual labour. The great majority of the intellectuals required by modern industrial societies are technical intellectuals, to administer and tool its collective enterprises. But there are also large numbers involved in the creation and dissemination of ideologies, which centre around what ends are to be considered rational and how choice can be made between competing ends. Ideologies seek to define certain interests and certain values and certain goals as legitimate, and have become increasingly integrated within, and in some cases subordinate to, the systems of technical rationality within advanced industrial societies. These intellectuals far outnumber the still surviving small prestigious coteries of traditional intellectuals who struggle to preserve elements of older, often pre-industrial forms of culture.

One of the most prominent of the new race of independent intellectuals, John Stuart Mill, devoted a large section of his essay, *On Liberty*, to arguing that only in those communities where opinion is free and rational argument and scientific research encouraged will progress in all things be swift and cumulative. The stifling of free criticism was regarded by many early liberals in this way, as not only illiberal and a denial of individual freedom, but inefficient and therefore irrational. Rational choice between ends and the search for the most rational means of realising ends would both be hindered. Because of their relative detachment from any social groups, Western intellectuals have often provided recruits for radical movements, and it is from the ranks of intellectuals that the fundamental critiques of Western society have come (although this should not be confused with fundamental challenges to it). Nevertheless, the great bulk of Western intellectuals have been conservative upholders rather than radical questioners of the dominant social and political order in the West, and have tended to follow rather than lead or anticipate social change. The dynamism of Western states has come not from the abstract rationalism of their intellectuals, but from the relentless pursuit of the intimations of technical rationality embedded in capitalist forms of economic and political organisation.

3
Liberalism

1 The political revolutions

In the modern history of the West the revolutions that erupted between 1776 and 1850 have a special place. Liberalism took its distinctive modern form and emerged as a universal creed quite as militant and ambitious in its claims and goals as many earlier religious doctrines. The full potential of the modern state was glimpsed for the first time, and the idea of the state was further elaborated. A new terrain of political argument and political practice was established, a new set of issues, a new range of concepts. At the same time the very triumph of the principles of liberty and their transformation into the new ideology of liberalism was marked by the first appearance of a deep conflict between two wings of the liberal movement, one emphasising liberty, the other democracy. This established one of the major dividing lines in the new politics of the West, the democratic current already containing within it a political tendency that was to contribute much to socialism.

The two most characteristic and influential ideological doctrines of the modern world first take shape in the revolutionary era at the close of the eighteenth and early nineteenth centuries. The dominant systems of ideas in the modern industrial West were elaborated in a world that was not industrial but still overwhelmingly agrarian, had few large cities, and where cultural interdependence (especially when based on a common religion) was still more important than economic interdependence through trade. It is hardly surprising that the utopian hopes and moral principles enshrined in liberal and socialist doctrine should have been severely tested by the enormous changes that have accompanied the spread of industrial capitalism, modern technology, and modern politics.

To understand liberalism the best place to start is the great revolutions themselves and the declarations of principle to which they gave rise. The American Declaration of Independence of 1776 and the French Declaration of the Rights of Man of 1789 were both followed by the drawing up of written constitutions intended to be foundation documents for the new states. They became the models for the multitude of constitutions and charters of states, as well as international bodies, like the United Nations, that have since been established. Yet although these constitutions first expressed liberal principles in their universal and familiar modern form, the liberal movement did not start with these revolutions, nor were these revolutions its first success. The English Revolution, which began with the civil war in 1640 and ended in the political settlement of 1688, produced the first modern state based on liberal principles, and English liberty was much admired and envied in the eighteenth century. Why then did the British state not support but actively oppose the revolutions in both America and France?

The reason lies in the character of the liberty that had been established in England. The driving force of the early liberal movement in Europe was the struggle against arbitrary power exercised by kings, and the legal privileges of the landed nobility. In England the first was of greatest importance, but in the course of the successful challenge to it, the conditions of the second were also destroyed, and important individual rights and liberties were conceded. The realm of liberty for 'free-born' Englishmen came to rest in the eighteenth century on a number of specific rights which for the most part were not legal rights and were not justified in terms of universal rational principles, but were established and maintained as unwritten constitutional conventions. Edmund Burke called it an 'estate of liberty' which was inherited by each generation and bequeathed by it to the next. These liberties included the freedom from arbitrary arrest, arbitrary search, and arbitrary taxation; equality before the law, the right to trial by jury; a degree of freedom of thought, speech, and religious belief; and freedom to buy and sell. This private sphere of liberty was protected from arbitrary state interference, it was argued, by the balance between the monarchy and the two Houses of Parliament, the Lords and the Commons, in which each checked the other, although in certain matters, particularly the raising of taxes, the House of Commons reigned supreme. The Commons was held to be representative of the people despite the tiny size of the electorate which elected the members, and despite the anomalies that had accumulated by the end of the eighteenth century. Many of the new industrial northern towns had no representatives at all, many seats were in the gift of particular landowners, others had lost all their constituents but continued to enjoy representation. (One constituency had even disappeared under the sea.) But it was claimed in defence of the old system that every significant community and interest had a voice in the Parliament, which was therefore able to act as a Council for the whole nation and could deliberate on the policy that best served the national interest.

What counted in this theory of representation was not the form of government so much as its result — liberty. Political arrangements that promoted the liberty of the individual citizen from arbitrary government were good arrangements, whatever abuses and anomalies existed. Edmund Burke, an eloquent defender of the British constitution, argued strongly that representation of the people did not require 'mathematical' or quantitative representation — the adding up of individual opinions or interests. Members of Parliament, he asserted, were not delegates for sectional interests, but representatives who could and should make up their own minds about what constituted the national interest. Parliament was

> not a congress of ambassadors from different hostile interests; which interests each must maintain, as an agent and advocate, against the other agents and advocates; but Parliament is a *deliberative* assembly of *one* nation, with *one* interest, that of the whole; where, not local purposes, not local prejudices ought to guide, but the general good, resulting from the general reason of the whole.

The reality was rather less than the ideal. The Whig constitution of eighteenth-century England preserved a set of liberties but restricted political participation to the propertied class and actual government to one section of it. The major liberties that were prized and inviolable were the general interests of this class, in particular the right to determine the level of taxation to be levied on its members, and secondly the security and expansion of their property. Parliament was little concerned with legislation – the one exception being the flood of acts legalising enclosures of common land, on which the fortunes of the English aristocracy in the eighteenth century so greatly depended, and which helped eliminate the peasantry as a political force.

What emerged from the English experience, nevertheless, were two crucial principles – government by consent and civil liberty. The first meant that the state was conceived as a partnership between government and people, expressed in a contract. If governments broke the contract, the people were freed from their duty to obey. Government was not regarded as all-powerful or all-important, but as a convenient and necessary device for securing certain objectives, chief among which was the maximum freedom of citizens to pursue their private affairs as equal members of civil society. Civil liberty meant above all two things: the absence of government interference and control in economic life, and religious toleration. As Locke put it, 'The business of laws is not to provide for the truth of opinions, but for the safety and security of the commonwealth, and of every particular man's goods and person.'

This Whig system rested on the full acceptance of a social hierarchy that protected great inequalities of wealth and position. Whilst its spirit was against legal privilege, it also underwrote the existing distribution of property and made ownership of land the basic requirement for political participation. This caused few ideological problems for Whig thinkers since, as in most political argument before the modern age, they sought to justify their principles and conclusions by appealing to historical precedents. The strongest justification for English liberties in the eighteenth century was held to be that such liberties had once been enjoyed by Anglo-Saxons before the Norman Conquest of

1066. Traditional liberties were being reasserted rather than new ones claimed.

Greater problems were encountered when the movement for liberty began to base its claims not on precedent or biblical authority, but on the rights of man. The idea that rights belonged to individuals as individuals in the state of nature and therefore prior to their entry into society cast liberal thought into its now familiar, universal form; its claims were not for this group or this nation in this time and this place, but for all human beings at all times in all places. If the idea of natural rights was valid, then states everywhere should be organised to recognise them and protect them. The rhetoric of rights has been resounding around the world ever since.

Once the argument is couched in such universal terms certain consequences follow. If all have natural rights, all human beings are equal in at least one fundamental sense. If government is instituted to protect the natural rights of its citizens and if its authority rests on their freely given consent, this implies that all citizens should have the right to participate in choosing the government. One of the most important natural rights of individuals is the right to own property, and the protection of property is one of the main reasons for instituting government. What then is to be done about the division of civil society into those with and those without property? Are the propertyless to enjoy the same political rights as the propertied and to be given the opportunity of challenging politically the distribution of property that arises spontaneously in civil society?

These problems come to the fore in the American Revolution   a revolution fought in accordance with the sound Whig principles the colonists had learnt from Locke and other leading English defenders of the 1688 settlement. The colonists demanded an end to arbitrary government from London; their most pressing grievances were the taxes they were forced to pay, despite having no representation in the Westminster Parliament, and the various measures, in particular the Navigation Acts, by which the British controlled American trade to their own advantage. No taxation without representation was one of the most popular slogans of the Revolution. But the colonists and their English supporters like Tom Paine went further in basing the claim for independence from British rule on the rights of man. As Thomas Jefferson expressed it in the original draft for the American Declaration of Independence:

> We hold these truths to be sacred and undeniable; that all men are created equal and independent, that from that equal creation they derive rights inherent and inalienable, among which are the preservation of life, and liberty, and the pursuit of happiness.

In his very influential pamphlet, *Common Sense*, published in America in 1776 on the eve of the outbreak of the War of Independence, Paine used the doctrine to great effect to argue that the only obligation that bound citizens to a government was whether that government was fulfilling the functions for which it was instituted. All attempts to justify obedience on the grounds of hereditary right, ancient tradition, or scriptural authority, he rejected as plainly inferior to the freely given consent of a community of free men.

Nevertheless, despite the rhetoric, the leaders of the American Revolution were substantial men of property, as the leaders of the English Revolution had been, and they were concerned to limit the scope of the Revolution. They wished for an end to British rule and arbitrary government, and the creation of a republic which would rid itself of the last vestiges of legal and political privilege, but they wished to keep the propertied classes as the dominant and most influential group in the new republic. They favoured therefore a franchise which would be restricted to those who owned substantial amounts of property, and a constitution that would protect property from any risk of confiscation. In addition they wanted the rights of existing property to be disturbed as little as before. The clearest example was the retention of slavery by the southern states. The rights of man, so loftily proclaimed in the Declaration of Independence, were not extended to slaves, a contradiction between the doctrine and the practice of American liberalism not resolved until the Civil War of the 1860s, and even then only partially. The constitution itself emerged, once independence had been won, as a complex system of checks and balances. Decision-making power was divided between a President, who was not at first elected directly by the people; two Houses of Congress, only one of which was to be elected directly; and a Supreme Court, whose judges were appointed, not elected, and appointed for life. The Supreme Court was charged with interpreting the constitution and was given the power to declare particular laws unconstitutional. The constitution could be altered, but only by a two-thirds majority in both Houses of Congress, which then had to be ratified by three-quarters of local state legislatures. Specific individual liberties were protected by a later Bill of Rights which became part of the constitution. The architects of the constitution saw their task as keeping to a minimum the participation of the mass of citizens in government, whilst ensuring that the government remained responsive to the wishes of the people and in particular to the wishes of the propertied classes. The social hierarchy of wealth was to remain intact. There was to be no place for an aristocracy of birth in the new republic, but every opportunity for an aristocracy of wealth.

Both Britain and America established states in the eighteenth century in which what was most highly prized was liberty — the rights of property and a degree of toleration for religious belief. This liberty was protected by constitutional arrangements that were designed to make governments representative of the community and responsible to it for their actions, but at the same time minimising the political participation of all except those who already dominated civil society through their ownership of property. As Edmund Burke explained, a well-ordered state had to encourage both ability and property, but since ability was 'active' and property 'inert', there was always a danger that if ability were given too much rein, governments would invade the rights of property. Hence it was necessary to prevent this by giving property a position from which it could block any incursions that threatened its interests. If property was impregnable, ability would then become willing to serve it. It was a timid doctrine but it suited the restrained liberalism of the landowners well enough.

The French Revolution was more far-reaching in both its ideas and practice, which explains why it made such an impact upon contemporaries, and why it has come to be viewed as such a major event in modern history. So much development was compressed in such a short time that, like the Russian Revolution after it, it furnished models and arguments for a whole new range of political beliefs, programmes, and ideals. Those who led the Revolution at the outset had ideas that were broadly similar to those of the American revolutionaries, and even of the English Whigs. The aim was to establish a constitution for government, to promote and preserve liberty, check royal power, and abolish privilege whose source was legal or political. This phase of the Revolution was summed up by the Declaration of the Rights of Man which stated that all sovereignty rested essentially in the nation, and that the aim of all political association was to preserve the 'natural and imprescriptible rights of man'; it provided for the separation of powers in government and the rule of law, and declared that free communication of thought and opinion was one of the most precious rights of all. These principles found further expression in the French constitution of 1791 which guaranteed a long list of natural and civil rights; all citizens were to be admissible to all positions and employments 'without other distinctions other than that of virtues and talents'; all taxes should be levied on all citizens according to their ability to pay; and the same offences should be punished in the same way without distinction of persons.

A number of factors, however, prevented the French Revolution becoming simply another experiment in liberal constitutionalism initiated and controlled by the new men of property and their allies in the Third Estate. The much greater resistance of the first two estates (the orders of the nobility and the Church) whose privileges were being attacked, the outbreak of counter-revolutionary war, and perhaps especially the popular pressure from the mass of urban poor and artisans in Paris (the sans-culottes), radicalised the regime and in doing so opened up quite new political horizons. The question of democracy came to the forefront, the creation of a community based upon the political equality of all its members. If all men had natural rights and the state existed to protect those rights, all men should have a say in choosing the government and participating in politics.

The new constitution, proclaimed in 1793, was at the time the most democratic in the world; three million Frenchmen were enfranchised under it. By then France had a revolutionary government led by the radical wing of the Jacobins — the Montagnards. The monarchy had been abolished (the king was later to be executed), and a republic declared.

Embroiled in a war against the absolute monarchies of Europe and their English ally, who were seeking to overthrow the Revolution, the Jacobins launched the Terror in Year Two of the Republic (1793–4) against their political enemies within France. At the same time they strove to turn the republic into a true 'community of equals' by imposing price controls and other interventionist measures in an attempt to share out, as far as possible on an equal basis, the goods available for consumption. The ideal of liberty — the organisation of state power to protect the sphere of private life in civil society — was qualified by the ideal of democracy, a community based on political equality in which government might intervene in civil society to defend the interests of the poor against the rich. From this it was only a short step to arguing that liberty and equality could only by fully realised if inequalities in civil society were abolished, particularly the inequality that stemmed from ownership of property. This was the position taken by Babeuf and the Society of Equals, one of the early forerunners of socialist ideas. In their manifesto, in 1796, they demanded 'real equality': 'We declare ourselves no longer able to endure that the very great majority of men should toil and sweat at the service and at the good pleasure of a tiny minority.'

The Jacobins were overthrown by the coup of Thermidor in 1794. Babeuf's conspiracy was easily put down. Under the Directory and the military dictatorship of Napoleon that succeeded it, liberty, the freedom of civil society from government interference, was re-established, although constitutionalism and democracy were both suspended. Even liberty, however, remained a revolutionary and universal creed in the political circumstances of absolutist Europe where royal, clerical, and aristocratic power was still so strong, and many of the gains of the Revolution were not reversed but consolidated and made permanent under Napoleon's rule. The *Code Napoléon* became the basis of

French law and was one of the clearest statements of liberal principles ever drafted. It proclaimed the freedom of civil society (in particular the freedom of economic enterprise), and defined the duties of the state in protecting it. It continued the tendency of the French state to centralise political power by weakening all intermediate groups and associations, a tendency that had existed before the Revolution, and that was to be so strongly attacked by Alexis de Tocqueville. It also accepted the principle enshrined in the Declaration of the Rights of Man that the basis of sovereignty should be the French nation. It thus foreshadowed the idea of the democratic nation-state, the basis for so many later French and European constitutions. Whether such nations were best represented by a single leader or by an assembly of elected representatives was to become an important issue in later liberal thought.

2 The constitutional state

Liberal constitutionalism continued in the nineteenth century as one of the main strands in liberalism, and remains one of the major components of Western political thought today. It was broadened to include a notion of representation that lessened its conflict with the idea of democracy, though this did not remove it altogether. Liberty in the form of definite civil and political rights was still presumed to be the main purpose that government was established to secure. Democracy was admitted not as an end in itself, or as a particular kind of state, but as one means among several for choosing those who have to exercise executive functions in a modern state. This method was granted to be superior to most others because of the legitimacy that was conferred on the party or group that formed the government by winning a free election. But liberty remained more important than democracy. The safeguarding of the private sphere from arbitrary government intervention was still the chief good sought from politics.

The theory in which these ideas found fullest expression in the course of the nineteenth century was the German theory of the *Rechtstaat*, the state founded and bounded by law. These laws were presumed to be of a particular character — laying down general rules for the conduct of all the associations and private activities within civil society, but refraining from prescribing how they must be conducted in detail. This ideal meant that legislation was to be separated as far as possible from administration. By confining itself to the framing of general rules the legislature would give the greatest possible freedom to the members of civil society to develop in whatever direction they chose. They would have to make their choices within a set of rules, such as the law on contract, but all such rules would be known in advance and would be general in form. They would not have to contend with the daily interventions and decisions of officials able to exercise their own discretion over the lives and choices of private citizens.

A government of laws rather than of men became the slogan of this kind of liberalism. Everyone was equal before the law, but unequal in their endowments, abilities, inheritances, opportunities and the use they made of them. The role of the state was to remove obstacles to the dynamism of civil society. Government should have as few responsibilities as possible and the best kind of constitution was therefore one that ensured governments were limited in what they could do. A common device was to separate the powers of government, typically between an executive, a legislature, and a judiciary. The legislature would be the sovereign body, directly elected from the people, which would decide the kind of general rules that should be enforced, and vote the necessary funds to maintain the agencies that could enforce them. The executive, armed with the mandate of the legislature and the revenue from taxes, would be charged with enforcing the laws and protecting the security of the whole community. The judiciary would interpret the laws in any clash between the executive and a private citizen or in any case where the legislature had passed a law which was in breach of the constitution.

The last case indicates the importance that such devices as written constitutions and Bills of Rights have often played in constitutional liberalism. If the courts are charged under the constitution with interpreting its provisions, this is intended to provide a major check to the ambitions of legislatures or executives. Similarly other devices can be employed to ensure permanent and structural conflicts of interest between the legislature and the executive; and the legislature itself can be divided into two houses or chambers, giving each some kind of veto over laws that enact major changes and originate in the other. Finally special provisions (such as two-thirds majorities) can be written into constitutions to make changing their provisions extremely difficult.

The aim behind all such devices is to disperse power, to weaken government in certain fields, so as to reduce its willingness and ability to intervene in detail in civil society, to protect the liberties of the individual from encroachment, and to force government to concentrate on performing the functions assigned to it under the constitution. On the question of what individuals should do with their liberty, opinions have differed, but not on the question of whether they should have it at all. The single most unifying theme in liberalism has been the struggle for individual liberty, freeing the individual from controls whether imposed by government, by other individuals, by custom, or by superstition. This has given liberalism a universal and a subversive aspect, since it seemed to undermine the legitimacy of all social authority, whether of kings, priests, or fathers, in the name of the rights of the individual.

Yet liberals remained alert to the dangers of unchecked liberty, which was why so many of them opposed democracy. Preserving liberty has been regarded as a highly precarious undertaking, requiring expertise and understanding, and this explains the strong elitist, and occasionally authoritarian, strain that runs through liberalism, notwithstanding its rhetoric about individual rights. This stems in part from its concern with the rights of property but in part also because liberalism is a rationalist ideology and places great importance on science. This means that it gives a privileged status to certain kinds of knowledge, knowledge that has been arrived at in a way that has been approved as scientific, through satisfying the criteria for inductive knowledge (observation, measurement, prediction, and experiment) which test ideas and theories against reality, or rigorous logical deduction from first principles. If the world has a true objective character that can be known, then there exist objective facts about the world that should guide the policies and plans of individuals as well as governments. From this standpoint rationality is not arbitrary but depends on processes of calculation. What is prescribed by the methods of rational calculation may conflict with what is demanded by representatives of the people. Rationalism and democracy have become incompatible for many modern liberals, and it is a conflict that was there at the outset, even in the idea of the *Rechtstaat* itself. For if this is indeed the best and most rational form of state for modern society, the form that can best preserve liberty and promote the fullest possible development of every individual, then it is too important a good to be left subject to the caprice of ignorant and ill-informed democratic electorates. Government becomes too important to be left to the governed.

Hence a real problem emerges for liberalism if the liberal constitution is for whatever reason refused by the people, or if the democratic majority encroaches on the rights of minorities, or of particular individuals. The advocates of liberal constitutionalism have generally held pessimistic views of human nature, believing that individuals being naturally rapacious and self-seeking, will plunder and murder one another with impunity and relish if they are not restrained by law, and if law is not backed by the coercive powers of the state. The problem then is what if a majority of individuals, acting through democratic institutions, vote to 'plunder' other members of the community, expropriating their property by using the very coercive powers of the state that were instituted to protect property? Might not such governments be as arbitrary and tyrannical as those of royal absolutism? This familiar liberal dilemma reverberates down to our own time, as the search has intensified to find ways by which government can be kept limited and liberty made safe.

This is the reason why the idea of a balanced or mixed constitution, in which there is a division and separation of powers, rather than a concentration of powers, figures to such an extent in the writings of liberal constitutionalists. Constitutions are designed to limit as much as to unite, and to protect the various associations, interests, and regions that make up civil society from arbitrary interference by government. Federalism itself is a further device of liberal constitution-making which seeks to break up the centralised power of a unitary state, and give the federated regions both some internal power and some veto over decisions made at the centre.

The fundamental principle from which all this flows is that the state should be subordinated to society rather than society to the state, because the state is only one among all the various associations of civil society and should not be allowed to subjugate and dominate all the others. Individuals and groups have rights that the state must respect, otherwise citizens are released from their duty to obey. This strand within liberalism appears deeply hostile and suspicious towards the state and is often spoken of as the philosophy of laissez-faire — the belief that that government is best which governs least. Government is restricted to a few basic functions: external defence, internal order, the stable management of money (the life-blood of civil society), and the enforcement of laws on contract and property. This minimal state of the liberal constitutionalists became dubbed the nightwatchman state, because it had so little to do, and it has certainly exercised a profound fascination within liberal thought.

Nevertheless the impression can be misleading. Although liberal constitutionalists advocated limited government they did not advocate weak government. On the contrary all liberal constitutionalists were believers in a strong state in certain areas. Indeed they argued that the very freeing of the energies of civil society required a strong and efficient state to prevent liberty from turning into anarchy. So whilst liberal constitutionalists have often been highly suspicious and fearful of state power, they have also been obliged to recognise that the liberty of the individual which they prize so highly cannot exist without a strong state. Otherwise property is not safe, contracts are not secure, competition is not fair and open, the value of money is uncertain, freedom to believe, write, speak, and associate is not protected, and the community itself may fall prey to foreign invasion.

It is no surprise therefore to find that one of the most influential schools of modern liberalism, utilitarianism, which thoroughly embraced laissez-faire economics, should also have been the source of proposals for far-reaching administrative reforms of the government, designed to make government more efficient and more powerful rather than less. Some later liberals have argued that Benthamism paved the way for the collectivist, interventionist state and should be struck out from the liberal constitutionalist tradition.

Bentham himself, however, was an indefatigable architect of constitutions and the commitment of the early Benthamites to laissez-faire economics was undisputed. Whatever the subsequent use to which utilitarian arguments were put, their first purpose was to justify a programme of administration and constitutional reform on the one hand, and economic laissez-faire on the other.

The major gulf between utilitarianism and some other branches of liberal constitutionalism lies in the doctrine of natural rights. Bentham described the doctrine of natural rights itself as nonsense, and the reference in the French Declaration of the Rights of Man to 'imprescriptible natural rights' as 'nonsense on stilts'. In its place he proposed to use the utilitarian ethics developed by some French Enlightenment thinkers — the doctrine that everything could be assessed in terms of its *utility*, the amount of pain or pleasure it afforded. If all human choices should be expressed in terms of utility it meant that utility was in principle measureable — there were no qualitative only quantitative differences between them. Individuals could make rational choices between the various alternatives facing them in such a way as to maximise their utility, and therefore the sum of their satisfactions. In a market economy the measure of utility was money.

The doctrine had two consequences. It indicated that only individuals could calculate how much utility any action or commodity had for them, so they should accordingly be left free to pursue their own interests in their own way. By maximising their own utility they would maximise their own happiness. At the same time, the doctrine prescribed that governments' actions should be guided by the principle of ensuring the greatest happiness of the greatest number. Policy should be judged by measurable consequences in terms of social welfare, and not by whether it conformed to some abstract notion of rights or justice. This implied that governments should and could make their own calculations about the choices made by all the utility-maximising individuals in civil society, and frame legislation accordingly.

This formula was intended to promote the cause of laissez-faire economics because it was assumed that only the freest possible rein given to individual competition in civil society could maximise individual liberty, hence any laws or practices that hindered that liberation would fall foul of the principle of the greatest happiness of the greatest number. By dispensing, however, with the fiction of natural rights, and with the whole tradition of natural law and its distinction between nature and society, the idea of an inviolable private realm was lost. If the greatest happiness of the greatest number demanded it, governments might need to intervene in civil society. Benthamism was fiercely individualistic; at the same time its conception of knowledge and rationality left open the possibility that what would ensure the greatest happiness of the greatest number could most securely be calculated by administrative experts. If an individual was fully rational should he not want what the government calculated he should want? If he were not fully rational, whose calculations should be allowed to carry greater weight? In this way Benthamism may be said to contain the seeds of the paternalistic and elitist politics pursued by the central bureaucracies of modern states everywhere, the essence of which is the overruling or discounting of subjective preferences in order to realise objective, social needs. Early Benthamites may not have expected any such conflict to arise, but it is a conflict deeply embedded in the structure of modern politics and of modern science, because of the inherent tension between the principles of individualism and rationalism. Science, for example, is a collective enterprise resting on objective rules and criteria whose results may conflict with the results of the free and therefore arbitrary exercise of individual choice and judgement.

In the early nineteenth century, however, Benthamism was one of the currents in the increasingly dominant ideology of liberal constitutionalism — and that meant limited government and economic individualism. The principle that came to embody the economic policy of liberal constitutionalism was free trade. If government could merely remove the obstacles to free trade both inside and across national frontiers, then the natural dynamism of an exchange economy would create wealth. The free trade religion was elaborated following the rise of Britain to commercial and industrial superiority by the middle of the nineteenth century, using methods guided by principles that were often anything but free trade in inspiration. It was widely regarded by other nation-states as an ideology, a further example of British hypocrisy, intended to throw a veil over the calculated pursuit of British national interests. But although the phrase 'free trade imperialism' accurately captures the policy of the British state, free trade was also believed in by liberals like Cobden and Bright as a means of undermining the nationalist ambitions of nation-states by encouraging cosmopolitanism (the word means literally free from national limitations), and making nations so interdependent that war and military budgets became unthinkable. Imperialism and protection were long regarded by liberals as the work of illiberal and reactionary political forces and as the direct cause of wars.

Internally free trade was a policy that if adhered to meant no government interference in contracts, even when these involved the employment of children. So long as contracts were fair and there was no cheating and no undue pressure in agreeing them, the liberal argument ran that in so far as individuals were responsible and rational they must be allowed to decide for themselves where the balance of advantage lay for them between different courses of action. Many liberals criticised bitterly the earliest infringements of free-trade principles, such as the British Factory Acts, which limited the length of the working day and the employment of children in certain occupations, and regarded their opposition as being based on humanitarian principles. As Herbert Spencer expressed it: 'The welfare of a society and the justice of its arrangements are at bottom dependent on the characters of its members.' This meant that if governments provided welfare benefits, or legislated to limit hours of work or improve conditions in factories, they would be protecting individuals from the consequences of their actions and this would weaken the moral basis of the liberal order. Spencer again stated this bleak doctrine in its starkest form: 'Is it not manifest that there must exist in our midst an immense amount of misery which is a normal result of misconduct, and ought not to be dissociated from it?' Free trade and the moral responsibility of individuals to help themselves found further embodiment in the principle of sound finance, the idea that strict economy in expenditure should be the

principal aim of finance ministers everywhere. This idea was
once strongly connected to the restricted property franchise,
since those who owned property elected the government and
paid the taxes that supported its activities. The link in the
minds of men of property between taxes paid and benefits
received was naturally close. In the nineteenth century, since
the sphere of government was small, the main target for
liberal reformers was the burden of the military budget used
to finance wars and colonies. In the twentieth century,
although the military budget in many states has grown
enormously, it is the welfare budget that attracts most
attention from the new free-market liberals. On strict free-
trade principles all government expenditure beyond that
necessary for the performance of the basic functions of
government hampers individual energies, reduces satisfactions,
and consequently is a great burden on the whole society.

Many liberals could see evils that arose from unrestricted
economic competition, but they regarded them as inescapable. Many remained highly pessimistic about human nature
and were therefore cautious about what could be expected
from the majority of human beings. Only a lengthy process
of education would improve the moral character of societies.
In societies as they were, taking short cuts to reach desired
goals would bring disaster. John Stuart Mill, who was sympathetic to many of the ideals of socialism, still warned
about forcing the pace of social advance. The problem, as he
saw it, was that human beings would only be willing to work
and take responsibility in economic enterprises if they had a
direct personal stake in them. He doubted whether working
for the common good would be a motive that was held
sufficiently strongly or widely to make economic production
as efficient as it was at the time he was writing (the middle of
the nineteenth century). He defended the market economy
on the grounds that it recognised the importance of self-
interest as a motive in human affairs, and that it allowed
many important things to be done and to be done efficiently,
which would never be done at all, if the altruism and social
conscience of individuals were relied upon. Mill did not
glorify self-interest since it could so easily turn into selfishness, and he hoped that altruism would one day become so
general that reliance on self-interest in economic affairs

would not be necessary. If this happened, then the organisation of societies along socialist lines could become the precondition for the development of the individual personality,
but until such time he believed that the institutions of private
property and free competition would have to be retained.
Other liberal supporters of the market order were more out-
spoken.

The aim of the early utilitarians was to reform administrative and political arrangements in accord with the simple
criteria they proposed — maximising the sum of individual
'happiness', and letting each individual judge where his
interest lay. In England this made them strong allies of the
campaign to change the basis of the electoral system and to
streamline the legal system. In the unreformed English
Parliament representation was based not upon individuals but
upon communities and corporate interests. The principle of
representing individual opinion (one man one vote) was
labelled the mathematical principle by its opponents, because
it meant that every individual was entitled to a single vote
and because it aimed at making every vote count the same. If
this principle were followed through, the whole electorate
had to be divided up into equal electoral districts, so that
every representative represented roughly the same number of
voters.

Once accepted, the principle has proved unstoppable, as its
opponents predicted. Attempts to restrict the franchise by
maintaining a property qualification, as in the early United
States, or a sex qualification, as in nineteenth-century Britain,
or a racial qualification, as in present-day South Africa,
contradict the principle of individual representation and in
the majority of states where liberal constitutionalism has held
sway all such restrictions have been abolished. The utilitarians
justified extending the franchise and basing the electoral
system on the individual citizen because they believed that
government would be made more efficient and more useful
to society if it was made subject to public opinion. Public
opinion was conceived as the sum of the opinions of the mass
of private individuals in civil society who were busy pursuing
their own private interests and maximising their utility
unhindered by government.

This way of posing the problem was often satirised by

opponents of the utilitarians because of its naivety and the rather restricted conception of human nature on which it was based. Macaulay in his attack upon James Mill offered in its place a straightforward historical defence of a franchise limited by property ownership, and ridiculed Mill's arguments for democracy because although Mill subscribed to the principle of one man one vote, in practice he wanted a democracy dominated by the people he felt closest to, the middle class. So he proposed all kinds of exclusions (including women and everyone under forty), which would have effectively denied the vote to roughly eighty per cent of the electorate.

A more sophisticated presentation of the utilitarian position was given by Mill's son, John Stuart Mill, who drew on ideas of Alexis de Tocqueville to focus attention on the dangers inherent in the new mass basis of representative government that was coming into being as the franchise was extended. The dangers existed so long as the mass of citizens were not sufficiently informed and rational and committed to the values of liberal constitutionalism, particularly the safeguarding of the division between a public and a private sphere. Similar fears prompted other liberals and conservatives to cling to the principles of a liberal constitutional order and reject the extension of the suffrage. It seemed intolerable to them that the liberal order should be threatened by admitting to a say in government decisions the representatives of those who had never believed in and were often profoundly ignorant of liberal principles.

Mill took a different line which was to shape the whole development of the liberal doctrine. He argued that the liberal order would only be secure and could only be justified if it actively encouraged full participation by all citizens in its institutions. Such participation would itself educate and inform the citizens and incline them to endorse basic liberal values. Such a belief was not based upon the narrow, utilitarian conception of human nature and its restrictive notions of what was useful and what was not, which Mill had learnt from his father and from Bentham, but upon a much wider conception of human individuality and the means to the full realisation of the potential of every human being, which he had developed out of his reading of romantic writers like

Coleridge. The principle of individualism in Mill's hands ranges far beyond the realm of economic relationships and becomes an advocacy of free choice in all matters of social life where the lives and interests of others are not adversely affected. In this way the principles that were used to challenge political absolutism and justify a private realm for the pursuit of economic interests, come to be used to challenge moral and social absolutism as well, and to threaten many traditional values and established institutions. What Mill and others did was greatly to extend the notion of the pursuit of individual happiness in the utilitarian tradition by beginning to identify the chief obstacles to human freedom as those social codes which unjustifiably restricted the full development of individual personality.

This kind of approach pointed to the need to begin the emancipation of groups, including women, who were submerged within civil society and denied full citizenship, and to relax social controls in accordance with the criterion Mill laid down:

> The sole end for which mankind are warranted, individually or collectively, in interfering with the liberty of action of any of their number, is self-protection. That the only purpose for which power can be rightfully exercised over any member of a civilised community, against his will, is to prevent harm to others. His own good, either physical or moral, is not a sufficient warrant.

Nevertheless, although Mill looked forward to a progressive improvement and enrichment of human societies through the steady unfolding of the capacities of its members, he was extremely cautious in advocating change. Just as he defended the retention of the market and distribution based on market exchange in economic affairs, so he advocated the exclusion of illiterates and those receiving public assistance from the electoral roll, and a system of plural voting, which would give someone in the professions up to six times as many votes as an unskilled worker. The intention was to ensure that those with education and property had as much weight in the political system as the working class in order to rule out what he called 'class legislation' by any section of the community.

He further suggested that legislation should not generally issue directly from the democratically elected Parliament but from a legislative commission, staffed by experts, who should decide on rational grounds what laws were needed and what form they should take, although power to enact laws would still rest with Parliament. Even in the hands of its most famous exponent liberal constitutionalism approached democracy with care.

3 The theory of popular sovereignty

John Stuart Mill's attempt to reconcile liberal principles with the circumstances of mass democracy placed him firmly in the liberal constitutionalist tradition. A second strand within liberalism took democracy as its starting point, the realisation of liberal values was secondary. Its proponents were not called liberals but radicals or Jacobins. Although it drew inspiration from some previous democratic theories and movements, the new democratic movement was much more universal in its scope and its claims. The American and French Revolutions had both begun with declarations of liberal principles but Edmund Burke as loudly praised the first as he roundly condemned the second. What frightened him, as well as the propertied classes of all Europe, was the democratic element present from the start in the French Revolution, and which briefly (in 1791-4), seized control.

At the time of the Revolution democracy was understood primarily as the ancient Greeks had defined it — a form of class government, rule in the interests of the poor and the oppressed, a highly unstable form of government which soon gave way to anarchy and then a new re-establishment of order, because the poor and their representatives were unfitted to rule. What was learnt by radicals from their experience of modern revolutions in which vast masses participated, and what had already been perceived by Rousseau, was that the nature of the modern state and modern civil society had undermined the old basis of social cohesion and political allegiance. At the same time the possibility had arisen of constructing a community of equals, which would overcome the divisions and conflicts of civil society and create the conditions for a just society commanding the loyalty of all its members; an ancient dream, but one that enters the modern world with new force and lies at the root of many of its political movements.

The radical democratic tradition rapidly diverges from liberal constitutionalism because it treats the political association of individuals that forms the state not as a means to the satisfaction of individual ends and purposes, but as the highest goal itself of social existence. The participation of all in politics is not desired because it makes government more efficient, but because only in this way can individuals fulfil their true nature by being absorbed into a network of loyalties and obligations that override considerations of individual self-interest. The feeling is rekindled that the political association between the members of a society is not just more important than other associations, but the supreme and indispensable one. Private life in civil society is an inferior existence.

Yet despite its apparent conflict with liberal constitu-tionalism, the democratic tradition shared the same roots in individualism, so that many thinkers like Tom Paine embraced both sets of ideas. The notion of individual natural rights, of a fundamental equality of human beings that belonged to the nature of things, was the starting point for the ideal of a republic of equals, a political association that explicitly recognised human equality. John Locke was one of the fore-runners of these ideas with his notion that every individual had a natural right to labour and to appropriate the fruits of the earth. A community of honest toilers in which everyone owned some property could provide the kind of conditions for a harmonious community. Locke himself did not draw radical conclusions from this principle. Feeling the need to justify the unequal distribution of property that existed, he sanctioned an unlimited right to appropriate, a right made possible, he thought, by the invention of money which allowed servants to be employed. This expedient doctrine was never very convincing. Much more so was the idea that if this right were stripped away, and individuals were dependent only on their own labour, they could only appropriate what their own exertions could produce. Unequal division of property and the existence of a large section of the community that was propertyless, seemed to contradict the principle of the natural equality of all men. The state of nature was at odds with the state of civil society.

In such circumstances the political ideas of the radicals began already to move beyond the liberal idea of protecting existing property rights. Instead of defining a private realm which should be inviolate, they began to question the legitimacy and justice of the large inequalities that flourished in such a private realm. Such inequalities came increasingly to be seen as incompatible with the state of nature and as direct obstacles to the realisation of a harmonious political order, because of the conflicts of interest they created between individuals. Liberal constitutionalism was not indifferent to inequality, but the equality it sought was formal legal equality, which was compatible with very considerable inequality of property, income, inheritance, and opportunity. The radical tradition began to concern itself with overcoming the inequalities inherent in civil society so as to create a morally cohesive society, a society that was classless because everyone belonged to the same class and none enjoyed privileges.

A persistent ideal in the modern history of Western political thought has been the kind of community that appeared for a time to be taking shape in the United States, the community of artisans and farmers, the small producers, where all work on their own account, control the quality and speed of their own work, exchange their products freely in the market, enter into contracts voluntarily, and so are independent and self-reliant. In such a community of equals, since the basis of society is democratic the political form is not just liberal but democratic also. This means that concentrations of power and wealth in civil society which are quite legitimate and to be expected in the liberal constitutional world, are undesirable and need breaking up in the radical one. The right to own property is still fundamental but it is a limited right. Whereas liberal constitutionalist regimes are compatible with the preservation of archaic procedures and privileges, as most obviously in the case of Britain, radical democratic ones encourage openness, plainness, and the absence of titles and privileges, and the undermining of all traditional authority and prescriptive rights. The critical examination of all social arrangements in the light of reason is given fresh impetus when special privileges and advantages have no longer to be justified and protected.

In the American Revolution the liberal and the radical rhetoric are side by side and often in the same mouths. This was partly because, except in the slave economy of the south, American civil society was as close as any community in the world at that time to the radical ideal. Hence Paine and Jefferson could in part celebrate what already existed, whilst warning of the dangers that might befall if the democratic basis of American society were lost. This is why Jefferson in particular edged toward advocating a limit on the amount of property any individual could hold, and why he distrusted and opposed (before he became President) the commercial and industrial policy of his political rival, Hamilton, which was aimed at giving full scope to commerce and finance and the amassing of great fortunes.

The radical ideal of democracy has proved more emotive than the liberal constitutionalist ideal which has either been extremely vague or relatively restricted in its appeal. The radical ideal promised participation to all not just in material goods, but in how the community was governed. It reflected a belief in the basic equality of the citizens and in the undeniable sovereignty of the people. It is an image that has since been appropriated within the broader liberal tradition and used to justify arrangements in the United States and elsewhere that have little to do with the kind of small-scale, morally integrated, independent producer communities Jefferson and Paine favoured. Nevertheless it has become commonplace to commend liberal democratic regimes as though they actually embodied this ideal, when the social and political basis for such societies and such states has long since vanished.

Powerful it proved too in the French Revolution in the hands of the Jacobins. The phase of liberal constitutionalism was rapidly succeeded by the phase of radical democracy. The phase was not welcomed by some of the Revolution's warmest admirers, notably Thomas Paine, who spent some time in prison during the Terror as a result of his opposition to the measures of Robespierre and the Committee of Public Safety. He lamented to Jefferson: 'Had this Revolution been conducted consistently with its principles, there was once a good prospect of extending liberty throughout the greatest part of Europe; but I now relinquish that hope.' The speed of the political development threw all into confusion. Robespierre and the other leaders worked consistently to express what they saw as the only true basis of the new republic — the equality of all citizens. As Robespierre proclaimed:

Democracy is a state in which the people, as sovereign, guided by laws of its own making, does for itself all that it can do well, and by its delegates what it cannot . . . . Democracy is the only form of state which all the individuals composing it can truly call their country . . . the French are the first people in the world to establish a true democracy, by calling all men to enjoy equality and the fullness of civic rights.

This theme echoed again and again in his speeches: 'Royalty has been destroyed, the nobility and clergy have disappeared and now the reign of equality is beginning.' Given the structure of French society such a principle was revolutionary in a radically new way. It recommended a politically directed reorganisation of French society to exclude privilege and minimise inequality. Robespierre frequently denounced those who, as he put it, 'want to build a Republic only to suit themselves and their interests, whose intention it is to govern in the interests of the rich and of public officials.' The real patriots were those who 'seek to found the Republic on the principles of equality and the general interest of all'.

Opponents of Robespierre and the French Revolution from the liberal constitutionalist tradition have often seen the cause of Robespierre's actions in the writings of Rousseau. But much more immediately important were the pressures created by the outbreak of war with the absolutist regimes of Europe. It was the need to wage revolutionary war against the rest of Europe that brought about the democratic republic and the Terror of 1793. The Terror claimed 27 000 lives in a population of 20 million but is engraved on the liberal conservative imagination in a way that the often much greater terrors of counter-revolutionary regimes later in the century are not.

More significant than the Terror for later developments were the measures by which the Jacobins organised the society for war: conscription, rationing, the placing of the whole community on a war footing, and the attempts to enforce equality of consumption and equality of treatment for all citizens. In the midst of it all a new constitution was promulgated. It had provision for universal suffrage, it guaranteed the right either to work or to support by the state, and the right of revolt; it abolished slavery and all remaining feudal rights without further compensation. It proclaimed the happiness of all as the aim of the government. When the Jacobins fell, their constitution fell also, and a new constitution was proclaimed, denounced by the radicals as a new aristocratic constitution which fastened the chains of the people once more, instead of breaking them.

The figure who broods over the Revolution is Rousseau. He cannot be either praised or blamed for the course of events, but they certainly highlighted how deeply he had grasped the character of civil society and its politics. He pioneered a new conception of popular sovereignty. Starting from the familiar contrast between the natural and the social condition of man, he argued that the only legitimate basis for state power was an agreement or contract made between all the individuals who were associated in the state. This social contract was not to be understood as a contract between a government and its people made in the distant past, in which the people surrendered their sovereignty in exchange for protection. In Rousseau's view the people could never surrender their sovereignty, it was inalienable, and the social contract was therefore an agreement which was forever being renewed. A legitimate state would be one in which the people participated as citizens in the regular exercise of their sovereignty. Where they did not, the government had become a despotism and its right to command obedience was at an end. The problem as Rousseau defined it was 'to find a form of association which will defend and protect with the whole common force the person and goods of each associate and in which each, while uniting himself with all, may still obey himself alone and remain as free as before.'

The state Rousseau sought had to be as absolute as Hobbes' *Leviathan*, but had still to rest on and preserve individual freedom. This could be done, Rousseau thought, if states were governed in accordance with the *general will* of the community. How was this general will to be discovered? By adding up individual preferences and taking the majority view? Rousseau argued that this procedure would only produce the 'will of all', a sum of selfish interests. In civil society individuals pursued their self-interest, satisfying their wants, and gratifying their appetites. Rousseau's concept of moral freedom was expressed in his statement that 'the mere impulse of appetite is slavery, while obedience to a law which we prescribe to ourselves is liberty'. This meant that he viewed the relations of individuals in civil societies as slavery, the domination of physical appetites. But he regarded human beings as capable of a much higher moral life where they would choose not what satisfied their own interests, but what promoted the good of others. The sphere for this higher moral existence was the state. A state composed of moral individuals in this sense would be ruled by the general will, because individuals would desire not what was good for themselves, but what was good for the whole community. Posing the problem in this way meant that Rousseau had to acknowledge that where individuals failed to perform their duty as citizens, the expression of the general will would not be a true general will but would be distorted by the intrusion of considerations that were self-interested, and therefore limited. At any one moment the view that most accurately reflected the general will might be held not by a majority but by a minority of the citizens. Rousseau offers no clear solution to this dilemma of deciding when a will was general, and therefore reflected the common universal interest, and when it was not, and reflected only a narrow sectional interest, but he posed more sharply than any political thinker before him the problem of creating in modern circumstances a morally united and cohesive community, which is founded upon individual freedom and individual responsibility. His ideal was the democracy of a small-scale community of artisans where, though executive powers were delegated to a government, supreme control over legislation was still exercised by the entire body of citizens. Unlike Jefferson and Paine, however, he was not much concerned with the role of his citizens as artisans or with the ideal of personal independence when it was secured through the production and exchange of commodities. He disliked private property and all aspects of civil society which hampered the full absorption of the individual into the life of the state. What he achieved was to show that the sovereignty of the modern state rested on a democratic basis — the equality of all citizens. As Karl Marx was later to put it, 'Democracy is the resolved mystery of all constitutions'. The only possible basis for making the government of the modern state legitimate was democracy. Whereas Hobbes and Locke had explored the negative character of the states' relation with civil society, treating it as a means to realise the ends of private individuals, Rousseau states its positive side, and in the starkest possible terms. He perceived the dynamic principle that has governed the evolution of the modern state — its claim to mould the lives of its members because it was democratic and rested in principle on the participation, not just the votes, of all its citizens.

4 The state as an ethical idea

There are many important points of difference between Rousseau and Hegel, but they were alike in attacking the conception of the modern state which viewed it as a contrivance to satisfy the purposes of the individuals who composed civil society. Hegel believed that the creation of civil society was the achievement of the modern world, but he strongly denied that the modern state could be understood simply as an extension of civil society, an external framework guaranteeing free individual activity. Hegel indeed objected to the simple-minded notion of the 'individual' which dominated so much liberal thought, and formed the basis for liberal thinking about economic and political problems. Hegel argued instead that society, the social network of institutions, beliefs and relationships existed prior to any single individual, so that the problem of individual rights and individual freedom could only be understood in the context of an actual society. He was against treating civil society as though it were the whole of society instead of just a part, because that meant ignoring other crucial dimensions of human existence.

Hegel's mature theory of the modern state, presented in *The Philosophy of Right*, started from an analysis of the human will. Individual actions were either self-interested in the sense that individuals were seeking to satisfy their needs, which meant asserting their right to appropriate material things, or they were altruistic, in the sense that individuals were recognising their common situation and acting according to their conscience and to ideas of what was right. But both these subjective aspects of the human will were absorbed and had to be understood within the context of what Hegel called 'Ethical Life', the objective moral and institutional order of society. In modern society this had three great divisions — the family, civil society, and the state.

The family was a form of human association in which human beings were not primarily independent persons, but members of a particular unit. The typical relationships between members of families were altruistic, in the sense that they were governed by affection rather than simple self-interest, and members of families would act so as to benefit other members without equivalent benefits being given in return. Members of families did not exchange equal value for equal value, as commodity owners did in the market, because they were treating relationships not as means to other ends but as ends in themselves. For the sake of family ties members would act in ways that were irrational when judged against the severe utilitarian standard of their own self-interest. Nevertheless family relationships were particular, not universal, because members felt loyalty and acted altruistically only in relation to the members of their own families, not of all families.

Civil society, the second sphere of Ethical Life, presented quite a different picture. This was the world of individuals emancipated from the controls of their families, their religions, and their political systems, free to pursue their own interests in their own way. Co-operation and interdependence were achieved through individual competition and self-reliance. Benevolence, self-sacrifice, unselfishness — these were values and motives out of place in civil society. Here individuals related to others primarily as means to their own ends. All individuals had to strive to offer a good or service which satisfied the needs of others, but the purpose in offering it was not to satisfy others' needs, but to satisfy one's own. The more the demand and the less the supply of the commodity which individuals could offer, the more success they would have in civil society. The result in Hegel's words was that 'in the course of the actual attainment of selfish ends . . . there is formed a system of complete interdependence, wherein the livelihood, happiness, and legal status of one man is interwoven with the livelihood, happiness and rights of all.'

Hegel described civil society as the sphere of 'universal egoism' which he contrasted with the family, the sphere of 'particular altruism'. What he argued was not that there was a sudden eruption of selfishness and egoism in the modern world, on the contrary he believed that these two spheres of universal egoism and particular altruism were permanent features of human social existence and human nature. What was new in the modern world was the degree to which these two aspects of Ethical Life and individual motivation had become separated institutionally, so that individuals took on a number of roles which were played out in different institutional spheres. Every individual was required to behave in one way as a member of his family and in quite a different way as a commodity owner in civil society.

The third, and the highest, sphere of Ethical Life was the state, the sphere of 'universal altruism'. Here again, what Hegel emphasised was that, like the family and civil society, the state was not separate from individuals. Properly conceived, it was an extension of human nature and human potentialities, because it was another way in which individuals could relate to one another. The rise of the modern state for Hegel did not mean that it came to dominate the family and civil society. On the contrary, the state only reached its full development when the family and civil society were strong and independent. Only individuals who accepted their duties as members of families and had developed their personal independence as property owners and members of other associations in civil society, were ready to be citizens of the state. Nevertheless to be a citizen, a member of a state, was the summit of Ethical Life as Hegel conceived it, and it was because the state made possible the full moral and human development of the individuals that composed it that it could demand complete loyalty, even to the extent of requiring the sacrifice of an individual's life in war. Individuals related to the state altruistically because in obeying its commands and paying its taxes they did not consider their own self-interest, but the objective interest of the whole community. This is why Hegel called the state universal and rational, because it was founded not on what divided but on what united human beings.

Hegel's account of the modern state was remarkable for its range and its anticipation of so many modern developments, and in particular for his understanding of the tension between the roles every individual had to play, especially between the role of private bourgeois in civil society, and the role of citizen in the state. He regarded the modern state as the association between human beings which made possible the highest realisation of human freedom, but he acknowledged at the same time serious problems which it created. Chief of these was the natural tendency for civil society to polarise between extremes of wealth and poverty. Hegel thought the possession of private property essential for the development of every individual's personality, just as he thought the enjoyment of civil rights by all members of the community the indispensable condition for them to achieve the sense of counting as persons in civil society. It followed that if any large section of the community were denied civil rights, on religious or racial grounds, for example, or were propertyless, and had no realistic opportunity of acquiring property, then the basis for their realisation of freedom as citizens was lacking. Hegel was concerned that both state and civil society should retain their separateness, otherwise the distinctive quality of modern life and the possibility of full individual freedom would be lost. This meant that solutions for abolishing poverty were ruled out, but he was at a loss to suggest how forces could arise within civil society itself to prevent poverty and to guarantee property to all its members. If poverty could not be overcome, it would be a source of continuing friction and instability and weaken the moral unity of the state.

A second set of problems concerned the way in which the actual institutions of the state should be related to civil society. Who should be entrusted with interpreting and executing the will of the nation, and how should the interests of civil society be represented? Hegel was as strong an opponent of mathematical representation as was Burke, remarking that universal suffrage especially in large states 'leads inevitably to electoral indifference, since the casting of a single vote is of no significance where there is a multitude of electors'. But the reasons for his opposition were quite different from those of Burke, since he despised the cult of tradition and the past as irrational. What he advocated was that members of civil society should be grouped in the associations that arose spontaneously (he called them corporations), and that these legitimate interests should be represented at the level of the state. State power itself would be in the hands of a universal class, a career bureaucracy. Its members, although belonging to families and to corporations in civil society, would also be imbued with a spirit of service and professionalism which would maintain their independence of all particular interests and allow them selflessly to serve the state. In this manner Hegel believed that a morally united yet internally differentiated community would be established which would make possible a balance between liberty and order.

5 Conclusion

Liberalism was the doctrine which pressed the claims of the 'individual' to be free to pursue his own interest in civil society and to participate in deciding how his community was governed. This dual strand in liberalism reflected the institutional separation of state and society. One result was that liberalism came to endorse two contradictory methods of reaching binding decisions. On the one hand is the market of individual commodity owners in which the central economic decisions — what is produced, and how it is distributed — result from the impersonal movement of prices, reflecting the push and pull of the forces of demand and supply, which arise from a multitude of individual decisions. On the other hand is the state and the other institutions and associations of civil society, in which every individual has the right to one vote, and decisions are taken on the basis of majorities. Both methods are simple but both created difficulties in identifying a general interest that was more than just a sectional interest, something to which all liberals attached great importance. In the market the free play of market forces produced a distribution of income so unequal that the pattern of production which the impersonal market decreed as being the one that most promoted the general welfare was heavily biased in favour of those with high incomes. The market might be defended on grounds of efficiency, that it led to the highest possible output, but less convincingly on moral grounds, that it linked effort and need to reward. Market arrangements were also much easier to defend morally when every individual owned property or had a realistic opportunity of owning property and working on his own account. It was less easy to justify an economy in which the majority were dependent wage workers.

In politics whilst liberals accepted that the only rational, because universal, principle was democracy, they were much concerned about the weaknesses of democracy as a form of government for realising the general good if all members of the community did not have the degree of knowledge, education, and intelligence to vote and participate in an informed and rational manner. Proposals for various constitutional safeguards, or for strengthening the associations and corporations of civil society, or for developing a professional and expert civil service, were the main result, the forerunners of many later theories. The principles of liberty and rationalism proved more important to most liberals than the realisation of democracy. This was a weakness within liberal ideology which socialism was to exploit.

4
Socialism

1 The unfinished revolution

The antagonism between liberalism and socialism can be misunderstood. As a doctrine socialism is not so much a call to reject the principles of liberalism as a claim that it alone can fulfil them. What they have in common has sometimes been more important than what divides them. Both originated as responses to the bourgeois revolution – the rise of the modern state, the expansion of civil society, and the development of scientific rationalism. Both had their roots in the period when a capitalist order that was not yet industrial began to emerge, and both endorsed aspects of the new industrial society wholeheartedly as it took shape. If liberals and socialists have often taken up opposed positions, these are positions within a common framework of values and assumptions, a fact sometimes more obvious to those outside the Western experience than those immersed within it.

The starting point for examining the origins of socialism is often the Industrial Revolution in England, which began in the 1780s, and which created the new industrial civilisation: the factories, the means of communication, the urban centres, and the industrial proletariat. But as important for the character of socialism as a political doctrine was the French Revolution. Lenin called revolutions 'festivals of the oppressed' because of the sudden and dramatic release of unsuspected energies and imagination in peoples that had up to then been oppressed and passive. In the brief concentrated space of the republic before the imposition of Napoleon's military dictatorship in 1799, new hopes and old dreams seemed capable of realisation. The collective power residing

in the modern state when it was based on democracy, the will
of the whole nation, and the new morality of justice and
equality, led very swiftly to political notions that went far
beyond the limited programmes of the liberal constitutionalists whose primary concern was to safeguard property
and order. It gave rise to the belief that the age itself was
revolutionary, that the French Revolution was only the first
step in a continuing revolutionary process. It had raised
issues and problems which had not been settled; hence a
further revolution was necessary to complete the changes
that had been set in hand in 1789. As the manifesto of the
Conspiracy of Equals put it in 1796: 'The French Revolution
was but the forerunner of another much greater and much
more solemn revolution, which will be the last.'

The watchwords of the French Revolution — Liberty,
Equality, and Fraternity — were adopted as the watchwords
of socialism. What socialists attacked were not the values of
liberalism but the impossibility of realising those values in a
liberal society. The kind of liberty and equality enshrined in
the charters of the rights of man, so favoured by liberal
constitutionalists, was denounced as hollow and worthless
by the radicals of the revolution. Jack Roux, for example,
described freedom as an empty pretence when one class of
men could starve another with impunity. This idea was to be
repeated much later by the French writer Anatole France,
who drew attention to 'the majestic equality of the law that
forbids the rich as well as the poor to sleep under bridges, to
beg on the streets, and to steal bread'.

Liberal constitutionalists believed strongly in equality, but
it was a formal equality that they wanted — equality of
treatment for all before the law. They did not support
equality of opportunity, the principle of giving human beings
an equal start in the competition for life's prizes, and still less
any equality of results, the principle of distributing social
wealth and social power equally, so that all individuals could
have equal consideration. They expected and justified the
emergence and perpetuation of substantial inequalities of
wealth and position within civil society. This was the guarantee of individual freedom. Once individuals were made equal
in law, they were free to make their own choices and make of
themselves what they could, handing on the results through

their families. The race was then to the swift and the battle
to the strong. The outcomes were not the concern of the
state. The core of the early socialist position, developing out
of the notions of radical democracy, was that *formal* political
equality which existed alongside *actual* economic and social
inequality destroyed the harmony and contradicted the
purpose of the state. 'True' equality and 'true' freedom
depended on the realisation of the ideal of the modern state
in the actual conditions and social relations of civil society.
In this way the social question, how civil society was
organised, was brought to the forefront. How could a state
founded on justice and equality tolerate relationships among
its members that destroyed the cohesion, the harmony, and
the fairness of the society by permitting huge discrepancies
in wealth, material possessions, and opportunities?

This much came to be recognised by many liberals, particularly where opportunities were concerned. What distinguished the socialist response was the emphasis placed upon
private ownership of property as the basic cause of the evils
and injustices of society. For socialists the existence of
private property gave rise to a fundamental division of the
population into classes with opposed interests which made
differences in wealth, power, and opportunities not temporary
and accidental, but permanent and cumulative. Only when
this rift was healed and classes abolished could an integrated
and just society be created. For Babeuf the class division was
between rich and poor; for later socialists it was between
those who owned property and those who were propertyless.
But property now meant not just wealth, but ownership of
the means of production, a legal title that conferred control
over how the labour of the propertyless workers was
organised, and was therefore the basis for social and political
power.

The key notions of early socialist thought were all linked
to major social evils that were regarded as arising not from
human nature or human weakness, but from the organisation
of civil society under a liberal constitutionalist order. These
evils included poverty, exploitation, selfishness, and alienation. Poverty and exploitation were blamed on a division of
the social product which was both unequal and unjust, and
which forced the majority of the population to be dependent

for their livelihood on a minority; selfishness and alienation were blamed on a form of society which compelled individuals to pursue their self-interest in order to survive and turned all relationships between human beings into commercial relationships. All qualities and capacities, including the capacity to labour itself, were turned into commodities, and individuals lost control over what once belonged to them. Money was elevated into the supreme social power and the principal social bond between individuals.

Not all these themes are found in all socialist writing, but the mark of early socialist thought was always the relation of social evils such as these to the institution of private ownership and private control of the means of production, and therefore to the existence of class.

The Jacobin tradition of radical democracy, which many of the early socialists carried on, meant that they did not turn their backs on the state, rather they believed that state and society should become one. What was wrong with the state was that it appeared as a body of armed force oppressing society. The socialists wanted its separation from civil society to be ended, and for its basis to be not force — exercised in the interests of one class — but consent, the willing participation of all citizens in collective decisions and collective tasks. For 'real' equality to be established in civil society, equality of consumption and property and opportunities, all members of the community would have to participate directly in ruling the association. This would ensure that equality was maintained, and that the general will of the community did not degenerate into the particular will of those who ran the government.

Socialism is often loosely identified with collectivism, bureaucracy, and government control, but the origins of early socialist thought lay in these notions of radical democracy. Throughout the history of socialism there has been a broad range of libertarian and anarchist ideas that have been deeply opposed to collectivism when that term denotes the exercise of control over society by government. From a socialist standpoint, the real dividing line in modern Western thought is not between liberalism (or conservatism or individualism) and collectivism, but between those doctrines that regard private ownership and control of the means of production as a major evil and those that do not.

What determined the development of socialism as a doctrine was the practical linking of it to the interests and demands of a new class, the industrial workers. Radical democrats were conscious of the power of mass action — they had witnessed it in the French Revolution. They were conscious also that revolution could hardly come about unless forced through by the united action of an oppressed class fighting for its rights and the redress of its grievances. Few of them believed (in the first half of the nineteenth century) that the peasantry could become radical, however, and the urban poor were disorganised and, except in a few great centres like Paris, were small in number, and with limited power of resistance against professional armies. A new industrial working class was growing rapidly and becoming concentrated in great new urban centres. Since it was so important for the success and continued existence of the new industry, it began to appear as the force that might prise open the liberal constitutional order and lead to the abolition of private property and the reconstruction of society on rational and progressive lines. All socialists assumed that rationality and progress were closely identified and that social arrangements that increased human welfare were more rational and morally preferable to those they replaced.

2 The reaction to laissez-faire

Socialism as a doctrine of war between classes had an obvious appeal to the leaders of the new labour movements, but there was no inevitable reason why it should be adopted by them, and in some countries it made little headway (the United States is perhaps the best example). As a doctrine, however, it was never simply a sectional creed that defended and advanced particular interests, but a universal creed that sought to construct a rational order which would benefit all citizens. The basis of socialism's appeal to organised labour lay in the sharp frontal assault it mounted on some of the social consequences of liberal doctrine, particularly the ethos and programme of laissez-faire. In practice governments that subscribed to laissez-faire principles, while abstaining in some areas, were still required to intervene intensively and continually in others — but an image of social neglect and indifference became associated with the term, in part due to the sustained propaganda barrage mounted by socialists. The abuses of the early factory system, particularly the over-working of both adults and children, the housing conditions in the new cities, the inadequate provision of security against unemployment, illness, accident, old age, and the neglect of health and education, were blamed upon the unleashing of economic individualism, and the pursuit by capitalists of their own self-interest with a minimum of legal checks or controls. The answer of the liberal constitutionalists, which has been used many times since, was given uncompromisingly by Herbert Spencer: 'Is it not manifest that there must exist in our midst an immense amount of misery which is a normal result of misconduct, and ought not to be dissociated from it?'

The practical and theoretical challenge to the system of laissez-faire preoccupied the early socialist movement, but it never lost its radical democratic strain. This was a source of considerable later tension between different wings of the movement. In general, the radical democratic tradition has stressed the basic socialist insight about the class nature of modern civil society — that civil society gave rise to a new form of class rule. What became the social democratic tradition was concerned primarily with the response to laissez-faire and the best way of managing industrial societies. The latter has emphasised redistribution of resources through government taxation and expenditure and more efficient production through government planning. Such an emphasis has united this kind of socialism with liberal democrats into the social democratic parties of the modern era, whose theory and practice have rested on the belief that the con-sequences of class society can be removed through measures undertaken collectively to restrain economic individualism. Uncontrolled individualism was the great social evil. As the French socialist Louis Blanc put it:

> The principle of individualism is that which, taking man out of society, makes him sole judge of what surrounds him and of himself, gives him a heightened sense of his rights without showing him his duties, abandons him to his own powers, and for the whole of government, proclaims laissez-faire.

This type of socialism sought to put man back into society, and to remind him of his social duties by encouraging collective regulation of economic life and social conditions through government action. It became particularly influential in France and England.

Making a sharp contrast between liberalism and collectivism, and identifying collectivism with socialism, means that both the democratic tradition in liberalism and later social democratic currents of thought have to be assigned to socialism. The difficulties in such characterisation are easily seen in the case of Saint-Simon, often taken as one of the first socialists. He was certainly no liberal constitutionalist, but he also stands a long way from socialism, since he had no belief in a fundamental conflict of interest *within* industrial society, hence no notion of class or of the need to abolish private property. He was a liberal who inaugurated a way of looking at industrial society and its problems which has been immensely influential, particularly in France. It certainly pointed towards collectivist solutions but it was never close to what was later understood as a socialist programme. In France Saint-Simonism became a religion for engineers and managers, for the new elites that embraced the ethos of the industrial society and were increasingly needed to run it. He was much opposed to unchecked individualism and the doctrine of negative liberty that flourished in England, and he believed the bad effects of individualism should be countered through a more collective organisation of society, rather than through the state. His ideas about industrialism as a new form of civilisation and his hostility to economic and social individualism on the grounds that it undermined social order and social consensus did influence many socialists, including Engels, but his thought as a whole belongs within the liberal and social democratic traditions.

3 Rationalism

That currents in liberalism and socialism should later merge is not surprising. The two doctrines were closely connected because so many of the basic assumptions they made were similar — about science and nature, progress and history, production and organisation. Rationalism was one such bond, and is often traced to its roots in the European Enlightenment, whose most notable feature was the importance assigned to the power of human reason. This was sometimes allied with great pessimism about the nature of man and the prospects for society, sometimes with great optimism about human perfectibility. But the sense of a new intellectual mastery and understanding which derived from observation, analysis, and experiment, and the conception of an objective material world whose laws could be discovered, became part of the consensus of Western thought. It meant that only those things counted as knowledge which could be shown to be rational according to the socially accepted criteria of reason. This challenge to the authority of traditional and religious knowledge and to all forms of knowledge not cast in the rationalist mould, has become, despite resistance and occasional outbreaks of irrationalism and mysticism, an enduring feature of the modern Western outlook.

There have been disputes within the rationalist camp over whether there are limits inherent in human reason, but not on whether the world can be understood in rationalist terms. The great dividing line in rationalism is not between liberalism and socialism but concerns the idea of progress and the meaning of human history. Those who have taken an optimistic view of human nature and human potential came to view the history of the human race as a history which had seen improvement and the unfolding of new powers, and which could be expected to continue along similar lines in the future, as knowledge increased and as social and political arrangements were altered so as to make progress easier. Universal harmony, universal happiness, were thought by the more optimistic liberals and socialists to be within reach.

Such thinking inaugurated a tradition of social engineering in which great emphasis was laid upon altering the social environment so as to produce a better and constantly improving society which would use its increasing material wealth to best advantage in the interests of the whole community. Government was often the chosen agency, but not exclusively; voluntary bodies, other associations and individuals were often regarded as just as important. Those who had a much more pessimistic view of human nature questioned the possibility of steady moral and social progress and put their faith in social engineering of a different kind, seeking to construct an external, coercive framework of law which could divert the selfish and destructive drives of individuals into socially useful channels. Such a policy aimed at limiting the evil in society rather than attempting to remove it, on the ground that nothing more was possible or safe. But the underlying belief in a rational order and a law-governed natural world remained. Both schools believed firmly that human agency could cause society to improve or degenerate. It was no longer Providence or God who were the arbiters.

The idea of progress was founded on the new intellectual discoveries, the most striking of which was the Newtonian conception of the universe, but it received confirmation and substance from material progress in the nineteenth century. The apparently limitless advance of human wealth did not settle the argument as to whether human nature was essentially depraved or essentially benign, but it established the idea of a secular historical development of the human race as the terrain for thinking about politics and society. Since industrialism and technology were the most visible signs of human mastery and human understanding of nature no branch of rationalism could disavow them. For all the disagreement and conflict over how industrial societies should be organised, the return to pre-industrial societies was unthinkable for the rationalists of all schools. The main opposition to industrialism as such within the Western tradition was to come from romantic currents of thought.

A final great bond between liberalism and socialism lay in the cosmopolitan and universal principles they both embraced. Both were universal systems of ideas — reason could not be confined within any national boundaries. What was true in Paris must be true everywhere. Before the rise of modern nationalism in the second half of the nineteenth century, liberals and socialists gave their primary allegiance to universal notions like reason and humanity. The German philosopher, Fichte, could declare in the early stages of the French Revolution that a just man was obliged to regard France as his true country, and Marx and Engels stated in *The Communist Manifesto* that the workers had no country. This made them the universal class, the potential representatives of all humanity. Such cosmopolitanism was an aspect of

the revolt of the individual and the revolt of reason against
the traditional structures of Church and state and the traditional forms of ideology. It became a distinguishing mark of
the new class of intellectuals which was everywhere pushing
to the forefront.

What is so noticeable in Western rationalism is that,
although there were some major philosophical divisions and
differences of emphasis, rationalism and the new philosophy
were conceived as involving not merely the discussion of the
best available means, but the acceptance of certain values as
self-evidently right. Cosmopolitanism, individualism, the
greatest happiness of the greatest number, the all-round
development of the individual, have all at different times
been defended as the embodiment of reason. A belief in
progress could be sustained if these central values were
coming closer to being realised in actual social and political
arrangements. Only much later did the moral and technical
aspects of rationality start diverging and pointing in different
directions.

4 Libertarianism

What needs emphasising is the extent to which the moral
values and moral climate of early socialism were anarchistic
and libertarian. Anarchism in its various forms was a crucial
seedbed for socialist ideas. The term anarchy conjures up
images of chaos, but is actually derived from the Greek word
meaning 'no ruler'. Many liberals as well as early socialists
shared the ideal of a self-regulating society, free of central
control and direction, and radical liberal thought was
anarchistic in rejecting all authority save the authority of the
individual's conscience. Principles such as the importance of
self-realisation, of individual autonomy for everyone, of
equal consideration and respect, implied the widest possible
toleration of individual differences, behaviour, and beliefs,
and have led to movements claiming equal rights and equal
status for many different groups, especially women.

Anarchists also believed that human beings were by nature
co-operative and benevolent, and that provided the state were
abolished and economy and society decentralised, societies
could function without conflict, without disorder, and without inequality. There was no need for any kind of centralised

political authority, which always distorted and destroyed the spontaneity and harmony of the relationships human beings established naturally in society. Anarchists helped pioneer co-operatives and libertarian communities, some of which were based upon the principle of equal exchange between private commodity producers, others upon co-operative production, whilst others still opted for self-sufficiency. In all cases simple small-scale arrangements were preferred as a better way of living to the complexity and enormous scale of modern industrialism. This was an important reason why anarchism as a political movement appealed so strongly to peasant communities in certain parts of Europe.

Some of the anarchist ideas and experiments in the nine-teenth century were similar to the kind of economic and social arrangements favoured by Jefferson and Paine, but all were undermined by the way in which industrial capitalism developed. Eventually this greatly reduced the political impact of many of these ideas, because the key question for socialists became how they should respond to the new industrial society and whether socialism should be a doctrine independent of liberalism or a development of one strand of it. In political terms there was the problem of whether socialism should be a doctrine of all classes engaged in production or only of the working class on the grounds that only the working class could represent universal interests and bring about the disappearance of all classes. The more the division of labour and the market was extended, the larger and more bureaucratic became the structure of its enterprises and its government. The organisation of industrial society and the struggle for power within it became the preoccupation of socialist thought, but as with liberalism, the early pre-industrial conception of simple co-operation between free individuals retained its moral legitimacy. Karl Marx was to weld these disparate ideas into a doctrine of compelling force.

5 The origins of Marxism

Karl Marx occupies a place within socialist thought for which there is no counterpart in liberalism. His work has proved so influential that it requires extended treatment. Marxism is the most important critique of liberalism in Western thought, and whereas most other socialist theories were eventually absorbed within liberalism, Marxism stands outside. Yet because it is a critique of liberalism it necessarily shares a large part of liberalism's outlook. Marxism is both the implacable enemy of liberalism and its heir, the doctrine that seeks to bury liberalism and to fulfil it. Arnold Toynbee described Marxism as the great Western heresy, a heresy that has so far failed to overturn the liberal order in the metropolitan centres of the West, but has become the official creed of regimes in other parts of the world, dedicated to the overthrow of Western power and Western domination, but not of the industrial system on which they are based. Liberalism and Marxism are the dominant ideologies in the modern world and no part of the world has remained entirely immune from them.

Marxism took shape as a doctrine in the course of critical and often polemical assessments of major theorists which the young Marx undertook during the 1840s. Engels, and later Lenin, described Marxism as a synthesis of German philosophy, English political economy and French socialism. Certainly Marx was deeply influenced by all three, but he was also influenced by many other aspects of Western thought, not least European literature and classical philosophy. His early intellectual development was a series of attempts to find a firm starting point for constructing a theory and a practice that could transform existing society.

In his early work Marx approaches all questions and all other systems of ideas from the standpoint of radical democracy. The overthrow of traditional authority, the Promethean revolt of the 'individual' against the absolutist states of old Europe, the universal claims in the ideology and rhetoric of the French revolutionaries, the power of rational thought – this heritage from the first great revolution of the modern era shaped Marx's outlook permanently. It was as a radical democrat and editor of a Rhineland newspaper that he challenged the censorship of the press imposed by the Prussian state and was forced into exile. It gave his socialism a libertarian bias that it never lost.

Marx's greatest talent lay in his ability to penetrate to the unstated theoretical assumptions at the heart of any piece of theorising. In his early work he was dealing with material in which the ideas and aims of radicals and socialists were not at all clearly defined. In criticising them in the light of the criticisms he was making at the same time of some of the fundamental liberal ideas advanced by Hegel and by the political economists, he worked step by step to the theoretical elaboration of a socialist standpoint which was independent of liberalism in all its shapes and disguises, and so could adequately define and advance the interests of the class of proletarians, whose interests were identical with those of the human species as a whole. Marx saw the industrial proletariat as the only possible agency in modern society for realising the society of equals which the radicals in the French Revolution had proclaimed.

Marx's theoretical labours and practical activities make little sense unless it is understood how they derive from the tremendous emotional and moral force which his early commitment to radical democracy gave his work, although he discarded its specific ideas and approach in his mature writings. The crucial political question for Marx was how a just community could be created amidst the conflicts and evils of early industrial society. The question he posed and spent his life answering was: did the character of this society and the way in which it was developing afford a basis for constructing the kind of social and political order which could go beyond the formal freedoms of the bourgeois state (which in practice gave very little freedom to the majority of the people) and achieve actual freedom, equality, and fraternity to ensure that all individuals developed to the maximum of their capability?

Given this political and moral standpoint Marx developed his ideas through a series of confrontations with the major contemporary intellectual systems of Western thought. As a rationalist, strongly influenced by the French Enlightenment, but still more by Hegel, he believed in the power of human reason but also in the objectivity of the material world. He differed from those rationalists like Hegel who believed that reason could only understand the world after a particular historical development was completed, and also from those, like the Young Hegelians, who believed that social conditions could be changed simply by acts of will and by changing the consciousness of groups and individuals. Marx never doubted that rational argument and analysis could help in the transformation of the world, but he argued that reason would only be effective if the conditions and limits to change were understood. These limits were not solely the products of human minds but were part of social reality itself, definite relationships between individuals, which individuals through their daily actions constantly reproduced. If these and the ideas implicit in them were to be transformed their historical origins and functions had to be grasped. 'Men make their own history', Marx wrote, in his analysis of the rise of Louis Napoleon, 'but they do not make it just as they please; they do not make it under circumstances chosen by themselves but under circumstances directly encountered, given, and transmitted from the past'.

It was for this reason that in some of these early debates Marx distinguished his position from that of the 'Utopian Socialists'. This name was originally given (by Engels) to Robert Owen, Charles Fourier, and Henri Saint-Simon. Both Owen and Fourier drew up schemes for co-operative living that were intended as alternatives to the competitive individualism of capitalist civil society. Owen was active in actually setting up such communities. Marx was not opposed to the ideals of common ownership and communal living, but he regarded such experiments as utopian because he could see no way that they could become general until the power of the property-owning class had been broken. As he argued in the Inaugural Address which he wrote for the First International in 1864: 'However excellent in principle, and however useful in practice, co-operative labour, if kept within the narrow circle of the casual efforts of private workmen, will never be able to arrest the growth in geometrical progression of monopoly, to free the masses, nor even to perceptibly lighten the burden of their miseries.'

For Marx the major obstacle to socialism and beyond socialism, communism, was the class nature of civil society, a fact that could not be willed or wished away, but that had to be overcome through a struggle in which the great majority of the people would be forced to take a part. Only then when private property was abolished would the basis exist for the kind of democratic, free, and equal community Marx and many of the utopian socialists wanted to see, a society in which the political economy of the working class (production for use by the associated producers to satisfy human needs) would supplant the political economy of the bourgeoisie (production for exchange through the market to maximise profits).

Marx's rationalism had another consequence. By resolutely (and probably more consistently than any other major Western thinker) refusing to account for social phenomena other than in rational terms, he excluded all explanations based on invoking the purposes of either Providence or God, or making metaphysical and unprovable assumptions about human nature. This meant explaining history as a wholly human process. As Marx put it, 'To be radical is to grasp things by the root, but for man the root is man himself.' Later in his life Marx was to hail the appearance of Darwin's work on the origin of species because it provided support for his own starting point. By accounting for the evolution of species as a process of natural history Darwin was able to dispense with the notion of a God who actively intervened in organic nature, just as Galileo and Newton had dispensed with it in their account of inorganic nature. Marx's ambition was to treat human history in the way that Darwin had treated natural history, as a process governed by laws which could be discovered by careful observation and analysis and which could be derived purely from the facts under study, rather than from any external force or principle.

Hegel too had broken new ground in his conception of the historical process as a wholly human process, passing through definite stages, and governed by principles internal to it. But he presented it as the progress of Mind, the World Spirit, whose different stages were so many different ways in which human beings had understood their own time. Marx instead placed the emphasis not on human consciousness but on the way human ideas and actions were related to the basic condition for human existence, the natural world. He came to see human history as a process of natural history, a process governed more by the interaction of human beings with their natural environment than by human consciousness and will. This is often misrepresented; Marx still placed great importance on consciousness and will. Given his political convictions, how could it be otherwise? He also insisted that human societies could not be analysed in the same way as the physical world. But as he wrote in a famous passage, he came to the conclusion that 'It is not the consciousness of men that determines their being, but rather their social being that determines their consciousness.' What Marx argued for was the examination of intentions, beliefs, and ideas in the context of the social relationships of each society. As he remarked in *Capital*:

> The Middle Ages could not live on Catholicism, nor could the ancient world on politics. On the contrary it is the manner in which they gained their livelihood which explains why in one case politics, in the other case Catholicism, played the chief part. For the rest, one needs no more than a slight acquaintance with, for example, the history of the Roman Republic, to be aware that its secret history is the history of landed property.

The result is that his early writings display a relentless search for the basic assumptions about human nature and human history which embodied the criteria of morality and the criteria of rationality Marx had adopted. By uniting moral and rational discourse at this level Marx believed he had founded simultaneously the basis for a scientific study of history, its various modes of production and social forma-tions, and a basis for judging the progress of human societies in terms of moral concepts such as justice and the capacities of the human species. The starting point he arrived at was the analysis of the basic structure of relationships between human communities and their natural surroundings which are necessary for their survival. Marx pictured human history and its stages of development as a process in which human powers and capacities had gradually unfolded. The basis upon which there had been historical development and historical progress was social labour. It was the way human labour was organised and its fruits distributed that had given rise to a number of different formations of economic society, the material basis on which had arisen particular forms of state, law, and ideology. Labour itself was the way human beings related to the world, the shaping of the world in accordance with their wants and the aims they set themselves in the light of the opportunities and possibilities which the natural world supplied.

Marx described labour in *Capital* as a nature-imposed necessity, independent of all specific forms of society because common to them all. Labour was a distinctively human characteristic marking human beings off from animals because it involved foresight and the conscious shaping of an environment, and because it was social — it was carried on within communities. Human experience for Marx, as with language itself, was fundamentally social. The opposition between individual and society was a false opposition because, for Marx, the individual could develop only in and through society. What he assumed in addition was that the human species was one and had a single history. This meant that there were no natural and permanent inequalities, no natural subhumans or slaves or nations or tribes, in Marx's conception of the human race. Such distinctions were all the product of specific social relationships and social formations. Yet despite the uniqueness of their different cultures, all social formations had certain features in common. All rested upon a definite way of organising the labour process — a particular mode of production. Human history could be analysed in terms of these different modes of production and the varied forms of society and state which arose on the basis of them.

Marx's theory of historical materialism states simply that all human societies in history are based upon a particular organisation and distribution of their labour. Without such arrangements they could not continue to exist — it is the basis of their life. Since the era of tribalism when property was held in common and human communities lived near subsistence, an era of class societies has emerged. The direction of the labour process and the appropriation of that part of the labour or its product which is surplus to subsistence requirements, is in the hands of a class that obtains exclusive ownership of a vital resource and maintains its ownership utilimately by force. This resource in the era of agrarian economies was land, hence the ruling classes of both the slave and serf modes of production were landowners whose position and consumption were dependent on their ability to force the subject class — whether peasants or slaves — to perform unpaid labour for them. In slavery this took the form of buying the workers themselves as property and as a result their capacity to labour for as long as they lived; in serfdom the peasants were tied to particular estates and obliged to spend so many days a year working on the lord's land and contributing certain payments in kind, as well as submitting to the lord's exercise of a great array of customary rights and special privileges.

One of the greatest misreadings of Marx has been to attribute to him the notion that human societies develop in a fixed and invariable sequence: tribalism, slave society, feudalism, capitalism, socialism, communism. A still greater misunderstanding is to suppose that Marx thought that every national social formation was destined to pass through the same sequence of stages in its historical development, which meant that no society could pass to socialism without first having gone through a feudal stage and then a capitalist stage. Rather than such a deterministic conception, Marx does make an important distinction between those modes of production that preceded capitalism and capitalism itself. Class relationships, for example, in pre-capitalist modes of production were relatively clear and unambiguous. So were the legal and political arrangements that enforced them and the ideologies that justified them. The way in which slave revolts and peasant revolts were suppressed gave a clear indication of the source and the control of social and political power. Nevertheless these earlier class societies all proved remarkably durable and none was overthrown directly by the revolt of the subordinate and oppressed class on whose labour it rested.

With the rise of capitalism a new problem emerged. Here was a new form of economic society in which state and economy seemed to be separated, the owners of industry did not rule directly as did Roman landowners or feudal barons, and the society possessed an ideology which for the first time denied that its society was a class society, and asserted instead that it existed to defend the rights of men, of all men — a phrase which was later extended to include women too. Life, liberty, and the pursuit of happiness were very different slogans from the ideologies of previous class societies which had sanctified slavery because slaves were subhuman, and

justified the great gulf between the idle nobility and the
oppressed peasantry because social differences were ordained
by God as part of the hierarchy that could be observed
throughout nature. Capitalism was the first class society to
deny that it was. Marx and the communists of the radical
democratic revolution, as well as many of the early socialists,
were convinced that it was, and Marx devoted some sixteen
years from 1851 onwards to showing how it was. His labour
produced the first volume of *Capital* and a mass of manuscripts, some of which have not been published to this day.
After 1867, his health broken, he was unable to finish the
massive work he had undertaken. But the foundations of the
most remarkable intellectual synthesis of the modern era had
been laid.

6 The production of commodities

The doctrines of *Capital* form the basis for Marx's claim to
have placed socialism on a scientific basis; to have grounded
it on facts and concepts developed out of a close study of the
social reality of capitalism which, whilst taking full account
of that reality, expose the limitations of all other conceptions,
whether liberal or socialist. In the first six chapters he analyses
the workings of the market, in the rest of the book he
analyses the sphere of production, first the capitalist labour
process, the way in which production is organised under
capitalism, and then the process of accumulation of capital.

He argues that capitalism can only be presented in liberal
doctrine as a society without classes because liberals do not
trouble to analyse the workings of the capitalist labour
process but concentrate instead upon the market, the sphere
of free exchange. For Marx, since the organisation of social
labour is the condition for the existence of every society, to
concentrate upon a different set of institutions is to systematically conceal the real determinants of social life. In the
market place he readily agrees, the claims of liberalism are
justified. It is as he puts it,

> A very Eden of the innate rights of man. It is the
> exclusive realm of Freedom, Equality, Property, and
> Bentham. Freedom, because both buyer and seller of a
> commodity . . . are determined only by their own free

will. They contract as free persons who are equal before
the law . . . Equality because each enters into relation
with the other . . . and they exchange equivalent for
equivalent. Property, because each disposes only of
what is his own. And Bentham because each looks only
to his own advantage. The only force bringing them
together, and putting them into relation with one
another, is the selfishness, the gain and the private
interest of each. Each pays heed to himself only, and
no one worries about the others. And precisely for that
reason . . . they all work together to their mutual
advantage, for the common weal, and in the common
interest.

In the market everything appears as a commodity, everyone
must be a merchant, an owner of commodities, and trade
them in the market. In the market only equivalent values are
exchanged. No one in principle is cheated (they may be in
practice); no one is coerced, no one is exploited. All of these
things may happen, but if they do, it is not the fault of the
market principle of free and equal exchange itself, but the
inadequacy of political and legal agencies in enforcing it.
Everyone is conceived as an owner of commodities, of
individual property, working on their own account, producing
for exchange and hoping to realise sufficient value in exchange
that will enable them to purchase in the market those other
use values necessary to satisfy whatever needs they have.
    Such a society will only function smoothly if there is some
mechanism by which the labour of every individual producer
can be connected and co-ordinated. Each producer can only
be sure of exchanging the particular useful article he produces
if he can first exchange that use value for a commodity which
is the 'universal equivalent' for all the commodities that are
produced. This special commodity which market economies
need is money — the commodity whose function is to express
the exchange value of all other commodities. Possessing
money an individual possesses the key to unlock the productive wealth of society. Money commands the labour of all
the isolated individual producers in the market because all
must have money in order to satisfy their needs. So money
becomes the social bond, the force that connects individuals

together in a market of independent commodity producers. It is, argued Marx, the great leveller of status and hierarchies, because it allows a price to be put on everything, and therefore for everything to be ranked on a single scale.

In the early chapters of *Capital*, Marx laid out the organisational principles governing the ideal societies of some of the radical democrats, the community of independent artisans, and showed how even in such a society individuals would find themselves ruled and controlled by anonymous and impersonal forces — money and the market. These forces arose out of the way their economic life was organised. As individuals they were isolated, their economic livelihood insecure because the distribution of social labour between different occupations and kinds of work was being organised through the competitive market rather than directly by the producers themselves acting under the guidance of a co-operative plan. Yet it was not a class society and extremes of wealth and poverty would be unlikely to develop. Every producer depended on selling into the market and buying from it in order to obtain the necessities for life, but no producer could be sure that what he produced would always be saleable. There might be a glut and the price might fall dramatically. The commodity the individual had produced and on which his very existence depended might suddenly have no exchange value — a situation he could not have foreseen and for which he could not be blamed.

Marx was aware that the radical democratic conception of an artisan community was nowhere realised. Modern civil society everywhere exhibited great extremes of wealth and poverty and whilst the majority of the population were without property in the form of land or tools or money, a minority possessed all three. Yet it still remained a puzzle how a class which owned capital could so use its wealth in a market economy to preserve and extend its capital. Marx argued that an individual capitalist would have no incentive to use his money to organise production unless he could be sure of retrieving it and enlarging it. But from where in the process of the production and circulation of commodities could come this addition to his capital?

Some of the early socialists took their lead from Locke, Adam Smith, and Ricardo, who all regarded labour as the source of wealth and value. If that was so, these socialists reasoned, then labour was entitled to the whole of the product. The share going to landlords as rent and to capitalists as profit was clearly a deduction from the total forced from the workers by the landlords' monopoly of land and the capitalists' monopoly of machinery and raw materials, backed up by their political control of the state. This theory was given plausibility by Locke's argument that each individual in the state of nature possessed the capacity to labour and the right to the fruits of his labour. Some of the early socialists used such arguments to assert that social justice demanded that societies be founded on the principle of equal exchange, in the belief that this would make the distribution of income and wealth roughly equal too.

This theory was however rejected by Marx, because it treated the exploitation of the workers as no more than an unjust distribution of the social product. Marx continued to assert that the actual distribution regarded from the standpoint of the market was perfectly fair. What was wrong was not the principle of distribution through the market, but the relationships in the production process itself. Capitalists like other commodity owners exchanged equivalent for equivalent on the market and received back a greater sum of values, of money, than the sum they parted with at the outset. They had to find on the market a unique commodity, a commodity whose use value was to create value itself. This commodity is labour power, the capacity to work, the human faculty which, Marx reasoned, alone creates both useful things (use values) and the possibility of exchange because the expenditure of a definite amount of labour-time is something that is common to the production of every commodity. No individuals are propertyless under capitalism because even if they have no product or service to sell, by lacking the means to produce them, they still have their capacity to labour, their labour services, which they can sell on the market to the highest bidder like any other commodity. The difference is that under no previous form of economic society had labour power itself become an individual commodity.

Marx showed that what is required for a class society to arise on the basis of a system of free and equal exchange between independent individuals is firstly, the concentration of hoards of money capital in the hands of a class of capitalists, and secondly, a free labour force — free to sell their labour power, because they are no longer tied to particular landowners or slaveowners, but free also from any ownership of property which could make them genuinely independent of capital. If land is abundant, for instance, a capitalist economy might quickly be transformed into a community of independent small-holders. For capitalism to exist, there must be a labour force whose members are obliged to sell control over their labour services in order to buy the necessities they need to live.

By selling their labour services to capitalists they make over the use of them for a specified period, they *alienate* their labour power. To alienate something means primarily to sell it, but the term also carries the meaning of loss, estrangement, and dispossession. What struck Marx so forcibly when he began reading the works of liberal political economy was that no distinction was drawn between the buying and selling of ordinary commodities and the buying and selling of labour power. For Marx labour power was not just another commodity like any other useful article or service — it was the life activity of each individual. 'As men express their life,' he wrote, 'so they are.' To alienate labour power as a commodity in return for wages was to place individuals under the control of a social power — capital — that would then subject them to its will and purposes. An alien and alienating world would arise on the basis of the productive activity of free men. Individuals would find themselves alienated from the product of their labour and from the activity of labouring itself, and therefore from the possibility of a true communal life.

The buying and selling of labour power Marx therefore analysed both as proceeding in accord with liberal ideals of market freedom and market equality, and as creating the basis for a new class society by subjecting workers engaged in production to the dictates of a social power which, although arising out of their actions, is not subject to their control, but on the contrary controls them. The market is the indispensable means by which the power of capital over the production process — the collective life activity of society — is achieved and maintained. Marx emphasises, however, again and again, that the real class struggle takes place not in the market place but in the sphere of production. Prices in the market are set by the forces of demand and supply. The worker comes to sell his labour power for wages. He receives what is due to him. He is not cheated in the wage bargain. Capitalism would be a very insecure mode of production if it had to rest upon a constant repetition of bargains that were unjust and one-sided in practice, although required to be equal and fair in law. The real struggle takes place in production itself. The workers have contracted to sell their labour power. But they have in principle only agreed to sell it to produce enough value to cover the wages that have been advanced. The interest of the worker is to work only for as long and only as hard as is necessary to replace to the capitalist the wages he has paid out. The capitalists naturally view it rather differently. If all they are to receive back is the wages they have paid out, they would have no incentive to advance their capital at all. Their interest is to ensure that the workers, during the time that they have sold their labour services to capital, produce more commodities than are needed to cover the wages advanced. In this way the working day is divided into two — a period of necessary labour when the workers replace the value of their wages, and a period of surplus labour when the workers create a *surplus value*. If this can be realised by selling the commodities that have been produced, it will give the capitalists a profit that will increase their total capital, and cause it to accumulate.

This fundamental conflict of interest, Marx argues, is continually reproduced in the capitalist mode of production. Each class stands on its rights. The workers claim the right not to produce more than is necessary to make good the value of their wages. The capitalists claim the right to full control and maximum use of the commodity, labour power, which they have freely bought on the market. As Marx puts it, 'Between equal rights, force decides'. A long and bitter struggle ensues over how long the working day must be and how intensely the workers can be forced to work during it.

For Marx the source of class conflict in a capitalist society is not primarily over the distribution of the economic surplus through the market, but over how that surplus is produced. His argument is that the labour process is a collective enter-

prise, comprising the life activity of all the individual members
of the society. A class organisation of the labour process
means not only that there is an unjust distribution of resources,
but also that individuals are prevented from controlling their
own lives and their own labour. Human individuality and
creativity and autonomy are all sacrificed to serve the needs
of production in the interests of capital.

It is in this way that Marx makes the concept of class so
basic to his concept of socialism. Equal relations in the
market place are not enough to establish a socialist society.
Only when the unequal relations of power in the production
process are transformed can the basis for a free and democratic society be created. The motives and beliefs of individual
capitalists and workers are secondary in Marx's account.
What is primary are the social relationships of production
which once established rule the actions of all. If philanthropy
is pushed too far by one individual capitalist he will cease to
be a capitalist. The pressures of market competition will see
to that. Marx's theory is therefore not about good or bad
men but about good or bad social arrangements. Individuals
are agents or bearers of social relationships which as individuals they cannot alter.

Marx attempted to show that capitalism was the latest in a
series of class societies, but also that it differed from previous
ones in several important respects. It possessed an inner
compulsion to expand production; the state appeared separate
from the economy; and its legitimacy derived from market
arrangements that enshrined the universalist principles of the
rights of man. Most important of all its development facili-
tated the growth of a 'class-in-itself' which Marx believed
could become through political organisation an active force
aware of its common interests. Such a class, a 'class-for-itself',
could transform the social relations of production and
establish the first free and classless society on a basis of a
level of production of use values which, whilst it would not
abolish scarcity, would greatly reduce its dominance over
social and economic organisation.

7 Accumulation

From his analysis of the class relationships of the production
process under capitalism, Marx identified the force that

propels capitalism forward, making its material progress unique in human history. It is because the agents of capital if they are to remain capitalists must constantly strive to preserve and extend the individual capital they control, that unleashes an unrelenting search for the methods that will best achieve it. In no other mode of production do such constant pressures for economic rationality exist. It meant that in its initial phases, when it was becoming established, capital fought ceaselessly for the extension of the working day and for full control over the labour services of its workers during it, and bitterly resisted modest proposals in the England of the 1830s to restrict the hours for certain groups of workers, including children. Marx commented that in its search for new reserves of surplus labour capital tended to push the working day towards the physical limit of the natural day:

> Capital is dead labour which, vampire-like, lives only by sucking living labour, and lives the more the more labour it sucks. The time during which the worker works is the time during which the capitalist consumes the labour power he has bought from him. If the worker consumes his disposable time he robs the capitalist.

Such a process had definite limits, however. In order for their labour services to be available the next day, workers had to sleep. Similarly the speed and intensity at which workers could be made to work had eventual physical limits. In addition, there was the resistance of workers to their exploitation. During the long development of capitalist relations of production a key question was the formation and training of a labour force adequate to the needs of capital accumulation. The same problem has existed wherever capitalist social relations have developed. The eighteenth century is strewn with pamphlets and books complaining about the idleness of the poor, and their reluctance to work, and drawing up schemes for ensuring that all those unemployed would be forced to seek work, only paupers receiving public welfare. One such scheme envisaged that paupers would be confined to a 'house of terror', where a strict regime of labour would be enforced so as to discourage any other able-bodied individuals from seeking public support. Marx noted that the working day proposed for these houses of terror was actually less than that which ruled in the 'houses of terror' of European industry in the first half of the nineteenth century — the new factories.

If capitalists had been confined to increasing the working day in order to get their hands on more surplus labour, capitalism as an economic system would not have developed social wealth beyond a certain point, however efficient its houses of terror were for extracting the maximum surplus labour out of its work force. What transformed the picture, however, was the development of an additional means of increasing surplus labour — raising the rate of exploitation not by increasing the length of the working day, but by decreasing that part of the working day for which the worker worked in effect for himself when he was replacing the value of his wages. The value of these wages was fixed by the amount of food and clothing and other goods necessary to keep the worker alive and reproduce his labour power. But the time spent producing these could be reduced if the productivity of workers could be increased, so that they produced more in the same hours of work. This could be done by giving them better machines to work with and constantly subdividing the production tasks in the factory. In this way technological discoveries could be systematically harnessed to aid capital in its insatiable thirst for more surplus labour. The enthronement of rationalism at the centre of the capitalist mode of production creates one of the crucial driving forces of the modern world.

Where workers have organised successfully into trade unions, or where they are scarce, this method of raising productivity has predominated over the method of increasing surplus labour by extending the working day. Under such a system the focus of class struggle shifts to the operation of the machinery itself and the consequences its introduction has for the work force. Marx argued that it established a process of accumulation whose tendency has been gradually to expel living labour from the production process altogether, replacing workers by machines, the product of living labour in previous production cycles. This is not a smooth process but develops through a series of cycles which begin with a period of boom in which labour is eagerly sought and all available labour is engaged, leading eventually to a rise in wages and other costs, a saturation of investment opportunities, increasing competition and a sudden collapse of profits. The result is a slump, widespread bankruptcies, a steep rise in unemployment, and a fall in prices, including the price of labour, wages. Such slumps allowed capital to be reorganised, as well as rebuilding what Marx called 'the industrial reserve army of labour' (which often amounted to one-quarter of the work force in the slumps in the European economies in the nineteenth century). This was the pool of unemployed which would be available for re-engagement once capital accumulation started again.

Marx predicted that over a run of ten-year cycles the industrial reserve army would tend to rise. But he also argued that in any case the raising of productivity through improved technology and more specialised division of labour did not guarantee capitalism a limitless future of expansion. The process did have limits, but they were limits that would only be fully encountered when the capitalist mode of production had established itself throughout the whole world and raised levels of production to unimaginable levels. The reason for these limits lay in what Marx termed the tendency of the rate of profit to fall, a concept which expressed theoretically the precariousness of profitability in capitalism as an economic system, as it reproduced itself on an every expanding scale and progressed to ever higher levels of accumulation. He predicted that although in absolute amount profits must increase, in relative terms they would tend to decline. Strenuous efforts would be made to offset this decline, including continual search for new technological innovations in labour-saving devices, and the extension of capitalist production to hitherto untouched parts of the world where labour forces were plentiful and weak. But ultimately the same exhaustion of investment opportunities that were sufficiently profitable, the same increased burden of maintaining vast concentrations of capital in fixed plant would recur to threaten profits, but this time on a much greater scale. In their quest for ways to avoid declining profitability, the agents of capital would have created an interdependent world economy, raised social wealth far above all previous historical levels, concentrated and centralised capital in a few hands, and transformed a labour process based on individual production and exchange into a socialised process based on vast collective enterprises.

Marx believed that this capitalist system and the state which protected and maintained it were heading for increasingly severe crises as a result of the laws of its own development. Capitalists could not avoid employing fewer and fewer workers producing more and more, or concentrating production in larger and larger units, or introducing every innovation that offered a cut in costs, or expanding wherever costs were lower. The end result was a system whose continued profitability was no longer secure and whose social basis was more and more precarious because of the growing organisation of the proletariat, but which had made possible a future classless society which would enjoy for the first time mastery over nature rather than subordination to it.

Marx's insights into the objective trends of capitalist development were unrivalled; his political ideas (discussed in chapter 7) did not receive such systematic treatment. What he emphasised, however, was that the universal revolution proclaimed by liberalism had turned out to be a revolution in the interests of the bourgeoisie, and the inauguration of a new system of class rule. Socialism, therefore, could only be based on a society that abolished classes. It required a social, not just a political, revolution. That meant ending the subordination of one class to another in the system of production itself. This could not be accomplished from above, but had to be the result of the collective action of the working class itself because only then would its democratic character be assured. Marx saw clearly that only the abolition of the wages system would finally end the rule of capital, but he did not imagine that wages, commodity production, and the division of labour, particularly that which had arisen between intellectual and manual labour, could be suddenly abolished on the morrow of the revolution. What he envisaged was a period of transition, which he called socialism, and which would follow the conquest of political power by the working class and would realise much of the programme of the early socialists. The aim of the workers' state would be to ensure that exchanges were equal and that every citizen enjoyed equal rights. This entailed, as Marx acknowledged, that rewards would be unequal: 'Equal right is still here . . . a bourgeois right . . . an unequal right for unequal labour. This right is thus in its content one of inequality, just like any other right.'

Only in a communist society would different principles of social organisation emerge, which Marx summarised by adopting the traditional socialist slogan, 'from each according to his ability, to each according to his needs'. Marx did not discuss in any detail the incentives to work in such a society, or how its economy might be co-ordinated, or how needs would be measured, but his hopes for a free society in the future clearly rested upon his expectation that the amount of labour necessary to maintain human societies in existence, the amount of *compulsory* labour, had been greatly reduced by capitalism and would be still more reduced under socialism. This realm of necessity would never be completely abolished, but by reducing it to a minimum a society of freedom based on free time for all its members to develop their interests and their talents, could come into existence. As he wrote in the 1850s:

> On the basis of communal production, the determination of time remains . . . essential. The less time the society requires to produce wheat . . . the more time it wins for other production, material or mental. Just as in the case of an individual, the multiplicity of its development, its enjoyment and its activity depends on economization of time. Economy of time, to this all economy ultimately reduces itself.

5

Politics and industrial society I: the national question

1 Introduction

The French Revolution marked a decisive moment in the history of modern Western thought, the point at which the Western ideology was first enunciated in its full scope. Yet the society it foresaw and which it proclaimed was almost nowhere in existence. The industrial bourgeoisie was remarkable for its absence, agriculture and agricultural communities dominated economic life, and absolute monarchies controlled most of Europe. The most 'progressive' and 'liberal' government in Europe before 1789 was that of Great Britain, still ruled by the landed interest. In these circumstances it is hardly surprising that the political experiments of the revolutionaries in Paris should have unleashed a Reaction of great virulence.

The forces arraigned behind the Reaction – Crown, Church, and Land – seemed more than sufficient to ensure its triumph against the fragile new doctrines of the Enlightenment and the Revolution. Yet from the start the conservative forces saw themselves on the defensive, a perception that proved one of their more accurate judgements. The new doctrines were securely anchored in the great social and political transformation that had begun throughout Europe. The French Revolution alerted ruling classes everywhere to the danger; but it was already too late. The separation between state and society already accomplished paved the way for the rise of capitalist industry, the triumph of popular sovereignty, and the inexorable spread of scientific rationalism. Although the supremacy of industrialism, however confidently proclaimed by Saint-Simon or Marx, looked distinctly improbable in 1800 and even in 1850, many of the wildest speculations of its early prophets and analysts have been fulfilled beyond even their expectations. Liberalism and socialism have triumphed. The agricultural economy and the absolutist states have vanished; a new society and a new politics have emerged, and new ways of understanding them. As Alexis de Tocqueville wrote, 'A new science is necessary to a new world.'

A new world. It arrived much more slowly than its advocates wanted and its opponents feared. It is only in the twentieth century that industrialism has become dominant in many areas of the globe. In the process first Western civilisation and then all other civilisations have been dismembered and radically transformed. In every country this process has produced a great resistance, but nowhere has the resistance been entirely sufficient to prevent the transformation taking place.

In the course of building modern states and industrial societies liberalism and socialism have undergone substantial modification. What originated as creeds of revolt against authority, inequality and injustice, have become the officially approved ideologies of established regimes. In their origins they were crusading doctrines rooted in the new philosophy, the new economic relationships of civil society, and new images of political association. They shared common assumptions about the power and legitimacy of reason, and the desirability of economic progress, and the possibility of transforming human societies and human beings for the better. They were universalist and internationalist in the sense that their principles were cast in a form which applied not just to this group or that group, this nation or that nation, but to all individuals everywhere. They were doctrines of universal humanity.

Their eventual triumph, however, was not quite as it had been imagined. Industrialism triumphed, but not in a form which many of the early devotees of industrial progress would have welcomed. Popular sovereignty triumphed, but in a manner which raised new divisions instead of leading to universal peace and brotherhood. Science triumphed, but amidst growing fears about the consequences of its methods and its practical applications for the very survival of the species. The optimism of the Western ideology has steadily been overlaid by a new pessimism and disenchantment about the world which it proclaimed and which it helped to bring into being, and this has occurred the more that industrialism has developed and its character has been understood. The unity between the moral concerns and objectives of the Western ideology and its commitment to rationalism has weakened.

This is the way in which the European Reaction, sometimes called the anti-Enlightenment, has had its revenge. As industrialism has progressed, so the confidence and coherence of both liberalism and socialism as moral doctrines have waned. Both have been assailed by increasing doubts as to the validity and worth of their assumptions and central beliefs. Industrial societies have turned out to be far more complex than was imagined, and the Western ideology often far too shallow to cope with the new context and new problems that have arisen. The easy passage to a world of peace and plenty which the Western ideologists expected, has been savagely belied and mocked by the greatest wars and atrocities in the history of the race, and by the appearance of unimagined contrasts between wealth and poverty in different parts of the world. The Western revolution has created a world economy and a world politics but it has also caused world problems to multiply. Just as Pandora in the Greek myth injudiciously opened the box which allowed all the ills that plague the world to escape, so Europe, by opening the sealed box of rationalism, has unleashed forces which few see any prospect of controlling. Rather they now control mankind. For many Western thinkers in the twentieth century even hope, the one blessing which still remained in Pandora's box, has fled.

2 Nationalism

It is in this setting that we must examine nationalism — one of the central features of the politics of industrial societies and one of the crucial moulders of modern Western social and political thought. The idea that human communities form a nation, that the nation is a suitable and in some accounts the only focus for political loyalty and collective life, is an idea that, whilst not originating in the French Revolution, was enormously amplified by it, and became a major force in all subsequent politics. In the Declaration of the Rights of Man it was stated that sovereignty rested upon the nation. Tying popular sovereignty to the nation fused nationalism and democracy in an apparently irresistible combination. The new political association founded on the will of the people soon developed in every country its distinctive symbols, its flags, its music, and its history. It created bonds of common feeling and common loyalty which could unite the great scattered mass of citizens in the service of a common cause — the nation, their own nation, the embodiment of the new revolutionary principles of liberty, equality, and fraternity.

In declaring this principle the leaders of the French Revolution were doing no more than pointing to a central feature of the kind of state that had been emerging. If the state was to become 'the official expression of civil society' and the guarantor of order and security in civil society, its claim to obedience and authority had to be based upon the relationship between government and the whole people. Applying this principle to existing states with definite territorial boundaries meant that the bounds of the association became the bounds of the nation, and the state a nation-state.

States had pursued 'national' interests before and invoked national feeling and fought national wars. What was novel about the rallying of the French nation around its new republic was the attempt to create a perpetual mobilisation of energies and loyalties, a total commitment to the cause of the nation-state and its success. The dynamism inherent in the modern state, its capacity to demand and to enlist unstinting popular effort and sacrifice, was first demonstrated by the revolutionary armies that repulsed the attack of the armies of absolutist Europe and then overran vast areas of the continent. Goethe watching the Prussian defeat at Valmy in 1793, a victory which preserved the republic and prevented an early royalist restoration in France, declared, 'Here and on this day begins a new chapter in the history of the world'. What struck him and other observers was how an armed people despite the turmoil and confusion of the internal upheaval in France, was still able to overcome the great professional armies of Europe. The tremendous increase in power and collective organisation which nationalism could bring a state or a political movement was displayed.

The ideal of the armed people in revolt against injustice and arbitrary power was the early liberal image of nationalism, and as such passed into socialism. The idea developed that every nation had the right of self-determination. Such a doctrine pointed at the heart of the great absolutist empires — Austria and Russia in particular — which contained so many separate nationalities. It ran right against the traditional doctrine of Western statecraft and diplomacy, which recognised only the existing boundaries of states. These had come about through a multitude of chance events, and were held to correspond to the evolution of common interests and institutions within a particular area. The reorganisation of states along national lines, so that every community which could claim to be a nation because it possessed its own language, its own traditions and culture and so a consciousness of its separate identity, could claim the right to self-determination, the right to form its own political association, its own state — such an idea was anathema. The statesmen of the great empires, the *multinational* states, recoiled particularly sharply.

Ever since the French Revolution nationalism and the idea of self-determination have been important principles in the Western ideology and have caused generations of liberals and socialists to sympathise with and encourage movements of national liberation and national unification. The overthrowing of traditional structures of authority, the building of a new order, a conscious and confident people establishing a new nation in which the ideals of the Enlightenment could be realised and the full energies of the people unleashed — such sentiments echoed through all the great national struggles of the modern era. All doctrines within the Western ideology have been united in emphasising the importance of carrying through the democratic revolution in every national social formation.

Nationalism has another side, however. It not only became an expression of some of the deepest convictions of the revolutionaries. The form of the modern state and the character of civil society and modern industry allowed other possibilities. It was to become one of the major vehicles for the Reaction, since nations could be mobilised around

different features of national life. Instead of nationalism
being a celebration of Liberty, Equality, and Fraternity, it
could also celebrate Monarch, Church, and Land. There was
no reason why nationalism and the bourgeois democratic
revolution should be confined to those features of national
life which revolutionaries thought progressive, or why the
nation should be defined so as to exclude the privileged
orders of the absolutist state, the aristocrats and the clerics.

The history of the European Reaction was therefore not
just a moment in the history of ideas, but was linked to the
counter-mobilisation by the traditional forces in Europe, the
defenders of the old order against all the trends and challenges
that were represented most forcibly by the French Revolution. Nationalism became a set of ideas for justifying all the
nation-states of the modern world and could be used to enlist
the support and commitment of citizens behind the most
oppressive as well as the most progressive regimes. The
character and institutions of the modern state, it was discovered, did not have to express either liberal or socialist
values, but could be organised against them. This became one
basis for parties of the Right in the modern era.

Liberal and socialist hopes for a harmonious international
order developing spontaneously out of a world of 'new'
nations were gradually disappointed. One idea put forward
by a line of liberals from Kant through Cobden to Joseph
Schumpeter was that wars and national divisions were created
and maintained because traditional states were often ruled by
a militaristic landowning class, bent on extending its territory
and enhancing its prestige. The growth of markets, it was felt,
placed societies on an entirely new economic foundation.
Instead of struggles over a limited resource — land — there
was the prospect of unlimited progress of material production. Trade would create relations of mutual dependence
which would foster understanding and reduce tension. No
one would go to war if they stood to lose much economically.
Wars and empires where they occurred in the modern world
were blamed on the continuing power of the old ruling
classes.

Socialists shared the liberal belief that the mobilisation of
nations was aimed chiefly at destroying the old world and
building the foundations for the new, and that in the new

world national divisions would speedily crumble because national republics would lay the basis for international co-operation. The creation of a world economy and world interdependence by capitalism would establish the material conditions for world socialism. The class allegiance and common interests of the workers across national frontiers were expected to prove more powerful than national allegiance and national interests.

Both theories have had to recognise, particularly since 1914, the persistence of war and the intensification of national divisions. In that year a major European war of unparallelled ferocity and destruction broke out between the most advanced European states; states who received the enthusiastic support of their labour and socialist movements and their mass electorates. Their actions destroyed the Second International — an alliance of socialist parties, one of whose main purposes had been to prevent armed conflict from occurring between the imperialist powers because it would be workers from all nations who would be the chief victims, the cannon fodder of the dispute between the ruling classes of different nations.

Both theories had to come to terms as well with a world economy and world political system which were marked by persistent, not merely temporary, imbalances in wealth and power. Not only was this preventing the creation of an equal material basis upon which a harmonious world order could be established, but was actively shoring up instead the national aggression and national ambitions of the most powerful nation-states in the world system. This problem was dealt with by socialists in their theory of imperialism. The theory marked the abandonment of the optimistic expectation that the growth of the world economy would automatically create the basis for socialism; and it often carried with it pessimistic conclusions about the likelihood of revolution occurring in the West, because of the way in which the pattern of domination and dependence between nations that had been established gave a privileged position to the working class in the metropolitan countries. It was held to blunt the will to revolution and provide a basis for class collaboration.

3 The anti-Enlightenment

By the end of the nineteenth century, the two leading European imperialist states, Bismarck's Germany and Victorian Britain, had both in different ways successfully mobilised popular support behind their institutions and policies, and were on the brink of a total all-out war for mastery of the world. Such an outcome was hardly foreseen by the thinkers who spearheaded the intellectual revolt against the Enlightenment and the doctrines of the French Revolution. Most of these, men like Edmund Burke in England, Joseph de Maistre and Louis Bonald in France, and Savigny in Germany, were much more concerned with justifying and re-establishing the political and social arrangements of the old order in Europe, than with evolving new principles for turning the nation-state against its creators. Yet this is what they achieved, by contributing to a line of thought that emphasised that nation and society took priority over the individual, and that radiated tremendous hostility to all the dominant ideas and values of the Revolution. This revolt against reason, which has inspired a wide range of political movements and doctrines, including many kinds of conservatism and fascism, first took shape as a defence of the old order in Europe.

It is important to remember, however, how much shadow boxing was involved in these early encounters. Europe in 1815 was hardly a continent that basked in the warm sun of liberty and rationalism. Industrialisation had barely begun and the activities of scientists were little noticed. The cake of custom was still set hard. What the writers of the Reaction attacked were the doctrines of the Enlightenment which had so recently been the occasion for the momentous and terrifying experiment in Paris. Not just the doctrines of the revolutionaries were assailed, but the whole individualist and rationalist tradition stretching back through the eighteenth-century Enlightenment to seventeenth-century thinkers such as Locke and Hobbes, Leibniz and Descartes. This great intellectual tradition, which had dominated European thought for so long, had suffered numerous brushes with established political and religious authority. But until the French Revolution it was not understood what a total transformation it heralded, what a complete undermining of institutions and beliefs it threatened. Confined to a few groups of intellectuals easily contained within traditional structures of authority, and resting on the slow unchanging material basis of agricultural production, the practical implications of the new doctrines were little grasped.

The European Reaction developed as a direct response to the practical challenge of the French Revolution. The doctrines that came under most attack were the doctrines of individualism and natural law. One of the most effective weapons of the liberals had been the concept of the sovereign individual, existing in a state of nature, free of social ties and obligations. The 'natural' needs and interests of individuals were made the criteria for judging whether social arrangements were just or useful or likely to promote security or happiness. The idea that rights and law and human nature could be derived not from an existing set of social practices and relationships, but from an intellectual analysis which abstracted from these and announced that the natural individual and natural rights and natural law were more real than what existed, this was the prime target for attack. For the Reaction, society always preceded the individual. The individual was unintelligible except in the context of the social institutions and groups to which he belonged. Societies were not made up of individuals but of families. Members of these families were related in a complex network of relationships in a variety of associations. There was a hierarchy of authority within each family and each association, as well as a hierarchy of families, at the top of which stood the institutions and offices of the state, and at the summit, the monarchy. The conservatives denied fiercely that the state was a political association in which there was a direct relationship between the government and the mass of individual citizens. The view of Hobbes and Rousseau that the claims of all intermediate associations between the state and the individual should be swept away in so far as they produced divided loyalty was denounced as tyrannical. The idea of absolute sovereignty to which such notions of political obligation led, was bitterly attacked because it meant subordinating the authority of the family and the authority of the Church to the authority of the state. In a well-ordered society the spheres of each group and association should dovetail — a hierarchy of authorities, but one in which each higher authority respected the sphere and autonomy of the lower.

Such notions, which revived important elements of medieval political thought, reflected a *pluralist* rather than a *unitary* conception of politics. Society was composed of a large number of overlapping groups; no claims to authority and loyalty were absolute except in their own sphere, and even there rested not on rational principles but on inherited customs. What was prescribed by past practice was what was right, not what was prescribed by individual reason. This doctrine justified resistance to change undertaken on rationalist principles, and celebrated traditional practices and institutions. It encouraged opposition to attempts to centralise as well as to democratise political power, where such attempts, as in the French Revolution, involved attacks on important social institutions such as the family and the Church.

What the writers of the Reaction disliked most about the Revolution was the series of decrees aimed at emancipating the individual from the social controls and authority of fathers and priests. The laws abolishing primogeniture (the rule which laid down that the whole estate of an individual should pass to his first-born son), and entail (the rule making an inheritance inalienable, so forcing it to be handed on in a manner already determined), and legalising divorce, were seen as threatening the foundation of family life. Families were not associations which individuals had any right to leave, and family property was not the right of any individual to dispose of because it had to be preserved intact and handed on to future generations. The patriarchal family was organised around the authority of the head of the household and required a strict division of labour between the sexes, and the subordination of women and children. Such extended families, which often included apprentices and servants as well as other relatives, were in many respects self-sufficient communities because they supplied the needs of their members over a wide range, including subsistence, health, and education. Any moves that undermined the family undermined the foundation of social order.

Similarly with the Church. The assaults on Church property and power during the Revolution were regarded as blasphemous. The aim of the revolutionaries was to create a secular state in which no religious association would have any privileged status. Church law would be subordinate to civil law. The state would be sovereign and the Church could claim no higher authority — it could not act as a supreme court in judgement on the actions of the civil power. This idea that the state had the right to overrule the Church on questions of religious doctrine and social morality, and to intervene if necessary in the internal management of the Church, was fundamental to the idea of the modern state. Its opponents, in their hostility to the doctrine of popular sovereignty, came close to asserting that the Church should have an authority greater than the state, so that if the state pronounced divorce legal, the Church could pronounce it illegal. At the very least the right of the Church to determine questions of social morality was claimed, as well as the obligation of governments to respect its decisions. The idea that a secular state, claiming to represent the people, could thereby claim sovereignty over such institutions as marriage was completely rejected.

Many of the writers of the Reaction, particularly in France, were Roman Catholics who found in the French Revolution a new reason to hate Protestantism. The Revolution was regarded as the realisation of the principles of Protestantism in the social sphere. By emphasising the sovereignty of the individual conscience in matters of faith and morals, Luther and Calvin, it was argued, had undermined the unquestioned authority of the Church hierarchy to decide such matters and had opened the way for authority to be challenged in other spheres as well. Behind such notions lay the doctrine of original sin, the idea of a basic and ineradicable evil in human nature which could only be restrained by social institutions like the Church and the family keeping individual drives and desires in check. Once free the individual from tight control over his appetites and his intellect, disorder and destruction would follow, because unchecked egoism, unbridled arrogance, and unrestrained licence would flourish. In this sense the Revolution was regarded merely as the culmination of the process that the Reformation had started two centuries previously. The Counter-Reformation and the Counter-Revolution marched hand in hand. What had begun as an internal doctrinal dispute within the Christian religion had widened into a struggle between the traditional order and the modern secular liberal state.

The French Revolution was the crucial event in the formation and development of modern conservatism because it concentrated the minds of the defenders of the old order in a way that nothing else had done. It alerted them to the danger and it created quite new divisions in political opinion. Edmund Burke who was a Whig, an advocate of liberty and a defender of the claims of the American colonists, became the first major European thinker to denounce the Revolution, and the categories he developed intuitively to defend the established order in England against the attack of the English radicals and those who wanted to reform the constitution, greatly influenced subsequent conservative thought throughout Europe. He emphasised the prior claims of society over the individual. Societies evolved, they were not created or decreed; they were partnerships between the generations; the living, the dead, and those that were still unborn. Violent sweeping change was out of place; only gradual piecemeal change was tolerable. Historical tradition and historical precedent were far more important guides than natural rights because human societies were extremely complex organisms which had evolved over a great span of time. To tamper radically with any existing institution was to engage in something the consequences of which could not be foreseen. Human reason was necessarily a frail, imperfect instrument, which could produce only limited understanding, and since society and nature were still shrouded in mystery, and would always remain so, the utmost caution had to be employed in altering anything, lest something irretrievable should be lost. Like de Maistre in France, Burke thought unreflecting prejudice and dogma a better guide in politics than abstract reason, because the former embodied practical, traditional wisdom.

What alarmed Burke about the French Revolution was not so much that the French revolutionaries wanted to establish liberty, he was a believer in liberty himself, but the way in which they were proposing to go about it. Instead of seeking precedents from the past for the changes they wished to make in French institutions, particularly the placing of limitations upon royal power, the revolutionaries looked only to the future. They wished to wipe the slate clean and make a new beginning, framing their constitution upon the inherent rights of man. Burke argued that such a man and such rights had nowhere existed. All that had existed were different communities, each with their own history, customs, and traditions. To tear up the past and trust to reason could only bring disorder and disaster.

In the course of his rambling polemic Burke rejected universal principles fashioned from natural law, logic, mathematics or any form of general reasoning as a basis for political doctrine. Such principles violated the historical uniqueness of each national community. National traditions and national circumstances were more important and more powerful than universal principles. This notion was an insight into the nature of the state system in Western Europe which was to form the basis for the conservative resistance to liberalism. Since the transition to modern industrialism was nowhere so fast or complete as the liberals and socialists confidently prophesied, and is not even complete today, there existed a great accumulation of traditional institutions, relationships, and beliefs which could provide the basis for political movements opposed to modernisation along liberal lines. The patriarchal family, the Church, the landed aristocracy, the ancient universities, the monarchies, the military organisations, were all bastions which could be held against the tide.

The Reaction did not stop the Revolution, or the creation of the modern world. It was contending not merely with some misguided and pernicious moral doctrines, but with the process of rationalisation itself, the whole complex of changes in political, economic, and ideological relationships that had struck such deep roots. Burke defended the unreformed English constitution and the powers and privileges of the landed interest, but these were being undermined far more swiftly by the explosive development of industry than by the activities of the constitutional clubs and the English Jacobins. On this question the spokesmen for the Reaction were divided. Burke himself was an economic liberal, fully accepting Adam Smith's precepts about free exchange, and could not see in that principle a far greater challenge looming to the national institutions he cherished than in alien 'French' doctrines of the rights of man. The laws of commerce, he once wrote, are the laws of God. If economic laws pushed wages below subsistence this had to be accepted.

The real change the Reaction brought was not in halting the Revolution, but in significantly altering the direction it took and the content it possessed. Eventually all states were forced to modernise; none was able to seal itself off from modern science and technology, modern industry and modern politics. But the manner in which modernisation was undertaken differed widely. The liberals assumed that modernisation required the overthrow of the traditional order and the construction of new states and new nations. It became more and more the case, however, that old states and old nations began to modernise, without undergoing a political and social revolution first. Revolutions from above in the hands of the landowning and military elites in states like Germany and Japan meant that these states became equipped with modern industry and technology which were used to reinforce rather than overturn parts of their traditional social and political structure. Capitalism and modern technology proved compatible with a wide variety of regimes.

The mobilisation of old nations for modernisation under the sacred banners of Crown, Church, Land, and Family, involved stressing what divided nations rather than what united them. Since each nation was a living organic community with its own unique path of evolution and its own unique historical customs and traditions, it followed that the divisions between nations were absolutely fundamental and could not be wished or willed away. Every nation had its own destiny, its own life, its own culture, and required its own living space.

What the conservatives discovered was that nations were forced to modernise because to avoid modern industry was to condemn the nation to inferior status. But they also found that such mobilisation as was required in order to achieve modernisation could draw on the energies and emotions latent in the traditional society to create a powerful nationalism that was both ideologically opposed to the liberal ideology whilst embracing the fruits of industrialisation. In such a manner conservative defences of the old order helped in the creation of national cultures that promoted the growth of the nationalist and imperialist mass movements of the modern era. The Right was unable to prevent modernisation but it succeeded in making Nation and the symbols and institutions of nationhood one of the great organising principles of mass politics in the modern state.

The success of the Right was assisted by a notable feature of the modern state as it has evolved. Nowhere did it have the character envisaged by some of the early radical democrats, the direct democracy of the assembled citizens, the re-creation of the ancient Greek polis. The size of modern nations and existing states meant the continuance and steady expansion of the specialised agencies — military, bureaucracy, judiciary — which had come to characterise the state. The relationship of these permanent agencies to popular sovereignty was through the formal system of representation laid down in liberal constitutions — the accountability of legislatures to voters through regular free elections, and the accountability of executives to legislatures or to the courts. The agencies themselves were held to be the servants of the legislatures but given their permanent role and their accumulation of expertise, they naturally developed their own view of the national interest which might or might not agree with the view of the national interest expressed through representative assemblies, free elections, and other ways of ascertaining the popular will.

These agencies naturally exerted a strong pull over the Right who saw them as the guardians of the nation's continuity, charged with defending its interests, maintaining its security and executing its will. This has meant that even where liberal constitutionalism has triumphed, the state apparatus has normally been identified with and staffed by groups identified with the political Right in every national social formation. Where the mass parties of the Right have not succeeded in winning control of the legislature this has sometimes meant a major clash between the elected government and one or more of the permanent agencies of the state.

The attack on individualism in the political and social sphere also involved a strong attack on economic individualism, particularly in some continental states. The defenders of the old order were frequently opposed to industrial capitalism because it appeared to give free rein to human selfishness, destroyed traditional communities, and produced extremes of wealth and poverty. Liberal political economy in promoting economic freedom prescribed only rights but not duties. Individuals might amass great wealth but they had no social responsibility, only an individual moral responsibility, to use it wisely or for the benefit of the whole community. All the individual was enjoined to do was to consult his own interest, to reckon up the balance of costs and advantages, and then to choose the best course of action for him, without troubling about the wider consequences for society. The theory assured him that the wider consequences were in any case already taken care of and would be beneficial.

The whole of conservative social thought rebelled against the notion of treating human relationships and roles in cost benefit terms that considered only individuals — their needs and their interests. For to do so meant that the great array of traditional institutions and customs would be found lacking since they involved many precious things such as love, honour, duty, faith, which could not be quantified and which would be excluded from the reckoning. There were fundamental ideological objections to the kind of unbridled economic individualism preached in England and practised in America. Nevertheless the fruits of the system of free exchange and modern industry could not be ignored. What developed in some countries, particularly in Germany, in opposition to liberal political economy was a system of national political economy which challenged the dogma of free trade, the heart of the policy of the leading industrial and commercial power, Britain. National political economy did not challenge the basis of modern capitalism, large-scale industry; it argued instead that it would be better to conceive economic 'individuals' not as actual individual companies and producers but as entire nations. It proposed a revival of mercantilist measures — protectionism, war, self-sufficiency — as the basis for national economic policy. Such policies were taken up by nationalist and imperialist mass movements and became a further means for attempting to consolidate the influence of conservative regimes over their subjects. Free trade was regarded by national political economists such as Friedrich List as merely the veil behind which the British state ruthlessly pursued its own national interests and exploited its particular advantages — the great productivity of its industries and their consequent dominance of world trade.

The liberal vision of a world economy which, in becoming more and more interdependent and crisscrossed by a multitude of individual exchanges and contacts across national frontiers, caused nation-states to become increasingly irrelevant, disappeared amidst a host of new nations and new empires, aggressively pursuing national advantage and fighting for control of territory, resources, and markets.

Alongside economics and politics the Right was also deeply disturbed about the effects of rationalism on traditional culture. The wholesale rejection of the past recommended by liberal doctrines, and the transformation of the kind of society which had given rise to Western culture in the first place, produced fears that the culture was being destroyed at its roots. This point of view was expressed by a long line of traditional intellectuals in the nineteenth century, among them Jacob Burckhardt, the Swiss historian, and the English poet and critic, S. T. Coleridge. The new rationalist doctrines, particularly utilitarianism and political economy, seemed extremely narrow and philistine because they turned all social activities and relationships into means rather than ends, and subordinated them to the 'cash nexus' – the power of money and the requirements of exchange. All distinctions tended to become quantitative rather than qualitative; if something could not be measured it was presumed worthless. In this manner ruthless egoism and short-run profit maximisation, and their counterpart, efficient administration, appeared to be destroying a great part of what human beings in the past had valued.

4 Gemeinschaft

The tension between the modern industrial society whose rationalist principles were busy invading every corner of social life, and the old landed community, the guardian of national culture and traditional values, impressed itself powerfully on many who observed it in their own lives, and it formed the basis for some of the enduring images and contrasts of nineteenth-century sociology. The most celebrated of all was the distinction between *Gemeinschaft* and *Gesellschaft* in the work of Ferdinand Tönnies, but the same basic contrast can be found in Durkheim, Weber, and Simmel. More recent sociologists have recast it as the distinction between folk and urban communities, and between the sacred and the secular. At its most general it is also the distinction between traditional and modern. The purpose of the distinction was to provide a framework for thinking about the momentous social change involved in the transition to modern industrial society. Whilst the process was accepted as irreversible, almost all Western sociological thought concerned with it, even by those who espoused liberal or socialist values, was tinged with nostalgia for the community, the values, and way of life that were disappearing.

The Gemeinschaft was the simple face-to-face community where human organisation and technology were on a small scale, and where social relationships were valued as ends in themselves rather than as means to other ends. The family was naturally the centre of this world and this type of community. The status an individual had depended on the status bestowed on him as a member of a family who had specific roles to play and specific relationships with all other members. This gave the individual tremendous psychological security, since his identity and status were not primarily matters of achievement and competition, but were largely bestowed and predetermined by accidents of birth and sex. The most important relationships individuals had with one another were blood relationships. Such networks of kinship made up traditional communities and the solidarity of these communities was then further reinforced by the ties of living in a particular place and by ties of friendship.

Such a community was based upon relationships that no single individual could alter. Every individual was born into a particular family with a particular history, living in a particular place, and these were the most important things about that individual. The ideal of Gesellschaft was just the opposite. It is the civil society of the political economists, the world of economic individuals each bent on maximising benefits and minimising costs, and holding nothing sacred (including family ties and moral principles) which stand in their way. The Gesellschaft state is peopled by the characters from Balzac's novels, those for whom everything is possible because everything is a matter of rational will, calculation, and ability. Such attitudes flourish best in urban societies because of their success in uprooting the family and traditional religious beliefs, and creating an impersonal, fast-moving, fast-changing society, bound together not by ties of blood or place or friendship, but by self-interest, by contracts, by the division of labour, in short, by the market.

The universal principles of the Gesellschaft state are impersonal because they apply to everybody and give no psychological or emotional security to its members. Every career for instance is to be thrown open to talent, but precisely because this imposes the same starting point on all individuals it ensures tremendous uncertainty and competition between all those individuals because of the constant risk of failure. The much greater dynamism and the explosion of material wealth which such principles encourage also raise permanent questions about the order, the legitimacy, and ultimate destiny of such societies. Such questions were not in doubt for traditional communities. But capitalist states with their populations concentrated in vast urban areas and their industry conducted on an ever larger scale have created a world in which these questions are forever present. The complexity of organisation, the scale of the man-made environment, and the character of technology have transformed these beyond all previous human experience. At the same time all traditional morality and values have been undermined not so much by rationalist beliefs and arguments as by rationalist practices, which have promoted in every individual the aspiration to enjoy a life style centred around ever greater consumption of material things.

The contrast between Gemeinschaft and Gesellschaft has been perhaps the single most influential distinction in modern liberal social thought in the last hundred years, because it reverses the optimistic evaluation of the new civil society by the forerunners of liberal political theory and liberal political economy. It is easy to see how in its exaggerated form such conceptions fed the imaginations of the Right. But the sense of loss was far more widely diffused — it was a strong theme in early socialist and anarchist writing, particularly that of Marx and Proudhon, and amongst many liberal thinkers, including John Stuart Mill. The disruption of traditional communities with their simple and direct relationships to the natural environment and their social solidarity and moral consensus was a deeply fascinating and alarming process. On one side it created the prospect of liberation from toil, from ignorance, and from oppression; on the other it uncovered new potential depths of evil and disintegration. This is why so many of the most convincing conservative responses were actually written by those like Emile Durkheim whose primary allegiance remained to the liberal values.

What has certainly emerged from much of the writing on the transition is a far more complex response than the simple opposition of Gemeinschaft/Gesellschaft allows for. Opposing traditional to modern society or rural to urban community, as though these were quite distinct, overlooks just how far modern civil society and the Gesellschaft state arose out of the traditional community. The ruthlessness of the agricultural landowners towards their own tenants, for instance, often exceeded the ruthlessness of the capitalist manufacturers. The philanthropy of the early nineteenth century landowners like Lord Shaftesbury, and Disraeli's Young England movement, inspired a strong political and ideological campaign against the conditions in the industrial districts. But as Marx commented in *Capital:*

> There is an old English proverb to the effect that when thieves fall out, honest men come into their own, and in fact the noisy and dispassionate dispute between the two factions of the ruling class as to which of them exploited the workers more shamelessly was the midwife of truth on both sides of the question.

He quoted the researches of the liberal newspapers into the wages paid to agricultural labourers on Shaftesbury's estates. Traditional communities in England were radically reshaped and in many cases destroyed by the landowners' application of rational economic criteria to the management of their own property, backed by the legal and physical powers of coercion; the agent of destruction was the dominant group within the traditional community itself. The concern shown by representatives of the landowners for the factory workers in the new cities was rarely shown by them for their own workers.

This may explain why the landed interest adapted surprisingly easily to the rise of industrial society. Peasantries often resisted tenaciously but landowners, the backbone of the old orders of absolutist Europe, acquiesced in the cause of national mobilisation, so long as this was under the auspices of Crown, Church, and Land, and maintained for them a privileged position, particularly in the recruitment of members of the public service. Styles of statesmanship differed but all conservative statesmen were agreed that the essential institutions of the old order must be defended whilst the growth of urban centres and capitalist industry were proceeding.

Despite their implacable hostility to the new rationalist ideology, the conservative supporters of the old order were selective in their opposition. They were more concerned to construct their own idea of nation and give a particular content to national mobilisation than they were to restore traditional community or block industrial capitalism. Even those nationalist movements of the Right which organised on a basis of mass opposition to large-scale capitalism, such as the fascist parties, were forced to rely upon large-scale capital both to achieve power and to pursue their policies of military mobilisation and national expansion. Nazi rhetoric, for example, celebrated all the romantic Gemeinschaft themes of German political culture, the values of blood and soil, the strength and warmth of traditional community. The more radical elements of the Nazi programme advocated the breaking up of the cities and large-scale economic organisations, a return to the simple certainties of agrarian communities. As with all parties of the Right the ideological rhetoric fell far short of practical accomplishment. The new nations the Right summoned into existence were not the old nations of pre-revolutionary Europe but capitalist and industrial. Nations, it was found, could increase their strength and become industrial and capitalist without becoming liberal in other directions and without endangering the privileges of the established elites. It was an important discovery and one which has had a lasting effect on politics in Western states.

6

Politics and industrial society II: the social question

A. National liberalism

1 The rise of modern industry

The creation of legitimate national political institutions became one focus for the politics of industrial societies; the relationship between government and economy was a second. However industrialism was defined and evaluated, one of its characteristics which could not be ignored was the very rapid and continuous enlargement of material wealth, and this made the character and control of the economy and the role of government within it an abiding concern of the politics and the theories of industrial societies.

As industrial capitalism became established more widely, so the categories of liberal political theory came to seem inadequate and the hopes of liberal revolutionaries unrealistic. Far from communities of independent and self-governing artisans and farmers being created, the monopoly of wealth and political power enjoyed by landowners under the old order was broken in the course of the bourgeois revolutions only for new concentrations of wealth and power to arise in the hands of the new lords of industry and finance. In many countries they made common cause with the landowners. The unmistakeable tendency of capitalism was to increase the scale of production both in terms of size of the capital and the number of workers employed, and the quantity of output and sales. Relentless competition and the cost advantages secured by the most efficient companies meant a constant process of attrition, the weak going to the wall during the periodic slumps that punctuated the forward progress of the economy. In industry after industry, output, sales, investment, and employment came eventually to be dominated by a few giant companies — huge collective organisations with their own internal bureaucratic structures and codes of discipline, run increasingly by professional managers rather than individual owners, and dedicated to increasing the efficiency of their ever widening operations.

An economy dominated by vast impersonal bureaucratic organisations was rather different from one dominated by individual independent producers. It meant that every stage of production had to be based on the co-operation of many individuals rather than being left to the inclination of single individuals, and this helped intensify the search for techniques that could raise the productivity of this new 'collective worker'. In this way, as production was concentrated in larger and larger plants, and control of these giant enterprises was centralised in fewer and fewer hands, an unmistakeable tendency emerged for labour to be expelled from the production process altogether, a tendency which pointed to eventual full automation of the labour process. Any technical process that could produce more cheaply than existing ones had eventually to be adopted, otherwise firms faced extinction. Having established an immensely complex division of labour within each factory and productive enterprise, capital steadily replaced human skills and functions by machines wherever it was profitable to do so. At the same time the functions of management and ownership tended to be split and the principal agents of capital accumulation became salaried managers in place of individual self-made entrepreneurs. Many owners were turned into rentiers.

Such developments have steadily restricted the principle of economic individualism, as it was understood by early liberal political economy. From the specialisation of individual artisans in their workshops and the exchange of goods between town and country dwellers, the division of labour came to involve vastly complicated exchanges between collective enterprises of ever growing scale — companies based on single factories, then many factories; companies covering one industrial sector, then many sectors; companies operating within a national economy, then transnationally. A set of economic relations which entails a great and still increasing degree of interdependence, not just in trade, but in

the way production is organised, has been established, span-
ning the whole world.

Within the boundaries of Western nation-states this social
character of production has also been reflected in two other
developments of far-reaching importance — the rise of trade
unions and the growth of the public sector. The first springs
from the resistance of the working force to the conditions of
work, including pay, which those controlling the process of
production attempt to impose on them. To the extent that
unions are successfully organised to defend the interests of
particular groups of workers, there is further interference
with liberal ideas of how a market economy of individuals
should work. The expansion of the state was stimulated and
shaped by the pressures for collective consumption and
investment of all kinds. Some pressures came through the
new democratic institutions and the new parties that were
formed once the vote was extended to a majority of the
people. But others arose as it was realised that the strength of
a nation-state rested on its national economy, and that if
accumulation and growth were to be as rapid as possible
within each national economy, many of the costs of that
accumulation had to be borne collectively. Education, health,
roads, ports, scientific research, energy, and many more,
became fields for public provision and investment, and
investment generally came under much closer public guidance
since it was increasingly seen as too important to be left
entirely to the material inducements of the market. An
expanding sector of public enterprise and public responsibility
was one result, and a growing penetration of the bureaus of
the state and the bureaus of private capital was another.

None of these tendencies developed all at once in every
sector or in every state. Nevertheless by 1900 the overall
picture was unmistakeable, and posed major difficulties for
liberal doctrine. The theme around which controversy and
practical politics centred in the new industrial society was
liberty and order. Two broad responses may be identified:
that of the national liberals or liberal conservatives, and that
of the social democrats. Both camps include a multitude of
groups who use other labels and many individual thinkers and
some parties cannot be wholly assigned to one or the other.
Nevertheless the division has proved an enduring one for

responses to the problems of managing industrial societies, and provides the basis for the most influential political ideologies and movements in Western states which have sought solutions within the framework of a capitalist economic order. What both approaches share has been the need to reconcile the clear separation of state and society in liberal theory with the evidence of their growing interpenetration.

2 Order and liberty

National liberalism or liberal conservatism comes in a direct line from liberal constitutionalism. Some of its modern exponents, such as Hayek, have contrasted the constitutionalist, individualist, and empiricist tradition with which they identify themselves, with the radical, collectivist, and rationalist tradition. The latter is then saddled with the blame for all the errors and misfortunes and crimes of the modern world. The central problem of industrial societies is seen as how liberty can be preserved and order maintained in them. This requires above all else that the market economy, with its institutions of private property and free voluntary contract, be protected because it is the most important sphere of individual freedom. Such a sphere is essential to prevent domination by the state. Like the liberal constitutionalists these national liberals emphasise the importance of the rule of law, by which they mean that laws should always be 'procedural' rather than 'substantive'; they should lay down only general rules which do not specify any individual or individual situation. The state has the duty to enforce these general rules, which are general in so far as they apply equally to all citizens, in a just and impartial way. It has no right to interfere in detail in the choices individuals make, the activities they engage in, or the wants they attempt to satisfy. But national liberals have also had to come to terms with the problem of mass democracy. Defending liberal constitutional principles and sound principles of economic management in states with a voting system restricted to those who own property and have a tangible stake in the country, is rather easier than in those where the principle of universal suffrage has been accepted, which gives an influence on government to those who possess no property at all other than their own labour power, and may therefore look covetously on the possessions of the rich.

Liberal constitutionalists were not oblivious to the dangers posed by democracy and the revolt of the masses. They worried about it a great deal, ever after it raised its fearsome head during the French Revolution. But liberal constitutionalists were also involved in fighting for the substance of their programme against the resistance of the traditional alliance of Crown, Church, and Aristocracy, and often needed the assistance of the masses they wished to keep in check. The gradual extension of the vote brought quite new problems of leadership and political strategy, since the constitution was now widened so as to make legitimate the demands and pressures of new social forces, in particular political movements based on organised labour which were often violently opposed to liberal principles. How in such circumstances could liberty be preserved? Would not democracy prove to be a system in which the rich were plundered by the poor, reason and science sacrificed to ignorance and prejudice, the wheel of industry and the progress of society halted, the essential checks created by private property to arbitrary and total state power removed?

The management of mass democracy became one major focus for liberal concern. Another was the growth of bureaucracy and administration. It was recognised that these were inevitable and irreversible, and that they flowed from the very rational, utilitarian, principles celebrated by the early analysts of civil society. There was no alternative to bureaucracy if large-scale organisations were to run efficiently and the activities of all their members were to be successfully co-ordinated. Yet in Max Weber's eyes, for example, it still represented an iron cage; the more industrial societies progressed, and the more complex they became, the greater co-ordination and planning they needed to run smoothly, hence the more they were forced to rely on bureaucracy, and the smaller became the sphere where genuine individual freedom and autonomy could still exist. Modern capitalism threatened to abolish the possibility of realising liberal ideals and to bring about, in Weber's phrase, the disenchantment of the world.

In this way the pessimism which had never been far removed from liberal thought began to seep back. In the twentieth century it grew to be a flood. The priority became to defend both the existing private sphere as a sphere of individual freedom, and to frustrate the larger and more ambitious schemes for social transformation. Progress was now seen as an illusion, and rationalism came to be distrusted, because it gave rise to planning and attempts at 'social engineering'. In this way many themes of earlier conservative writing of the Reaction were absorbed. Liberty was defended against equality, efficiency against equity, the private sector against the public.

This creed which has formed the content for so much of the political economy of the Right during the past one hundred years has often been espoused in conjunction with strong nationalist views. Nation and Liberty have not proved irreconcilable ideological principles. Indeed the ideal of a free economy and a strong state has proved a potent combination in more than one modern Western state. Liberals like Richard Cobden advocated free trade (which meant not just free movement of goods, but of labour and capital also), and minimal government, and were as opposed to government spending on war and colonies as they were to spending on welfare, on the grounds that both were an encroachment on the liberty of the individual and both entrenched vested interests and bureaucracies in the control of government policy. A few economic liberals with Cobdenite beliefs have survived, but not many. Far more common amongst modern economic liberals has been the condemnation of high public spending on welfare with support for high public spending on arms and highly restrictive immigration policies.

Economic individualism has remained a central value. The idea of rational economic conduct which was such a distinctive feature of the rise of civil society and the spread of market relations, was analysed in great detail by Max Weber and the sociological school he inspired. Capitalism for him was not a new mode of production but an orientation to economic activity, the search for the most efficient, therefore rational, means to produce use values, regardless of other considerations. Such an orientation he believed had always existed in human societies. What needed explaining was why it had become so dominant in modern societies. The answer, he suggested, lay in the working out in secular terms of the implications of Protestant doctrine. In Protestant doctrine good works could never guarantee the salvation of any individual since who would be saved and who damned was predetermined by God. Given the nature of hell every individual had a pressing need to know that he was one of God's elect. The psychological burden of this anxiety could be lightened by following a calling. This meant adopting an ascetic life style, abstaining from luxury consumption and sensual pleasures and leisure. Unremitting and unsparing devotion to work and duty provided for each individual Protestant the psychological certainty of salvation. In the economic field the consequence of the Protestant ethic, this compulsion to follow a calling, was to channel energies into making a success of enterprises. In this way commercial success itself came to be regarded as a sign of belonging to God's elect.

Weber did not offer his theory as more than an exploration of one factor that was important in explaining why a capitalist orientation to economic life had become so dominant. More interesting, and more important, was his discussion of how, once capitalism had become established, rational economic conduct became the standard for all social behaviour, and began to penetrate the whole society. Capitalist accounting practices – balance sheets, double entry bookkeeping, the exact calculation of profit and loss, the attempt to quantify, measure, and derive precise estimates of net advantages – such systems which in utilitarianism became the foundation for a systematic political theory, provided the basis for administration of large-scale organisations, including companies, armies, tax offices, churches, and finance departments. Such formal accounting practices became the routine knowledge of every bureaucracy, and the way in which the whole society was gradually subjected to the same utilitarian ethos (the balancing of costs against benefits) that had already come to dominate its business life. A principle and system that first flourished as the best available means for individual persons to maximise their self-interest became a general social principle and orientation, one which was put into effect by a new race of 'individuals', the giant bureaucracies of the private and public sectors.

This paradox of the modern world formed the crux of

Weber's thought; the principles of rationalism which enhanced and extended individual freedom and autonomy at the same time assisted the growth of organisations that radically curtailed them. That did not mean that he ceased to defend the private sphere or to believe in economic individualism. But awareness that economic individuals were no longer individual producers, single human beings, or single families, meant that the arguments for economic liberalism had to be revised. The individualist basis of liberal theory and of academic disciplines like modern economics (whose abstract models are built on the assumption of rational individuals who maximise utility), only disguises the shift that has taken place in this strand of liberal thought. So long as there is no monopoly in buying and selling, so long as there is competition between individuals, it does not matter whether these 'individuals' are single persons or huge corporations employing several thousand people. Each is conceived in law as an individual subject with rights and duties and a single independent will — able to make contracts, hire and fire, buy and sell commodities, own and dispose of private property. Politicians who use the rhetoric of economic liberalism to extol the small man, the independent producer, the self-reliant artisan and shopkeeper, implicitly or explicitly defend the interests of corporate capital too.

Monopoly is the great dread of this modern liberal school. What freedom there is can only be preserved through encouraging competition — competition between companies in the private sector, between government departments and between political parties in the public. If the world has to be bureaucratic, some vestiges of freedom can remain so long as there are sufficient bases of power that can compete with one another. This line of argument has been pursued by various pluralist schools of thought, which have emphasised the importance of conflict between groups and individuals to preserve freedom and prevent the emergence of any single centre of power which could then dominate government. The duty of the government is to preserve competition. Competition in turn preserves the independence of the government and leaves it free to formulate the national interest which emerges (somewhat miraculously) from the melee of sectional interests, including parties, over which it presides. Occasionally the principle of competition has been aimed at corporate capital itself, as in the anti-trust movement in the United States, but more frequently at the 'monopoly' powers exercised by trade unions and democratic governments. The first was regarded as a direct interference with one of the foundations of 'rational economic conduct' — a free labour market. If the price of such a vital factor of production was controlled, and still worse if the conditions under which it could be used in production were restricted, then the whole basis of a 'rational' calculation of costs and benefits could be upset. The belief that such rational calculations could be objective because they were based on the sum of preferences and choices of all individuals was central to modern liberal political economy. Trade union powers and privileges thus became a major battleground, for trade unions are the principal organised social force in industrial societies capable of resisting the uninhibited pursuit of capitalist rationality. Trade unions have therefore in many different states resisted the process by which whole categories of jobs and skills periodically become obsolete. They have also often fought attempts to incorporate all particular interests into a single national interest, defined and pursued by government. In so far as trade unions have been successful in their resistance they have always appeared to national liberals, and often to many social democrats as well, as an intolerable infringement of economic freedom, and have been condemned as a vested 'monopoly' interest obstructing progress and the national welfare.

The main protection against monopoly is still regarded in national liberal thought as the constitutional state, the framework of law which establishes and protects a market order, by enforcing equality before the law and safeguarding contracts and property. Every 'individual' is entitled to the legal protection within the framework of general rules that has been laid down. What is produced and how it is distributed are no concern of the law, and therefore no proper concern of government, whose only interest should be to enforce the law. If individuals are left free to pursue their interests in their own way within the general confines of certain legal rules, then all have the opportunity to do well, and failure and poverty become personal responsibilities or misfortunes, since everyone has a chance of mobility and success. The market order does not guarantee outcomes that are just or fair, the most worthless occupations and talents may receive enormous financial rewards, the most highly regarded a pittance. But such affronts to ways of judging what an individual deserves according to traditional moral principles are regarded as tolerable because of the compensating benefits a market order brings. In a market order, it is argued, almost every conceivable kind of human want can be satisfied and individuals have a considerable degree of freedom as to how they spend their income and how they divide their time between work and leisure.

3 Democracy

The more sophisticated of modern economic liberals have moved beyond any attempt to put forward a defence of capitalism by trying to justify modern economic organisation with the traditional moral arguments of liberalism. The principle of rational economic conduct has been fully accepted and so has its consequences, the commercialisation and bureaucratisation of more and more spheres of social life. The practical problem that remained, however, was whether wide popular support could be won for the principles of a market order, in particular the ideals of economic efficiency and economic liberty, and what kind of political order could be relied upon to uphold them. Once the electorate was no longer restricted to property owners, how could free trade, balanced budgets, and sound money, be protected from constant meddling by the unskilled and inexperienced representatives of the people?

These fears which run throughout the modern period in many different national traditions and have most recently been forcibly restated by Hayek, reflect the much greater importance that is attached by this current of thought to liberty than to democracy. Overthrowing political absolutism was intended to safeguard the sphere of liberty, not inaugurate the rule of the majority. Democracy was regarded as a principle that could undermine the liberal order because it unleashed forces that were ignorant and easily manipulated. One of the earliest and greatest analysts of the dangers of democracy was Alexis de Tocqueville, based on his observation of the workings of American institutions. He was no reactionary, for he regarded the modern revolution as irreversible, yet he still deplored many of its tendencies which he saw at work both in France and America, and which he argued were leading straight towards a new despotism which threatened to engulf liberty. This problem of how liberty can be safeguarded in a mass democracy makes him a forerunner of much later thought.

Tocqueville used the concept of democracy to refer not simply to the constitutional form of the state, but to the civil society on which it rested. What he observed was that once legal privileges separating different social groups were abolished, tremendous competition developed between individuals for status. Since the status and the identity which an individual enjoyed were no longer inherited or bestowed automatically they had to be competed for. So much individual striving, however, had the paradoxical result that, instead of developing each person's individuality, it tended to level everyone to a common condition. Fear of failure and exclusion meant that mediocrity and conformity were more encouraged and rewarded under this system than high individual achievement and extraordinary talents, and all individuals came to share the same basic conditions, experience, and opportunities. In this way a democratic society tended to become a mass society in which the better and more educated elements were submerged and afraid to show themselves. The chief causes of such mass societies, Tocqueville argued, were measures that centralised power and abolished the independence of all intermediate associations and groups such as Churches, families, and universities. Along with other pluralist writers he regarded groups which gave individuals a focus of loyalty in addition to that of the nation-state as a major bulwark of liberty, for it encouraged diversity and alternative bases of social power which would challenge the inherent despotism of the democratic nation-state, and its claim to enjoy undivided and absolute sovereignty.

This notion that modern political forms forced all individuals and groups in civil society to be both part of the sovereign, the general will, and at the same time made them utterly subordinate to it, the particular will that constituted the

government, became the basis for later theories of totalitarianism. The unprecedented claims of modern states to
represent the interest of all, and to constitute the highest
form of community possible, made legitimate opposition
precarious. On what grounds was individual or group opposition to the general will permissible? All modern regimes,
whether single party or multi-party, make totalitarian demands on their members to some degree, and all at times have
persecuted individuals or groups who have proclaimed their
conscience or their group identity to be more important
than the interests and commands of their government. The
kind of libertarian belief expressed by the English novelist
E. M. Forster in his celebrated remark that if he had to
choose between betraying his friends and betraying his
country, he hoped he would betray his country, has never
been tolerated by any of the great nation-states that have
dominated the history of modern Europe. 'My country right
or wrong' has been the rival attitude they have sought to
foster.

From the standpoint of liberal theory, therefore, totalitarian regimes are one form a modern state can take. The state
swallows civil society. One party, one group, in civil society
seeks an absolute political monopoly: it secures control over
the communication of ideas through books, newspapers, and
modern media, and suppresses all other political parties. It
seeks to destroy all independent and therefore rival bases of
power in civil society, whether private capital, trade unions,
the Churches, or the family. Civil society is atomised, its
organisations and voluntary associations are destroyed or
incorporated by the state, and it is reduced to the aggregate
of individuals who compose it. Their only important relationship is to the all-powerful state, whose authority is often
personalised as the authority of a single leader. Such regimes
enforce mass participation in politics, and their legitimacy
rests on their success in getting their citizens to see the state's
goals as their own. They normally require in addition an
extensive police apparatus and a network of informers to
maintain constant surveillance of the population. The concentration of production and centralisation of financial
control in modern capitalist societies give birth to a new
breed of military industrial Leviathans. As Jacob Burckhardt

argued in the middle of the nineteenth century in a passage which anticipates both the analysis and the experience of totalitarianism:

> I have a premonition which sounds like utter folly and yet which positively will not leave me: the military state must become one great factory. Those hordes of men in the great industrial centres will not be left indefinitely to their greed and want. What must logically come is a fixed and supervised stint of misery, glorified by promotions and uniforms, daily begun and ended to the sound of drums . . . . Long voluntary subjection under individual Fuhrers and usurpers in prospect. People no longer believe in principles, but will periodically probably believe in saviours . . . . For this reason authority will again raise its head in the pleasant twentieth century, and a terrible head.

In the modern theory of totalitarianism a simple contrast is drawn between totalitarianism and democracy. In the one the state completely dominates civil society; in the other civil society completely dominates the state. But the sharpness of the contrast can mislead. The legitimacy of democratic governments rests on invoking total claims of 'the nation' or 'the people', and the lines between the public and private realms are increasingly blurred. The democratic principle of popular sovereignty is heavily qualified because the formulation and implementation of government policy actually depend on a state apparatus that is everywhere hierarchical, bureaucratic, and secretive, just as the market principle of leaving everyone free to spend their income as they want is qualified by the degree to which tastes and wants are now guided and controlled by the intensive sales, advertising, and marketing strategies of the corporate sector.

Political and civil rights and liberties coexist uneasily with the way in which modern industrial societies are organised and run. They can be suspended in regimes that have one party and those that have more than one. Their institutional bases have become insecure, and certainly free markets have often not been sufficient to preserve them.

The awareness of this dilemma permeates national liberal

thought, which is concerned above all with how economic freedom can be safeguarded. The danger inherent in democracy is that regimes may be elected which set out to destroy the fundamental basis of the liberal order by attacking the institutions of private property and free exchange. Such a programme is designated 'totalitarian' and one response to it is to justify the suspension of political and civil liberties and the suppression of political opposition, if this is the only way of preserving economic freedom for private capital. 'Authoritarian' regimes of the Right that protect private property whilst suspending political freedoms are preferred to 'totalitarian' regimes of the Left that may interfere with property rights. If it were applied consistently, which generally it is not, this theory would label the Nazi and fascist regimes of the 1920s and 1930s authoritarian, and only communist regimes, where private capital was expropriated, 'totalitarian'.

Except in its blacker moments, however, national liberal thought has not primarily been concerned with how to justify fascism as a lesser evil than socialism, but with how to redefine the nature of democracy and find some principles for checking the aggrandising intentions of democratic legislatures. One major school of thought in America arose out of disenchantment with how democracies actually work, the observation that industrial societies do not function at all in the ways that many liberals once expected, and the realisation that there is no real point, or desirability why they should.

This 'revisionist' school of democracy is associated above all with Joseph Schumpeter, the Austrian political economist who settled in America; the central ideas derive from the theory of elites worked out by Vilfredo Pareto and Gaetano Mosca, and the theory of bureaucracy of Max Weber. Weber's work is the seedbed for modern liberal thought, particularly in Germany and the United States. He was strongly committed to liberal values and to national liberal politics, but, as already noted above, what is so striking about his thought was his pessimistic view that the necessary and irreversible way in which industrial capitalism had developed and would continue to develop undercut the possibility of preserving and realising those values. His problems and his concepts became the basis for a large part of modern sociology, particularly his discussion of bureaucracy and class. These ideas were also closely linked to his political perspectives.

He recognised the need for bureaucracy arising out of the division of labour, the constant subdivision of tasks and ever greater specialisation which separated the roles individuals were called upon to perform more and more clearly from one another. This division of labour was the basis for the great increase in social productivity on which all the achievements of modern societies rested. Bureaucracy was, he argued, the organisational principle of modern life — not just one way of organising an industrial society but the only way. Whether the society was capitalist or socialist made no difference. Not just economic enterprises but all enterprises — political, religious, and military — had to be organised bureaucratically. Bureaucracy meant the rational deployment of expert knowledge and the rational co-ordination of human activities for common goals. Rational meant adjusting means to ends as efficiently as possible. Bureaucracies are organisations of officials arranged hierarchically. Each group and each individual at each point in the hierarchy is assigned clearly defined and specialised tasks. They act and make decisions in accordance with rules that are both known in advance and written down. Officials are recruited and promoted primarily on the basis of merit, they cannot buy or sell their position. They are not independent property owners in their capacity as officials. Instead they regard their work as a career, a 'calling', and can expect to move up the hierarchy of their organisation in the course of their working life. As a result they tend to develop an ethic of service, duty, and altruism, rather than being motivated primarily by financial gain or self-interest. This orientation to work they shared with the capitalist entrepreneur Weber so much admired.

One result of bureaucracy was to institutionalise expertise. The accumulation of knowledge about nature and society was the result of applying the rational methods of enquiry pioneered by modern scientists. The more society was organised bureaucratically — its business firms, its government departments, its schools, its political parties — the more the fruits of modern knowledge could be rationally and systematically employed, and arbitrariness and inefficiency banished. The term, bureaucracy, has become synonymous with inefficiency, red tape, and waste, yet bureaucratic forms of administration and co-ordination are the only means by which inefficiency and waste can be kept under control, because, so Weber and his school argue, there is no other way of co-ordinating the huge numbers of individuals that must be co-ordinated in great collective enterprises if modern societies are to run at all. Societies where economic production is on a small scale, where education and health care are based in the family, and there is little urbanisation, generally lack bureaucracy. Activities are co-ordinated through the traditional relationships of personal dependence that exist between the leaders of the community and its members. But they are also societies which, with few exceptions, have low standards of living and low social productivity. The extent of bureaucratisation is one measure of the modernisation of traditional societies.

The more bureaucratised a country, the more attention is paid to expert knowledge and efficiency, and progress and welfare are increasingly defined in terms decided by experts. The whole culture becomes rationalist and utilitarian, searching out the cheapest and most effective means for the achievement of stated goals, and social goals themselves become defined in terms of the technical means that are available. In such a world democracy in so far as it increases individual autonomy, individual conscience, and individual choice becomes irksome, because only experts have knowledge and experience to decide. The mass of individuals are only welcome to exercise free will and free choice in the market place, where as individuals they can use their economic 'votes', their income, to consume the products continually created for them and choose a 'life style' within the limits of their resources. But they are certainly not welcome to participate collectively in the formulation of decisions throughout the great bureaus of private capital and government which maintain and service industrial society. It is too expensive in time, too wasteful in resources, and can lead to technically incorrect and inadvisable decisions.

Taken to their ultimate limit, such notions imply that industrial societies are best run without a democratic political system which may only hamper the work of the professional bureaucracies of government, and interfere in those of the private sector. Realities of government leave no room for untried and untested initiatives that surface through the democratic political process. Modern societies have been dissolving into numerous discrete and specialised spheres, each of which is now commanded and jealously guarded by its own expert bureaucracy.

The problem of bureaucracy which Weber discerned so acutely, threatened the liberal order of capitalism from one side; from the other it was besieged by the rise of socialist movements and the increasing use of politics to pursue sectional class interests. Social democrats wished to use the democratic principle of taking decisions by majority vote to authorise interventions by government in the economy and society so as to redress the ill effects of the market principle — giving access to resources and organising production according to the existing distribution of income. Weber's solution was to search for ways in which economics and politics might be institutionally separated. At one time he proposed the idea of independent parliaments which could be the training ground for strong national leaders. Their source of authority would be *charismatic*, rather than *traditional*, like the authority of kings and heads of families, or *rational-legal*, like the authority of directors of companies. Charismatic authority was enjoyed by leaders who could inspire a degree of loyalty, trust, and commitment in their followers that would leave leaders free to act in the way they thought best. In this way, argued Weber, responsible national leaders would emerge fully aware through their parliamentary training of the national needs and the complex interdependence of the national life, and able through their popular support to rise above the narrow sectional interests of pressure groups, and so represent the national interest. For Weber the national interest involved both the preservation of the capitalist economic system and the military strategic interests of the nation-state.

When German democracy was established in 1918 Weber lost his earlier faith in parliamentary institutions. He regarded the German parliament and its parties as totally dominated by economic interests, and came to advocate instead a strong presidential form of government in which national leadership would be provided by the direct election of a single charis-

matic leader who would then have the means and the freedom
to override the parliament and govern in accordance with
national needs. In this way he believed democracy could be
harnessed to safeguard the essential (even though increasingly
incompatible) liberal features of modern society which he
prized above all — economic rationality and individualism —
and to make them more secure by founding them on the
mobilisation of consent.

4 Stratification and elites

Another of Weber's major contributions to twentieth-century
liberal thought was his account of the different ways in
which industrial societies were stratified; how inequalities
between individuals and groups in civil society showed themselves and what consequences they had, particularly in
politics. He identified three major kinds of stratification:
class, status, and party. Unlike many earlier liberals he
acknowledged the existence of classes as an ineradicable
feature of industrial societies. But whereas the Marxists
defined class in terms of the social relationships of the
production process between capitalist and worker, Weber
argued instead that it was because different groups had
different market situations that classes arose. Workers
belonged to a different class from capitalists or peasant small-
holders because they were obliged to sell their labour power
in order to live. Such basic differences in market position
created groups with quite distinct 'life-chances', and arising
from this, different life styles — including income, education,
culture, and ideology. Because of their different positions in
the market economy of civil society, the material interests of
these groups were sharply opposed and gave rise to continual
political and social conflict, as each group sought to improve
its relative position.

The second kind of stratification — status — Weber argued
often cut across the stratification created by the market.
Every individual, regardless of his class position as defined in
the market, might also belong or aspire to a status group
whose principle of association was not economic interests,
but social honour and prestige. Whereas classes were often
fluid and their membership unrestricted, status groups
depended on criteria which excluded others from member-

ship. These criteria could be racial, ethnic, religious, or regional, or could be defined in terms of culture, life style, or achievement. The important thing was that the members of a status group felt that they belonged together. At their extreme they became castes, into which individuals were born, and from which they could not escape. Weber argued that despite the growth of markets and free exchange, status groups were extremely important in industrial society. Though they might at times reinforce class divisions, they might also counter them, and in some societies be far more important than class in determining the beliefs individuals held and how they acted. A good illustration of the distinction that Weber wanted to make is his description of the bourgeoisie of the medieval towns as a status group rather than a class, because of its life style and beliefs. These gave rise to the rational orientation which, in Weber's view, was far more responsible for the development of capitalism than any economic or class interests this group may have had.

The third principle of group organisation that stratified industrial societies was party, which Weber defined as groups created by the willingness of individuals to associate in order to accomplish some important collective purpose. These three concepts — class, status, and party — helped found an immensely influential way of looking at the social and political system of advanced industrial societies. The form-ation of political parties was obviously closely related to classes and status groups, since the relative importance of class and status in a social formation would determine what kind of party system arose — which cleavages and divisions would be articulated politically. Societies might range from a class-dominated politics at one end with the parties being identified with sectional economic interests, to parties representing particular regions, particular races, or particular religious and ethnic groups.

Whilst he recognised that the party system would mainly reflect the way in which each society was stratified, Weber also believed that the national interest had to be asserted over the sectional interests of society, whether these came from classes, status groups, or parties.

This part of his theory was developed in the analysis of elites. The elites which controlled the public and private

bureaucracies of the state apparatus and private industry
could be seen as a special kind of status group, the guardians
of rationality. They recruited normally on the basis of formal
educational achievements which required thorough immersion
in a highly organised minority culture and minority life style.
The elite theorists, most of whom like Pareto and Mosca were
impassioned opponents of democracy and socialism, argued
that it was impossible to avoid rule by elites, and that if a
socialist democratic revolution was successful, it would only
mean the overthrow of one set of elites and its replacement
by another. Elites might circulate, but some elite there had to
be. The revolutionary ambitions and hopes of democrats and
socialists were vain and utopian, impossible of realisation.
The division into rulers and ruled was a permanent feature of
all societies.

What made rule by elites in modern society inevitable was
the importance of specialised expert knowledge and the
centralisation of power and organisation. These two features
made any direct form of democracy along the lines of the
early trade union formula, 'what concerns all should be
decided by all', wasteful and inefficient, and at the same time
gave opportunities for active minorities to assume the direction of every organisation, regardless of how democratic its
formal constitution was. This *iron law of oligarchy*, which
was propounded by Robert Michels (a pupil of Weber's) and
Moisei Ostrogorski in the analysis of the new democratic
mass parties, suggested that policy and decision-making
would always be in the hands of a few leaders and officials.
This being the case a most important conclusion was drawn.
If oligarchy and rule by elites were inescapable, it followed
that the real choice and contrast was not between democracy
and bureaucracy, or democracy and elitism, but between
different kinds of elite domination. The character of the
elites and their accountability were what mattered, not the
fact that they were elites.

Out of these diverse strands the 'new' theory of democracy
has been fashioned. The most single influential statement of
it was provided by Schumpeter: democracy is that 'institutional arrangement for arriving at political decisions in which
individuals acquire the power to decide by means of a competitive struggle for the people's vote.' What Schumpeter did

was to strip the concept of its association with a particular
kind of policy (rule in the interests of the poor and the
oppressed), by transforming it into a formal device for
organising decision-making. Democracy becomes a means for
selecting and choosing between elites. It alters the context of
elite behaviour to a certain extent, but not the inevitable
presence of elites. As a means of choosing leaders democracy
can be employed in any large organisation or association and
has the advantage of conferring legitimacy on whoever
emerges from such an open contest for popular endorsement.
It becomes identified as the system of party competition in
which ideological and policy issues take second place to the
personalities and images of the leading politicians. Given the
highly centralised character of government and media in the
twentieth century, it is not surprising that democracies in the
West, following the American lead, have been increasingly
organised as political markets, a market of policies and a
market of votes, and have come more and more to resemble
the economic markets in which voters become the consumers
of policies. The parties act as entrepreneurs offering their
products through large-scale advertising and news management, and the mass electorates record their preference at
infrequent intervals as to which set of leaders should formally
preside over the giant bureaucracies of the industrial state.

   The twentieth-century analysts of democracy, particularly
the school which flourishes in America, far from deploring
the low level of political participation and understanding in
Western democracies, argue that the widely observed apathy
and ignorance is a feature of advanced industrial society, as
deeply rooted as the existence of elites. The participation of
the masses in the political system needs to be such as to make
the performance of the elites efficient without interfering in
detail with how they operate. Free and regular elections
ensure the former – the political elite cannot become entirely
closed or self-selecting. The organisation of the party system
ensures the latter. The domination of the mass parties by
their leaders also means that over time leadership groups are
evolved which have a proper understanding of the complexity
of the technical decisions that have to be made to allow
modern industrial society to run smoothly. Hence they
become the brokers between the demands of the public and

private bureaucracies and the demands of their own supporters, the latter reflecting ideological preferences, status
group demands, and class interests which are not always easy
to accommodate. What the parties exist to provide are not
programmes of action but alternative sets of leaders. Each
leadership team will be assessed through the media according
to how well they relate to the pressing national needs as
identified by the leaders of industry, finance, the military,
and so forth. Ideology has become a pejorative term in the
new theory of democracy because it has come to be used not
in a neutral way to indicate the fundamental ideas and
purposes of a social group or movement, but to denote a set
of ideas that conflict with the requirements for technical
rationality and optimum performance as these are defined by
the various elites of modern society. A party whose leaders
are too 'ideological' is given a negative rating compared to
those whose leaders are 'practical' and 'realistic'. In this way
democracy comes to be seen as a major source of irrationality
in modern life, reflecting and transmitting hopes, values,
feelings, and fears, which often conflict with the policy
consensus derived from expert opinion.

In Weber's thought there is still the tension between
technical rationality and individual liberty, which he incorporated into his methodology through the distinction he tried
to draw between facts and values. This tension has largely
disappeared in later thought. The criteria of technical rationality become the criteria for defining the national interest
and the bounds of the 'consensus'. The advance of democracy
made many theorists reluctant to employ simply a theory of
elite domination to explain how industrial societies maintained
order. The idea of consensus grew in importance as a result,
particularly in the United States. In the work of Talcott
Parsons, for example, which builds directly on Weber, the
coherence and stability of societies depend on their common
values and beliefs. Conflicting class interests can be more
easily accommodated within a social order provided the basic
principles and values of that social order are widely accepted
and the elites charged with formulating the general will enjoy
authority. In advanced industrial societies the meaning of
consensus has therefore come to be acquiescence in the goals
and decisions of the dominant elites in exchange for the

stream of material goods to shape private life styles that the industrial economy can provide. The belief that this consensus (at its height in the 1950s and early 1960s) was not ideological and that ideology was nearing its end was rudely shattered by events in the 1960s. But the imperatives behind technical rationality still exist, and so do the pressures to maintain and organise consensus in industrial societies.

B. Social Democracy
5 The new liberals

The principal alternative in the late nineteenth century to the emphasis upon Nation and Liberty developed by national liberals and liberal conservatives was the doctrine of the 'new liberals' and the social democrats. This tendency was strongly influenced by the 'positive' conception of the state, developed by a wing of liberal thought strongly influenced by classical precedents. Whilst recognising the separation of the state from society, these theorists believed, in contrast to the liberal constitutionalists, that it was the state that was the sphere of free choice and independent action and society the sphere of privation and dependence. Society was the arena in which human beings satisfied their physical needs and were governed by crude self-interest, and therefore scarcely rose above the level of animals. In the state, however, human beings were free to choose and deliberate and pledge themselves to goals that were higher than mere physical needs. As citizens they were able to develop the moral qualities which set them above other animal species.

This alternative outlook on the modern state ran counter to the principles of liberal constitutionalism with its emphasis upon individual rights, the protection of spheres of individual liberty, and the need to restrain government. It was no less individualistic, however. A contrast sometimes drawn between individualism and collectivism sees the nineteenth century as the century of individualism and the twentieth century as the century of collectivism, but it is wrong in suggesting that the dominant strand in modern liberalism is no longer concerned with the individual. The real difference is between a form of liberalism which conceives individualism primarily in terms of the exercise of individual rights, particularly as far as property is concerned; and one which conceives individualism primarily in terms of individuality, of guaranteeing the conditions under which all individuals can develop their abilities and control their own lives. From another angle the dispute in modern liberalism is about two definitions of equality, one stressing equality before the law, the equal treatment of all individuals, the other equality of opportunity, an equal start and prospect for all individuals, and consideration of their different needs not determined by ability to pay.

Social democratic thought evolved alongside the rise of organised labour movements and the extension of the franchise to the people. Instead of seeking ways by which the apparent dangers to liberal values and institutions posed by the entry of the masses could be averted, social democratic thought started from the problem of how laissez-faire capitalism could be transformed into an industrial society which could win the loyalty and secure the participation of the whole people. Only on the basis of equality and democracy, social democrats believed, could a common life for all citizens be created which could hold industrial societies together and make their institutions and relationships legitimate. To establish order, maintain progress, and avoid social conflict and class war, a social consensus had to be created which reached deeper than the consensus arrived at between elites and the permanent agencies of the state on how national policy should be conducted.

One theme animates the whole of social democratic thought — the means by which capitalism can be transformed into a post-capitalist society without sacrificing some of its major achievements. It is how a society which is depicted as being rent by class conflicts, unrestrained individualism and selfishness, and therefore by both social disintegration and by waste and inefficiency, can become one in which a basic harmony and community of interest have been achieved between the different social groups engaged in production.

The picture of unregulated capitalism and the need to correct its worst abuses was the driving force behind social democracy as a system of ideas. The grounds for action were argued partly in terms of the need to improve efficiency and partly in terms of the utilitarian commitment to maximise individual happiness and fulfilment. The argument for efficiency is most prominent in a tradition which leads from Saint-Simon, includes the Fabians and the Webbs, strongly influenced Engels, and has often attracted conservative nationalists. The argument for individual happiness and fulfilment was developed by thinkers as diverse as Emile Durkheim, Edward Bernstein (the first and foremost reviser of Marxism), and L. T. Hobhouse.

Saint-Simon remains a crucial figure. Although many of his writings do read like the views of a quite orthodox liberal, he did not share the liberal faith in constitution-making designed to safeguard liberty by means of external checks. He possessed a vision of industrial society as a new civilisation which would require new collective principles of organisation. These were to be provided not by the state and 'politics' but by the leaders of industry; the engineers, the scientists, and the artists. The old corrupt power-hungry state of soldiers, kings, aristocrats, and priests, would wither away, and the government of men would be replaced by the administration of things. What Saint-Simon meant by this phrase was that social relationships would no longer be relationships of power and dependence. He believed that there was a fundamental unity of interest between the different groups, such as managers, technicians, and workers, who worked in modern industry. Human societies, he argued, after a period of disorder, revolution, and the flourishing of 'critical' thought, were about to return to a new 'organic' period, similar to the Middle Ages, in which social harmony, social order, and social progress would be maintained by the universal acceptance of the values of industrialism.

Saint-Simon did not foresee the great conflicts between the two classes of modern industry that were to develop in the nineteenth century, but he did highlight some enduring problems for the way in which industrial societies were organised, problems to which social democratic movements were one major response. Saint-Simon's work was continued in France by a band of extremely active followers, including his former secretary, Auguste Comte, who conceived his task as developing a 'positive philosophy' which would be the new religion to bind industrial societies together. He systematised Saint-Simon's thought and extended its range. But the greatest sociological account of industrial society influenced by Saint-Simon was that of Emile Durkheim.

6 Anomie

The idea that the market order, so prized by the liberal constitutionalists, was itself the chief cause of growing disorder and conflict in industrial societies, was a familiar theme in conservative writing in the nineteenth century. In thinkers like Durkheim it becomes a preoccupation of liberal thought as well. Durkheim strongly rejected the abstract individualist approach of the utilitarians, because he argued that a society which simply left individuals free to pursue their own interests would quickly fall apart. The market succeeded in coordinating economic activity, matching needs to needs, not only because of the external guarantees of the state, but also because social relations were still governed by shared values other than those of self-interest.

One of Durkheim's abiding concerns was the problem of social order and under what conditions social solidarity was possible. Traditional societies, he argued, exhibited 'mechanical solidarity', they were made up of an aggregate of similar family units bound together by a structure of common beliefs — the *collective conscience*. In modern societies this collective conscience had been considerably weakened by the gradual emancipation of the individual from social and economic controls over his behaviour, and the cult of individual rights and individual freedom that accompanied it. The new economic freedom meant that social solidarity was no longer 'mechanical' but 'organic'. The chief agency of social solidarity now was not common beliefs but the division of labour, which rested on individual specialisation and functional interdependence; every individual was assigned a function which it was his duty to perform, and had to rely on others performing their functions if the society was to operate smoothly and all needs were to be met. Durkheim regarded societies based on organic solidarity as potentially superior to traditional societies. But modern societies were at present suffering so many problems and conflicts because the development of the new market economy and the subdivision of work tasks and increasing specialisation of jobs had not been matched by a corresponding development of the moral norms necessary to regulate it smoothly.

Much of Durkheim's work was therefore devoted to an exploration of the consequences of the kind of unrestrained individualism that was actively promoted by capitalism. In the market every individual was encouraged and required to compete, to aspire to the highest prizes, to seek unlimited appropriation of goods and wealth. There was no limit set to what any individual might achieve, and no social agreement on the kind of division of labour and division of rewards that was just. What resulted were great economic instabilities, financial panics, commercial crises, and perpetual struggles over the distribution of income. Durkheim called this situation *anomie*; no social norms existed to restrain individual behaviour; selfish and destructive activity was the result. Durkheim argued that human wants were essentially insatiable; to remove the social controls that alone kept these wants within bounds, to elevate money into the social bond by making it the universal medium of exchange, and therefore pecuniary gain the chief link between individuals, was to unleash human desires in a quite unprecedented way. Capitalism he regarded as a set of institutions which had freed individual behaviour in the economic field from moral regulation, and had therefore directly produced the rootlessness, the restless self-seeking, and the commercialisation of modern life. The lifting of the ban on divorce he considered had similar effects in the sphere of the family by encouraging unlimited sexual desires and experimentation, once individuals no longer felt they were tied to a single partner for life.

Durkheim diagnosed the need for stable institutions to regulate modern industrial societies and by keeping them orderly restrain expectations within limits where they could be realised. In this way individual autonomy and individual happiness would be achieved. Individuals would accept their place within the modern division of labour and the specialised function it allotted to them without regrets. If industrialism could be as perfect a moral order as it was a technical order, then both egoism and utopianism would be held in check. Industrial society would be able to promote material progress and individual self-determination at the same time. This elusive combination of efficiency and equality which Durkheim formulated is the heart of the programme and promise of social democracy.

7 The anarchy and waste of capitalist production

Social democracy, though not always under that name, has been the most influential political response to the problems created by the manner in which industrial capitalism has developed and by the arrival of mass representation. By the end of the nineteenth century irresistible pressure had begun to build up for 'collective consumption' — the provision by central public agencies of those goods and services which were not being provided through markets. This pressure came not just from popular demands for welfare and security, but also from business demands for support and subsidies, and also from those groups of intellectuals and administrators who became aware that the capitalist economy had reached a stage where it required greater central stimulation, co-ordination, and assistance if the pace and profitability of accumulation were to be maintained. These pressures have seen the gradual extension of public responsibility and the proliferation of new public agencies.

One major argument for the new collectivism was the need to eliminate inefficiency and waste. Many early socialists regarded the periodic overproduction and stagnation of the capitalist economy as scandalous. The sight of idle machines and unemployed workers during every slump in the trade cycle suggested that an industrial economy where all factors of production were fully employed, and production was uninterrupted and not subject to the stops and spurts of capitalism, would advance the material wealth of society much more rapidly. Competition was regarded as often extremely wasteful, leading to the kind of exaggerated behaviour so much in evidence on speculative markets and stimulating production in areas that were not 'socially useful'. Rational application of industrial techniques to produce the greatest amount at least cost could dispense with waste. Conflicts between workers and employers were seen as a further instance of wasteful competition. If all industries were publicly or co-operatively owned, the principle of public service could replace that of private greed and unite all parts of industry in the common task of production.

If an industrial system based on individual competition was wasteful, still worse was the inefficiency of the system. The wealthiest economies in history were tolerating huge discrepancies between rich and poor, and seemed to be organised to prevent the realisation of the human potential of their populations and therefore of a major productive asset. The slums, the inadequate education, the standards of health care, the provision against sickness, unemployment and old age, were for social democratic thought the chief aspects of the social question, and demanded remedy. All seemed to point to the fact that free market principles, the religion of economic individualism and laissez-faire, could not co-ordinate the vast interdependent organisation of modern industry. In many areas an extension of public responsibility was required and the setting up and funding of public administration which could provide the collective services the society required, and which it would not otherwise get.

In the individualist terminology of academic economics, the new concerns came to be expressed in the concepts of 'welfare' and 'social costs'. It was recognised that there were many cases where the costs and benefits involved in particular activities were not accurately reflected in the prices that were charged in free markets, and so did not accurately represent the total cost to the community. Goods like pure air and clean water which were consumed collectively could only be secured collectively. The extent to which certain other goods such as defence, and health, and education are 'public' goods in the same way has produced much controversy. In general social democratic thought has been sympathetic to the treatment of a wide range of goods as public goods which should therefore be provided on a collective basis by public agencies from funds raised through taxation. The national liberal preference, except in the cases of defence and public order, has been to make the basis of provision individual payment. This has become a major political issue in all advanced capitalist states.

So pressing was the need for some central co-ordination of industrial societies that public involvement has grown remarkably in the last hundred years. Whatever measure of state activity is taken, the importance of the state now lies not merely in securing the basic structure of law and establishing an acceptable form of money, but in actively subsidising, supporting, and organising industrial activity. Roads, schools, hospitals, ports, universities, and scientific research have all generally become collective burdens borne through the state.

In addition, the state has become closely involved in economic regulation. Its own size and spending grew to be so big and to have such a major impact on the economy that the kind of simple housekeeping remedies propounded by the Victorian advocates of sound finance and balanced budgets came to be seen by many as inadequate and damaging, since they both prolonged and worsened the periods of recession. The importance of Keynes in Western social and political thought is that, steeped in liberalism and academic economics as he was, he nevertheless recognised that a new set of principles and policies was necessary to cope with the form industrial societies had taken, with their extensive public sectors, their trade unions and their monopolistic corporations. He argued that the Great Depression of the 1930s was caused by a shortfall in demand which could not be remedied by the orthodox measures of deflation and cutting public expenditure, and did not *have* to be remedied by socialist measures of full-scale nationalisation, central planning, and redistribution of property. Instead the government could leave the bulk of the economy in private hands whilst taking responsibility for the overall performance of the economy, managing demand in such a way as to promote full employment, stable prices, and economic growth. Freed from the requirement to balance their books, governments could manipulate their own spending and revenue so as to produce desired effects on the total level of demand for goods and services.

Keynesianism discredited central planning amongst social democracts in Britain, because it offered a way of combining central direction and influence with private initiative and responsibility. The same formula with or without Keynes' direct influence was adopted in all Western states. Capitalism could be transformed into a regulated 'mixed economy' by enlarging the sphere of public enterprise, public spending, and public regulation. The abuses of liberal capitalism and an unfettered market order could be corrected, without resorting to the wholesale restructuring of society which social democrats had come to associate with the Bolshevik experiment in Russia. Bolshevik experiments were not needed in Western Europe because the social democrats believed that the modern representative state with its permanent central bureaucracy enjoyed independence from dominant interests and could be democratically controlled by the majority. Socialism could be secured through the ballot box by socialist parties winning the right to exercise control over the central administrative organs of the state. Mass political participation by the working class could therefore eventually bring the peaceful achievement of their demands. The modern state, far from being a barrier to the building of social democracy, in the way that the old absolutist states had been a barrier to liberalism, was the instrument and the framework within which the new goals could be won. The state could express and execute the general will of the community.

8 Equality

These ideas have nourished generations of social democrats. As a doctrine of efficiency and the need for rational central administration of industrial societies, however, the early reform programmes of social democracy often attracted the support of conservative forces who were hostile to the unregulated individualism of the market order. One particular source of concern in Britain was the poor physical quality of the population due to the conditions in which so many lived, and the effect this had upon the military effectiveness of the British Empire. Fabians like Sidney Webb, one of the chief authors of the British Labour Party's 1918 constitution, and imperialists like Lord Milner thought alike on these questions, Webb even remarking, 'How can we get an efficient army — out of the stunted, anaemic, demoralised denizens of the slum tenements of our great cities?'

But beyond efficiency and the charms of administrative order, the moral force behind collectivism was the doctrine of equality, the notion that the ideals of liberalism could only be fulfilled if individuals were given not just civil rights (the right to free speech, free association and fair trial), and political rights (the right to vote), but also social rights. Only if there were universal provision of certain basic needs such as education and health would individuals be in a position to develop fully as individuals. One of the most eloquent accounts of this new liberalism was given by L. T. Hobhouse. He declared that 'liberty without equality is a name of noble sound and squalid result', and argued that all true social liberty rested on restraint of individual interests and desires. It followed that restraints on unfettered economic individualism, such as legislation to supervise working conditions in factories and to legalise trade unions, were essential to give equal economic liberty to all citizens. Hobhouse also argued explicitly in favour of paternalism as a liberal principle: 'The state as over-parent is quite as truly liberal as socialistic. It is the basis of the rights of the child, of his protection against parental neglect, of the equality of opportunity which he may claim as a future citizen.'

The moral case for social democracy which was pressed by progressive liberals like Hobhouse and Tawney was that only if industrial societies were organised on the basis of an equality that went beyond abstract rights and signified equality of opportunity and an equality of basic condition, would they create a social order accepted as legitimate by all their citizens. Such a society would be held together by individuals seeing their duty to be the performing of their social duties rather than the pursuit of their self-interest. Some social democrats envisaged the replacement of private property by social ownership, whilst differing on whether all property should be held by the state or by co-operatives. In practice, however, and particularly after the adoption of Keynesian-inspired policies of economic management, social democrats have come down in favour of preserving private ownership alongside a substantial public sphere.

Private ownership of the means of production, free trade unions, free elections, and public responsibility for economic prosperity and social welfare, are the four essential ingredients of modern social democracy, and their combination has given rise to a number of problems. Social democrats believe that class conflict can be limited and contained provided governments assume responsibility for the economy and ensure through high taxation and high spending that collective welfare services are provided for all. Everyone is made to feel part of the same community and to experience the state as their state. In this way the class inequalitites of distribution are lessened. The trade unions too are given a firm legal status, and are involved more and more closely in the processes of decision-making.

At first glance the mixed economy approach of social

democracy might seem more suited to the way in which industrial societies have developed than the idea of a market order and strong state of the liberal conservatives. Yet the growing interpenetration of state and society since the end of the nineteenth century has posed problems for all schools of thought. The sharp separation between the principle of commodity exchange in the market and the principle of administrative rationality in the state has been gravely undermined by the encroachment of administrative agencies on so many areas previously reserved for the market. This was accompanied by the decline of parliaments and legislatures and the increasing importance of cabinets and executives which presided over the burgeoning state apparatus. In the simple notions of early constitutional liberalism the public and private realms were to be kept sharply separate, and individual needs were to be met by everyone being free to determine what they produced and what they consumed within the general rules of commodity exchange. Social and collective needs — including the general arrangements of society — would be the concern of those elected by the citizens to represent them in a national assembly.

As economic organisation grew, however, and the public sector expanded, so the separation proclaimed in theory became increasingly hard to observe in practice. The response of the liberal conservatives was to warn of the threat to economic individualism posed by the growing powers and activities of public agencies; the response of the social democrats was to welcome the new collective basis of industrial society as a means of reducing social conflicts and realising greater social equality. They looked for new forms of representation alongside the traditional parliaments so as to make the expanding government bureaucracy fully responsive to the interests it was supposed to serve. One familiar trend has been for government to extend the range of consensus wherever it can by drawing trade unions and other producer groups directly into the process of economic management. Underlying much social democratic theory is the notion that what has to be represented and what guarantees liberty in the modern state are social groups and corporate bodies. Durkheim again anticipated much social democratic thought in his recognition that the 'individual' was a creation of the modern state, and for the individual to have and to enjoy rights meant not that the area of state involvement in modern society would contract, but that it would need to grow constantly. At the same time he feared the development of an all-powerful state and argued for that reason that the necessary extension in the power of the state be counter-balanced by the growth of 'corporations' and secondary associations of all kinds. All citizens, he thought, should have experience of communal life other than through the state.

The balance between the state and other associations in individual societies has given rise to theories of corporatism. Corporatism literally implies incorporation − the welding of different interests and wills into a single will and interest. In the circumstances of modern industrial societies this could only be done by the kind of forcible suppression of the trade unions as independent organisations undertaken by fascist regimes. In the Western democracies trade unions, whatever their leaders have done, have remained genuine associations. As a consequence, many social democrats have seen the trade unions performing the kind of role in modern societies which the Churches performed earlier. They are the only bodies strong enough at times to resist the automatic imposition of the commands of the centralised state which flow from the consensus agreed between the bureaucracies that control the public agencies and the private companies, and which is given moral legitimacy by invoking popular sovereignty.

The dilemma and the weakness of social democratic regimes arises because as political movements social dem-ocratic parties rest directly or indirectly on the independent organisations of the working class, but as governing parties they preside over the modern highly centralised, highly interdependent nexus of government and large-scale industry. This dilemma takes different forms in different national societies, according to the kind of relationship between state and economy that has emerged and the way in which a national interest is created. Three broad patterns can be distinguished. There are those states, such as France, where the state apparatus has generally assumed a dominant and directive role; there are those like Germany and Japan where the links between government and business are extremely close, and other groups, including trade unions, play a secondary role; and there are those like Britain and Sweden where trade unions are stronger and economic management has rested in certain areas on a more or less formalised structure of tripartite bargaining. What is common to all these approaches, however, is the greatly enhanced role of the central state apparatus in the management of the economy and its concern, whether this is expressed formally through trade union representation or not, with creating conditions that maximise economic advance and minimise social conflict.

Combining the two has not proved easy for any of these states, because their ideological legitimacy came to rest heavily upon the ability of the governments to create and maintain prosperity. The ideal of a social democracy, resting on high public spending and therefore high taxation to provide collective goods, has never had the same moral appeal as the ideal of the market order. This has meant that the social democractic justification of the modern industrial state, the promotion of equality and the protection of trade union rights, has come under increasing pressure because of the difficulty of preventing expenditure outrunning the ability to increase revenue, maintaining high enough levels of profitability in the private sector, and avoiding the consequent struggles over the distribution of income.

How to maintain legitimacy and accumulation in the midst of a new world recession appears insoluble and has exposed the shallow nature of much recent social democratic thought. The comforting idea of a state that could satisfy the needs of all its members through a judicious mixture of public and private provision has collapsed. But attempts to find other means for managing industrial society have not proved easy. The tension between maintaining legitimacy and maintaining accumulation has steadily intensified the problem of maintaining democratic forms in capitalist societies.

7

Politics and industrial society III: the spectre of revolution

1 The Russian Revolution

Liberalism, which set out as a creed of revolt against absolutism, subsequently became the official creed of developed industrial societies. Its two main ideological strands, national liberalism and social democracy, provide the general stock of ideas from which most parties in the political systems of the West draw inspiration. The utopian element in liberalism remains but it is now overshadowed by the brooding pessimism of so much modern liberal thought, as liberal and social democratic thinkers contemplate the condition and prospects of industrial society.

The optimism and idealism that once characterised liberalism, the strong belief in moral and material progress, passed to Marxism in its various forms. Given the negative, pessimistic character of so much modern liberal thought it is not difficult to see why Marxism has acquired such a dominant position. It is the last great representative of the Enlightenment belief that a rational re-ordering of society is both possible and desirable, and can remove many of the ills and sufferings in existing human communities. Marxism has remained firmly attached to those cardinal values of the Enlightenment — rationalism (the belief in the power of human reason to provide understanding and find solutions) and universalism (the casting of its principles in terms that are applicable to all human beings everywhere). This ecumenical character of Marxism, its presentation as a doctrine of the human race as a whole, is one secret of its enduring strength, and it is what makes it necessarily a revolutionary and subversive doctrine with its ideal of a unified, classless, and democratic world society. As an explicit creed of the poor and oppressed it drew on precisely those energies which liberalism unleashed but grew to fear. Nevertheless Marxism is far from being a unified creed or movement. Marx's writings have been interpreted in almost every way imaginable and have had an enormous influence throughout modern Western thought; and as a political label 'Marxist' now embraces such a wide range of movements and ideas as to be almost as elusive as the terms socialist and liberal.

The central event for the understanding of Marxism, however, remains the Russian Revolution, just as modern liberalism requires a study of the French Revolution. Without the Russian Revolution it is possible that Marxism would have been absorbed within liberalism in the way that social democratic parties have been, accepting the legitimacy of modern nation-states. The success of the Revolution, the subsequent triumph of a party that espoused Marxism, and the adoption by the new Soviet state of Marxism as its official doctrine, gave a new practical impetus to the development of Marxist ideas. It transformed Marxism into the major creed of opposition to Western capitalism, it split the socialist movement almost everywhere, and it supplied a new doctrine and a crucial example for nationalists and revolutionaries in Third World countries who wished to modernise but not westernise their countries. Marxism was a profoundly Western doctrine, but because it also appeared as deeply antagonistic to prevailing liberal ideology and to Western states, it permitted both incorporation and rejection of Western ideas at the same time.

The appeal of Marxism as a Western yet anti-Western doctrine was reinforced by the fact that it was Russia, a Western yet at the same time non-Western state, where Marxism first triumphed. Marxism has, however, found the marriage between its universal principles and the national interests of particular states as hard as liberalism ever did. It did not remain a subversive, critical, and liberating doctrine for very long in the Soviet Union. It was used to justify the harsh, authoritarian methods employed by Stalin to industrialise and modernise Russia's vast economy, and was transformed into the official creed of the Soviet state, despite the inequalities and lack of many basic rights in present-day Soviet society. As a moral doctrine Marxism in its Soviet version became as threadbare and unattractive as liberalism.

The recognition (in certain cases belated) of the actual nature of Stalinism has caused huge tremors, splintering Marxist parties everywhere, and Moscow has lost its place as the undisputed centre of world Marxism. Yet the Russian experience remains central to Marxism, and it is the interpretation of that experience and of its significance around which so much of modern Marxism revolves. Like the French Revolution much was concentrated in a short span and many hopes were placed in the world's first workers' state. The overthrow of the most backward and repressive absolutist state in Europe, the bastion for one hundred years of European reaction; the almost bloodless seizure of power in Petrograd and Moscow; the taking of the land by the peasants; the battles fought against the armies of counter-revolution and the Western powers to preserve the young republic; the debates on how such an enormous backward country composed of so many nationalities and subject peoples could be modernised and the first socialist economy built; the great flowering of Russian art, poetry and architecture; all this, just like the French Revolution before it, fired imaginations in the West and divided opinion into sharply opposed camps.

2 Engels and the Second International

Marx's work, although one of the greatest intellectual achievements of the whole Western tradition, left many ambiguities and uncertainties for those who attempted to build socialist movements on the basis of his principles. In part this was due to the very incompleteness of the work. Only volume 1 of *Capital* was finished, volumes 2, 3, and 4 remaining in draft, and not even drafts were prepared of further planned volumes on the state and the world market, which Marx had referred to in letters. Never has such a powerful political movement arisen on the basis of writings which apparently contained so little systematic discussion of politics and the state. Marx's main political writings were *The Communist Manifesto*, written, when he was thirty-one, jointly with Engels; some pamphlets analysing events in France between 1848 and 1851, and in 1870; many articles and letters; and manuscripts like the *Critique of the Gotha Programme*, which analysed and criticised the programme adopted by the German Social Democratic Party (SPD) when it was formed in 1875. The heart of Marxism remained *Capital* itself, which was concerned with the analysis of the capitalist mode of production. Although it contained an implicit analysis of the state, the implications for politics had to be brought out by developing its method. *Capital* itself did not provide a political manifesto. It was conceived on such a grand scale, it constituted so fundamental a critique of modern capitalist society, its institutions, its ideas, its origins, and its future, and so novel an approach, that the intellectual effort was beyond most of its early readers, and its importance was not at first widely recognised. Like all great intellectual works it required interpreters for its ideas to become widely known and understood. Of all the early interpreters one stands out as by far the most important – Friedrich Engels.

Engels was a friend and intellectual partner of Marx from the early 1840s. In the 1850s he sacrificed his own intellectual ambitions and worked in his father's cotton firm in Manchester so that he might support Marx in London. After Marx's death he took charge of Marx's papers and edited and published volumes 2 and 3 of *Capital*. He was also the author of a number of important works (*Socialism : Utopian and Scientific; The Origins of the Family, Private Property, and the State*, and *The Dialectics of Nature*) which popularised the essential ideas of Marxism as Engels saw them.

The chief political problem Marx left unanswered was exactly how the industrial working class was to come to power and construct a socialist society. The confident predictions of *The Communist Manifesto* that society was more and more splitting up into two great camps, that the ruling class was growing ever richer and smaller, and the proletariat ever poorer and larger, had not been borne out by the time Marx died in 1883, and such arguments were in some respects belied by the much more rigorous analysis of capitalist development contained in *Capital*. Marx believed with many nineteenth-century radicals that the rule of the bourgeoisie would be short, and that the French Revolution would be eclipsed by a European Revolution that would complete what the events in Paris had begun. He was anxious

lest the Revolution should break out before he had finished
Capital, and half expected every commercial crisis to precip-
itate it. Such optimism proved unfounded. The time scale for
the unfolding of the potentialities of capitalism proved far
longer, and although Marx provided the theoretical means for
grasping this, he did not draw the implications in his own
scattered political writings, which remained rooted in earlier
notions. In particular he failed for the most part to analyse or
to anticipate the great forces of bureaucracy and nationalism
which had become so important by the end of the nineteenth
century, and which by then preoccupied advanced liberal
thought. To the end of his life Marx was an internationalist
and a believer in radical forms of democracy. But he failed to
relate these values to the obstacles in the path of socialist
movements created by the successful mobilisation of nations
and by the increasingly bureaucratic and centralised character
of organisation in industrial societies, which appeared to
undercut the small-scale, participatory, and libertarian
democracy favoured by all the radical democrats among the
early socialists.

This failure was made more serious by Marx's refusal to do
more than make a few general points about the future
character of socialist and communist society. He took for
granted that such societies would need to be founded on the
high level of development of material production and scientific techniques which had been achieved by capitalism. Marx
refused to indulge in speculation about the future, partly
because he wished to avoid what he regarded as the absurd
fantasies contained in many of the blueprints of the utopian
socialists, partly because he held that understanding followed
practical experience and could not precede it, and partly
because he believed that the new society was inseparable
from the revolution which would create it, so no one individual could predict in detail the forms it would take. These
were all good reasons but it meant that Marxism was extremely vague about how socialist societies would be organised
and how they would overcome some of the problems that
capitalism was increasingly encountering, problems which
often seemed to belong not specifically to capitalism as a
mode of production but to industrialism itself.

Engels' main contribution to the interpretation of Marx

and Marxism was to offer an account of Marx's views on history and the state which rapidly became authoritative. He linked Marxism extremely closely with science and the scientific movement, presenting it as the embodiment of reason, and Marx as the discoverer of the natural laws that governed the evolution of human societies, just as Darwin had discovered them for living organisms, and Newton for inanimate matter. In Engels' hands the dialectic tended to become a formalised and abstract method of enquiry separate from the material it was investigating, rather than a way of posing problems and presenting results. Whereas Marx never attempted to apply his method beyond the examination of historical events and institutions in the human world, Engels believed that dialectical materialism (as it later came to be known) was a universal method which provided the key to the investigation of all phenomena.

Engels therefore helped to reinforce the character of Marxism as a science of society, a body of objective knowledge, independent of moral values, which could be used to determine correct political practice, and to predict future economic developments. Engels helped to popularise the idea of Marxism as economic determinism — the belief that the economic factor was decisive, that a sharp distinction could be drawn between the economic base and the political, legal, and ideological superstructure, and that it was the economic base that determined (in the last instance, Engels tried to insist), the superstructure. When confronted with 'Marxists' who claimed that politics and ideology were simply reflections of underlying economic interests, he hastened in letters to qualify the notion, claiming that:

> According to the materialist conception of history, the *ultimately* determining element in history is the production and reproduction of real life. More than this neither Marx nor I have ever asserted. Hence if someone twists this into saying that the economic element is the *only* determining one, he transforms that proposition into a meaningless, abstract, senseless phrase.

One reason why Engels interpreted Marx as he did was that he was much more influenced by Saint-Simon than Marx was.

It was evident in the simple historical scheme with which he concluded *Socialism: Utopian and Scientific*. He distinguished three major epochs in social development: the epoch of medieval society, when production was organised for individual use and immediate consumption; the epoch of capitalist revolution, when production was organised collectively and for exchange; and the epoch of proletarian revolution, when the means of production which had already been socialised, became public property and both production and consumption were organised collectively. Capitalism was a necessary stage through which societies had to pass before they could achieve socialism, but whilst it created the preconditions for socialism it also prepared the means by which socialism could be established. It was a social formation riven by contradictions. Firstly, because the worker was severed from the means of production there was an objective antagonism and conflict of interest between the proletariat and bourgeoisie. Secondly, although the productive process itself was increasingly organised collectively in huge enterprises which co-ordinated great masses of workers, machines, and materials, the co-ordination of the whole economy was still left to the market and 'unbridled competition' between individuals. Thirdly, the consequence of this was on one side the continual displacement of workers by machines and therefore the swelling of the industrial reserve army of labour (the unemployed), and on the other, an unlimited and unplanned extension of production, leading to regular bouts of general overproduction, financial panics, and commercial crises. Fourthly, as production became organised more and more on a collective basis, this fact was recognised within bourgeois society by the development of public companies, where ownership and control were divorced, by the rise of monopolies and trusts, and by increasing state regulation and state ownership. Such developments were not socialist but they revealed that the bourgeoisie as a separate class of individual property owners had become unnecessary because all its social functions were performed by salaried managers and technicians.

Socialism for Engels would be implemented after the proletariat had seized the public power and inaugurated central planning. The contradictions of capitalism would be overcome — classes, the anarchy of production, crises, and the state, would disappear. These were all aspects of the central contradiction — that between the mode of production, which was social, and the mode of exchange, which was individual. The wealth of the community was created by social co-operative labour rather than individual isolated labour, yet rights to a share in that wealth, and property rights over its control and disposal were still individual. Socialism was a scientific rather than a utopian doctrine for Engels because its possibility was defined not by its desirability on moral grounds, but because both the material conditions (socialised production) and the human agency (the industrial proletariat) that would be needed to establish it were already present within existing society.

Put in this way the evolution towards socialism under capitalism became a necessary and inevitable process, because the primary emphasis was placed on how the socialised character of production would be complemented by the socialised regulation of exchange through central planning. Socialism, as Engels envisaged it, would put science in command; production would be rationally planned, and technology exploited to the utmost, which would allow a still greater development of the productive forces than had been achieved under capitalism. Once social production was firmly in the hands of the modern collective worker (the associated producers, especially the scientists and engineers) the need for the state would disappear, and the state would accordingly wither away. Engels used Saint-Simon's formula — the government of men would be replaced by the administration of things. This followed from his view of the origins of the state. The state arose, he argued, when human communities first became divided into classes. A separate power was needed to keep social conflict within bounds and to enforce the claims of the dominant class. Once classes were abolished, as under socialism they would be since property rights would no longer be individual, the need for a power separate from society would disappear. The need for collective administration, co-ordination and planning would, however, be much greater, but like Saint-Simon, Engels thought that industrial society could dispense with the repressive apparatus of the modern state.

Conceiving the state as the state of the dominant class, Engels was forced to recognise that the state often appeared, as in the regime of Napoleon III in France, to be independent of that dominant class and its interests. He argued that this was possible because as the division of labour progressed so the state power tended to alienate itself more and more from society and become an autonomous, centralised bureaucracy. But it followed from this kind of analysis that if the state power was detached from the dominant class there was a possibility that it could be peacefully won and controlled in the interests of the majority, especially if the need for socialism was daily becoming more evident. Since economic crises would get steadily worse, socialism would appear as the only rational and scientific solution to the problem of production, as well as the only policy in the interest of the great majority.

Engels therefore viewed the state as an apparatus of coercion arising out of the division of labour and the existence of private property; a specialised set of agencies acting to defend the interests of the ruling class of property owners, but also capable of acting independently. He wavered between counselling its overthrow and destruction and arguing that much of its machinery was essential to the co-ordination of a modern industrial society and could be taken over and used by the victorious proletariat. The inexorable growth in the power and organisation of the German Social Democrats convinced Engels at the end of his life that the transition to socialism would be a much more orderly and gradual process than he had envisaged when he was young. The enormous development of the productive forces under capitalism, including in particular science and technology, and the growing complexity and interdependence of industrial society made socialism the logical outcome. The speed with which the production process was apparently moving from an individualist to a collectivist basis gave rise to hopes that the socialisation of the relations of production could be accomplished peacefully in many countries. Private ownership, commodity production, individual competition, all were being rendered obsolete by the inexorable logic of modern development.

Such notions became Marxist orthodoxy in the Second

International before 1914, which saw the outbreak of the controversy over revisionism. The orthodox position of the SPD as enshrined in its Erfurt programme of 1891 endorsed a fatalistic view of capitalist development. Economic crises would necessarily become more severe, leading eventually to a breakdown in the capitalist economic system. Whether through overproduction of goods, stagnation, or a collapse of profits, the economy would cease to perform adequately. These deepening crises would be accompanied by ever greater concentration and centralisation of production, hence by ever greater monopoly; by the destruction of all middle rank occupations because of fierce competition, and by the increasing impoverishment and misery of the great mass of the population. Such trends would be accompanied by the ever more extensive socialisation of production which made socialism more and more necessary. Understanding the laws of capitalist development in this way meant that the chief task for socialists was to organise a powerful and disciplined movement of resistance to capitalism. Eventually it would take over once it was widely understood that no practical political alternative to it existed.

Such notions supplied one answer as to how socialism was to be achieved and capitalism overthrown. Capitalism was busy overthrowing itself. But two quite different assessments also emerged. The first came from Bernstein, one of the party's leading theoreticians, and through his earlier links with Engels a guardian of the party's theoretical tradition. He proposed *revising* Marxist doctrine to bring it into line with the actual practice of the German SPD and what he saw as the new character of capitalism emerging in Germany. He denied all the basic tendencies of development on which the SPD expectations of capitalist collapse and the inevitability of socialism were based. He argued that capitalism would evolve peacefully into socialism without violent crises, and that socialism itself was best understood as the complete realisation of democracy, the achievement of full political civil and social equality for all citizens. No polarisation in wealth was taking place, the material position of the working class was improving, new middle strata were emerging, there was no inevitable trend towards monopoly and centralisation, and no necessary connection between capitalism and war.

The strength of revisionism stemmed from the emerging strength of social democracy in late-nineteenth-century social formations, particularly due to the rise of trade unions. It was also espoused by many who wished to reject determinism and fatalism, and to establish socialism as a matter of conscious moral choice as to how industrial society should be organised, rather than a science which predicted the inevitable degeneration and overthrow of capitalism before socialism could be created. The basic idea of revisionist Marxism, as of all social democracy, was that the essential aims of socialism were liberal aims and could be achieved once democratic regimes had been established gradually, and then by piecemeal changes. No abrupt transfer of power from one class to another, no social upheaval, and no overthrow of the existing state had to take place.

Such ideas were resisted by orthodox ideologues of German Marxism, including Karl Kautsky, but also by a new radical wing which included Rosa Luxemburg. These radicals not only replied to the empirical criticisms made by the revisionists to certain Marxist tenets, they denied that socialist goals could be achieved within the limits of the political order of Germany, because establishing a democracy meant overthrowing the German state. Given the prostration of the liberal bourgeoisie before Prussian absolutism, this could only be secured through a mass revolution from below, led by the proletariat. A familiar slogan of the radicals, and of radical Marxism ever since, was that the only alternatives created by the nature of capitalist development were socialism or barbarism. No comfortable liberal middle way was possible. Rosa Luxemburg gave this a further twist by arguing that capitalism would inevitably break down, and in the course of breaking down would plunge the world into barbarism through the wars and brutality it would unleash. The only guarantee of further human and material progress depended on the proletariat intervening and successfully establishing socialism. In contrast to the passive wait-and-see political strategy of some of the orthodox Marxists, Luxemburg agreed with them that capitalism's breakdown was certain, but not that the victory of socialism was inevitable. That depended on whether the proletariat was well organised, well prepared, and well led, and seized its opportunities.

How the trends of capitalist development were interpreted was shown by the radicals to be of crucial importance for Marxism. The idea that expansion of the productive forces could not continue indefinitely under capitalism was the essential starting point for socialist political strategy. Without this assumption Marxism would necessarily move towards reformism, since there would be no purpose in preparing for insurrection and a final trial of strength with the bourgeois state if capitalism had regenerative powers and could ensure rising material standards of consumption for the majority of all classes. If such were the case the capitalist system would not suffer increasingly severe crises, the agents of the ruling class would not need to resort to coercion; the prospect of barbarism would recede. The strategy of using state power to win significant reforms and gradual change would be the perspective likely to command most popular support.

In this way the great divide between reform and revolution became established, based on contrasting evaluations of how capitalism would develop, a division that was to be enormously widened by the events of the First World War and the Russian Revolution. The remarkable collapse of the internationalism of the Second International in 1914, when the leaders of every national working class, with few exceptions, pledged full support for the national war effort of their respective ruling classes, produced the apocalyptic descent into barbarism which radicals had been predicting as the necessary result of the conflicts generated by competitive capital accumulation. The opportunities that were created for a successful proletarian intervention were only grasped in Russia and it was the triumph of the radical faction within Russian social democracy — the Bolsheviks — in the October Revolution and their ability to retain state power that permanently transformed the character and the doctrine of Marxism.

3 Leninism

Before 1914 the centre of Marxism was unquestionably Germany. The Russian party was small, forced to operate illegally and in a country where 90 per cent of the population were still peasants and capitalism was only beginning to establish itself. Yet it was the Russian interpretation of Marx

— Marxism-Leninism — that was to become the new orthodoxy. The group of Old Bolsheviks who developed Leninism,
amongst whom Lenin, Trotsky, and Bukharin were pre-
eminent, were European rather than Russian Marxists. They
saw themselves as part of an international movement, engaged
in an international debate, and active in an international
struggle. The notion of Marxism as an instrument serving the
interests of the Russian state was established by Stalin over
the bodies of almost every one of the original Bolsheviks.
Between the Marxism of the Bolsheviks and Stalinism there is
a wide gulf.

Marx had expected revolution to succeed first of all in the
most developed capitalist states, England and Germany. In
fact it broke out in a state which was only just embarking on
industrial development and had a tiny industrial proletariat.
But Marx and Engels had always insisted that the coming
revolution was not primarily national but international, a
tradition inherited and developed by the Bolsheviks. So
conscious were they of the backward state of Russia that
their internal debates were focussed around the question not
of how socialism could be established in Russia, but of how
the toppling of the Tsarist autocracy could trigger a revolution
throughout Western Europe. No sense can be made of Bol-
shevism if this international perspective is forgotten.
Certainly there were many Marxists in Russia who believed
that the backwardness of the country was such that the most
socialists should attempt to do was to support the liberal
bourgeoisie in making their revolution and introducing a
modern state, winning civil and political rights, and establishing a capitalist economy. Only on this ground could a successful socialist movement based on the industrial proletariat
arise, because only capitalism could create the preconditions
for socialism.

These notions that every national society had to pass
through certain stages of development before the opportunity
for building socialism arose reflected the deterministic and
fatalistic ethos of the orthodox Marxism of the Second
International and were quite contrary to the way Marx had
posed the question. The perspective of radical Marxists in
Russia was very different. They emphasised how all nation-
states had been inexorably drawn into a world political and

economic order in which self-sufficiency and national paths
of development were impossible. Events in one part affected
all others. The fact that Russia was the most backward state
also made it the most likely to collapse, given the growing
tension between the antiquated political structures of the
absolute monarchy and the interests of the rapidly developing capitalist sector. The scale of industrial operations,
particularly the size of the factories, the number of workers,
and the kind of technology employed, were often as advanced
as anywhere else in the world.

The radicals among the Bolsheviks judged that a revolution
would most likely occur at capitalism's weakest link, but that
once a break had been made in the chain of imperialist states,
the revolution would spread and become general. None of
them had any doubt that a revolution would occur in Russia.
The question was what the character of the revolution would
be and what attitude to it should be taken by socialists. If the
main task of the revolution was the achievement of democracy,
the establishment of a democratic republic and the freeing of
civil society, then an alliance should be sought with the liberal
bourgeoisie. But many doubted that the bourgeoisie was
either strong enough or determined enough to carry through
its own revolution. So the paradox emerged that the bourgeois
democratic revolution would have to be led in Russia by the
proletariat. But the problem then was whether the proletariat
having seized power, toppled the autocracy, and established
democratic institutions, should retire into legal opposition to
the new democratic capitalist order and hand power to the
bourgeois parties, or whether it should seek to retain power
and prepare for the second stage of the revolution, the
transition to socialism.

Lenin argued that the proletariat should lead the revolution
and should establish a revolutionary dictatorship of the
proletariat and peasantry, but he was extremely cautious
about the speed with which the revolution should proceed to
the socialist stage. Trotsky on the other hand, until 1917
outside the Bolshevik party, argued for a strategy of permanent
revolution. The democratic revolution would be led by the
proletariat, Tsarism would be overthrown, civil and political
freedoms declared, the monopoly of land broken, and the
land redistributed to the peasants. A democratic republic

based on broadly based individual property ownership would be created. Trotsky argued, however, that at the very moment of establishing the democratic republic, the proletariat would have to begin the task of building socialism, because in the circumstances of world imperialism no democratic republic could be maintained. Either the revolution had to proceed straightway to creating the conditions for socialism, collectivising the land and launching industrialisation, or else it would succumb to counter-revolution. Yet Trotsky acknowledged that to establish proletarian power in a society in which none of the preconditions for socialism existed meant the certain defeat of the socialist revolution, unless the infant socialist republic was aided by support from revolutions in the West. A socialist Russia was only possible if there was a chain of socialist states in Europe.

These ideas of permanent revolution, of uniting the democratic and socialist phases of the revolution, of seeing the Russian Revolution as one stage of a much wider European revolution, became the hallmark of Bolshevik strategy. Lenin was fully converted to them in 1917, partly as a result of observing the character of the Revolution which had erupted, partly because he had become convinced in his studies of imperialism that the necessary objective conditions for successful world revolution had been created by the imperialist rivalries of the leading European states which had culminated in the great European war of 1914. Imperialism represented a new and higher stage of capitalist development. The drive towards ever greater concentration and centralisation of production had resulted in the domination of national economies by a few giant trusts and a fusion of banking, commercial, and industrial capital into finance capital. The anarchic character of capitalist production had meant that competition on the world market was increasingly between national capitalisms, and their nation-states who fought for control of markets, raw materials, and labour power, had in the process divided up the whole world between them and constructed a number of vast empires. The origins of this new imperialism lay in internal problems of accumulation, the constant need to expand production and markets, which intensified national rivalries, assisted the growth of the military and bureaucratic state apparatus and led inexorably to armed conflict. A social system which could resolve its problems of economic production only by extending its political domination over other nations and regions, and ultimately by unleashing total war, was ripe for overthrow, and Lenin diagnosed that revolution would soon erupt throughout the chain of imperialist states.

These strategic principles were combined with Lenin's enormously influential writings on the party and the state. Lenin's conception of the party first took shape during the great split in the ranks of Russian social democracy, between Bolsheviks and Mensheviks (the terms mean majority and minority), over the drafting of new rules for the party organisation. Lenin was accused at the time and many times since of wishing to build a disciplined party machine of professional revolutionaries, recruited from the intelligentsia rather than from the workers, who would not be the instruments but the masters of the proletariat. The evidence for this view rests largely on a reading of *What is to be Done?*, the pamphlet on the organisation of the party published by Lenin in 1903, just before the split. But *What is to be Done?* has to be interpreted in the light of Lenin's later writings and actions, otherwise Lenin's thought is seriously caricatured, and he is regarded as an authoritarian centralist who fashioned the political instrument which led eventually to Stalinism. Trotsky's judgement in 1905 is often quoted:

> In inner-party politics these methods lead, as we shall yet see, to this: the party organisation substitutes itself for the party, the central committee substitutes itself for the organisation, and finally a dictator substitutes himself for the central committee.

This problem was not, however, peculiar to Leninism but was inherent in all socialist, and indeed all democratic, political activity in the kind of social formations that were emerging as capitalism developed. Lenin had a keener understanding of this than many socialists. He saw that the revolution had to be made by the industrial proletariat and the old state overthrown, but there was nothing that guaranteed that this could happen spontaneously and automatically. The class had to be organised and mobilised before it could intervene successfully, and this would have to be done against the fierce opposition of the ruling class, which would not willingly tolerate free trade unions and working class political parties, and in many states including Russia would actively repress them. Even where a high degree of organisation had been achieved and legal recognition for working class organisations secured, as in England or Germany, the problem still remained of what perspectives, what ideas, what ideology, should guide these powerful movements. In the British and French labour movements in 1900 Marxism and Marxist ideas had barely any influence. In Germany revisionist, orthodox, and radical ideas contended for a hearing.

Lenin believed strongly that in so far as Marxism was a science, it offered a standpoint which was true and objective, and which alone could guarantee an independent class policy for the proletariat, one which advanced the interests of the proletariat to the utmost and avoided subordinating them to the interests of other classes. Lenin therefore attached the greatest importance to revolutionary theory: 'Without a revolutionary theory,' he wrote, 'there can be no revolutionary movement.' It was only if the leaders of the working class understood and applied Marxism that they could hope to follow policies which successfully advanced the class struggle. This belief in the power of reason has been a central feature of Marxism and it was reinforced by Lenin who pointed out that Marxist ideas would not simply germinate of their own accord, spontaneously, in the proletariat. Marx had spent enormous theoretical labours in working out his ideas and like any science, its principles and how to apply them required considerable effort and study. With such effort the ideas that would dominate the labour movement would be ideas that dominated the rest of society — the ideas of the bourgeoisie.

Lenin's conviction that a sharp dividing line could be drawn between true and false ideas, between science and ideology, between those ideas which reflected Marxist principles and were true, and those which opposed or deviated from them, was one reason why so much of his writing takes the form of polemics against other Marxists and socialists. In his eyes it mattered crucially which ideas were accepted, since if an ideology was not socialist it must be bourgeois.

The basic social conflict was between proletariat and bourgeoisie, and their respective parties, a conflict which turned on
the question of whether industrial society should be organised
as a capitalist or socialist state, the dictatorship of the bourgeoisie versus the dictatorship of the proletariat. This simple
division was clouded by the existence of a third political
force resting on strata that were intermediate between the
bourgeoisie and the proletariat, the petty bourgeois democrats,
who believed in a structure of individual ownership and
production, the kind which formed the basis of simple commodity production. The petty bourgeois democrats drew
their support from the peasantry and non-unionised workers,
and intermediate social groups, and their ideology from
various strands of liberalism and early socialism. Lenin argued
that since their programmes were utopian, the effect of their
ideas and propaganda was necessarily to aid the dominant
class, the bourgeoisie, by drawing a veil over its real interests.
The greatest danger of all was that the political organisation
of the Labour movement should come to be dominated by
petty bourgeois democrats, who would completely lack the
will or the understanding to advance the struggle for socialism and confront the real sources of the continuing power
of the bourgeoisie.

With such conviction about the importance of Marxism
not just as one system of beliefs and values among others, but
as a science to guide proletarian strategy, Lenin stressed the
importance of organising a vanguard party, a party of socialists who would be entirely dedicated and loyal to it, and
would be fully educated in Marxist principles. Only in this
way could a firm and purposeful Marxist lead be given to the
proletariat. It was a vanguard party because the level of
consciousness and understanding of those active in it was
necessarily greater than those outside, who were far more
subject to the pressures and influences of bourgeois society.
But it was not intended to be a vanguard entirely divorced
from the proletariat. The majority of the Bolshevik vanguard
in 1917 were workers not intellectuals, and Lenin constantly
emphasised how close links had to be maintained with
workers' experiences and workers' struggles, otherwise he
feared the party would become bureaucratic and incapable of
responding swiftly enough to events. Nothing could be further

from Lenin's own ideas and practice than the notion that the vanguard could work out on the basis of its Marxist science what policy or line should be followed on any issue, then hand it down to be applied without question by the rank and file. The unity of theory and practice meant constant inter-action and learning from experience. Lenin himself was the first to overthrow accepted ideas when he judged they were no longer adequate. He was powerfully influenced by the revolution of 1905 and still more by that of 1917. As soon as he arrived in Russia and perceived the scale of what was taking place he decided that Trotsky's perspective of perm-anent revolution was correct, that the opportunity now existed for the Bolsheviks to take and retain state power on their own, and that the existing Bolshevik policy of support for those groups that were attempting to consolidate the new democratic republic was mistaken. He was initially opposed by the bulk of the Bolshevik Central Committee, who were wedded to the traditional policies and perspectives of the party.

Lenin's conception of the relationship between the party and the class it claimed to represent was thus far more com-plex than is often allowed. If it had not been, the Bolsheviks would not have taken state power. There would still have been a Russian Revolution, but it would have had a different outcome. Lenin's argument was not that the adoption of particular strategies and particular methods of organisation would make revolutions happen, but that when revolutions did break out, only that political group which was best prepared, most disciplined, and armed with the correct strategy, could understand what was happening and win mass support for its policies and leadership. On the basis of his study of Marxism, Lenin, like Luxemburg, expected rev-olutions to occur. Capitalism was so riven with conflicts and contradictions — particularly in its new and highest stage, imperialism — that they were bound to happen. The practical question was who would benefit? Would the revolutions lead to a consolidation of bourgeois rule, the emergence of new states, and the restructuring of the world capitalist economy? Or would the opportunity be seized for a victorious inter-vention by the proletariat to overthrow bourgeois rule and establish socialism? For the latter a disciplined party was essential, one which could act decisively. The principle of democratic centralism expressed the simple idea that the fullest possible debate on any proposal should be allowed within the party, but once the decision was taken, the right of opposition should cease, and all members should be obliged to carry out the agreed policy. A party that was wholly centralised would be bureaucratic and authoritarian, a party wholly democratic would be incapable of united action. Like many of Lenin's ideas, this was later perverted by the theory and practice of the Stalinists, whose commitment to centralism was rather more in evidence than their commitment to democracy.

Lenin's second major contribution was on the question of the state. Marx never wrote a systematic account of his view of the state, and the simple certainties of *The Communist Manifesto*, where the state was described as 'a committee for managing the common affairs of the whole bourgeoisie', gave little guidance to Marxists faced by the different kinds of state and regimes that developed in different countries. Was the state simply an instrument of class rule which had to be destroyed before socialism could be built? Or was it an instrument that could be wielded by whoever gained control of it? Could socialism be introduced by an elected government pledged to use the state apparatus to establish it?

Lenin inclined strongly to the first view. There could be no compromise with the bourgeois state. It had to be overthown. But what had to be overthrown was the state's repressive apparatus — the army, the police, the judiciary, and sections of the bureaucracy, the institutions that together ensured the dictatorship of the bourgeoisie. Other parts of the bureaucracy, however, he regarded as essential instruments for socialism, in particular those parts charged with co-ordinating the economy and managing credit and the financial system. Lenin argued that the repressive apparatus of the bourgeois state had to be destroyed before socialism could be built because of the way in which he conceived socialism. For him, as he made clear in a number of pamphlets written on the eve of the Bolshevik takeover, the destruction of the old state was possible and necessary because of the existence of a new state which was already in embryo — the soviets. Just as Marx had hailed the Paris Commune of 1870 as the first practical example of the revolutionary dictatorship of the proletariat, so Lenin saw in the radical democracy of the soviets a new form of political rule for industrial societies based on the participation of the whole population in the administration of the state. His solution to the distance between the parliamentary representatives and the people in liberal political systems was a state which was based on the widest possible involvement of the people in state affairs. Powers would still be delegated, and there would still be some permanent officials, but the state would no longer be separate from the people, because its functions would be carried out directly by the people. The practical principles of organisation which Marx praised in the Paris Commune, and which Lenin reiterated, including payment of public officials at workmen's wages, and making all public officials subject to election and instant recall, and the arming of the people, have not found much favour in the Soviet Union, but they were the programme of the radical wing of the Bolsheviks. The famous slogan that under socialism the state would wither away was a reference to the separation of the state from the citizens in bourgeois society, not to the state's function as such, which would now become the responsibility of every citizen. Those elected by the people to administer the state would be delegates directly accountable to their electors, rather than representatives as in a liberal assembly, accountable for their actions only indirectly and at infrequent intervals.

Lenin's hopes were not realised in Russia. The soviets which he looked to in 1917 as a popular power which would control production and distribution and secure the popular base of the regime were effectively destroyed by the pressures of the civil war between 1918 and 1921. The demands of the war economy for ever greater centralisation of command drove a rift between the party and the organs of popular power that was never healed. The Bolsheviks were confirmed in power but only at the cost of creating a state as distant from the people in certain respects as the one that had been overthrown, and with its own repressive apparatus. This was not an inevitable outcome of the Bolshevik enterprise; it flowed inexorably from the internal pressures of the civil war and the external failure of the expected European revolution. Those two developments did not alter the fact of the Revolution. The old order had disappeared for ever, the land of the old aristocracy had been seized and divided by the peasants, and capitalist property had been expropriated. But they certainly altered its outcome by decisively influencing the kind of regime that arose in Russia in the 1920s and 1930s. If the Bolsheviks had been defeated in the civil war or fallen victim to a counter-revolution in the 1920s the gulf between the Bolsheviks' first years in power and the regime installed by 1930 would not need remarking. The surface continuity created by the survival of the party and the continued use of Marxism as the official ideology obscured the extent of the change that had taken place.

The insight of the Bolsheviks was their appreciation of the nature of modern capitalism and the rivalries that were bred by imperialism. They recognised that the organisation of a world economy and the competition between existing nation-states for power, influence, and resources made the struggle against capitalism a world-wide struggle which reached far beyond Europe. They correctly identified resistance to Western political and economic domination as one of the major developments that would occur in the twentieth century. One of Lenin's principal innovations was his analysis of the national question and his attack on Marxists who regarded all nationalist movements as bourgeois and reactionary because they were said to weaken international proletarian solidarity. He argued that this was nonsense in a world composed of empires and subject peoples, and therefore of nations at different stages of political and economic development. He proclaimed the right of self-determination of all oppressed nations, which included all those within the Russian Empire; at the same time he acknowledged that the interests of the party and of socialism were paramount. Support for national liberation struggles could not be given uncritically by Marxists, but it still had to be given. The demand by an oppressed nation for its own state was an essential political demand, a demand of the democratic revolution which had to be respected. Only if the right of every nation to secede and form its own political community was granted could a secure basis be laid for international co-operation between proletarians of all nations, and the sources of national hostilities and national chauvinism be eradicated.

The Bolsheviks' misfortune, however, was to misjudge the prospects for revolution in Western Europe, which alone could have saved the Revolution in Russia. The dictatorship of the proletariat, which was envisaged by both Marx and Lenin as a temporary phase during which proletarian rule was consolidated and attempts to restore capitalism prevented, rapidly became the kind of dictatorship *over* the proletariat, about which many other Marxists had warned, and which preoccupied Lenin in the last years of his life.

It is often asserted now that Stalinism already existed in embryo in Lenin's early plans and conceptions in 1903, and that the Russian Terror was an inevitable outcome of Bolshevik ideas, just as the French Terror was an inevitable outcome of principles elaborated by Rousseau. It is about as sensible as arguing that the slave trade and the slave economy were an inevitable outcome of the liberal principles of economic individualism. If it were so it would be hard, without resorting to a belief in demons, to understand the world-wide appeal and impact of the Russian Revolution. For all its failings the Revolution embodied fundamental aspirations and unleashed enormous popular energies.

These aspirations lie deep in modern Western experience; the ideal of a society classless and democratic and free, a state controlled and administered by its members, an economy of abundance freeing human beings from endless toil. These ideals are nowhere realised in modern industrial societies, which is why the world's first socialist experience and attempt to construct a socialist economy still command attention. So do the great economic debates of the 1920s over how an isolated Soviet Union with a backward and overwhelmingly agrarian economy, cut off from foreign capital and from foreign revolutionary aid, could establish a modern self-reliant industrial economy and society laying the foundations for socialism. If despite all its crimes the Stalinist regime retained support for so long outside its borders, it was largely because of the powerful example it displayed of the first non-capitalist economy to industrialise and modernise itself. It is because of these features that the Russian Revolution has been such a major event for world politics in the twentieth century. As Lenin wrote on the eve of the Bolshevik takeover:

When every labourer, every unemployed worker, every cook, every ruined peasant sees, not from the newspapers, but with his own eyes, that the proletarian state is not cringing to wealth but is helping the poor, that this state does not hesitate to adopt revolutionary measures, that it confiscates surplus stocks of provisions from the parasites and distributes them to the hungry, that it forcibly installs the homeless in the houses of the rich . . . that the land is being transferred to the working people and the factories and the banks are being placed under the control of the workers . . . when the poor see and feel this, no capitalist or kulak forces, no forces of world finance capital which manipulates thousands of millions, will vanquish the people's revolution; on the contrary, the *socialist revolution* will triumph all over the world for it is maturing in all countries.

This was the real power driving the revolution forward.

4 Western Marxism

The Russian Revolution changed the character of Marxism because of the immense authority which now attached to the writings of Lenin and the leading Bolsheviks. The Russian experience of soviets, of the dictatorship of the proletariat, of the overthrow of bourgeois rule, became the inescapable ground for the discussion of Marxist theory and Marxist strategy. It split the socialist parties of the West irrevocably. A new International was set up — the Third — to link together the parties that looked to Moscow and endorsed Leninist ideas as the correct political interpretation of Marx.

The terms social democrat and communist became sharply differentiated for the first time, and although many social democrats, including the former 'Pope' of Marxism, Karl Kautsky, still called themselves Marxists and although there were still, particularly in the German, Austrian, and Dutch labour movements, important political interpretations of Marx that rejected Lenin's ideas, the survival of Russia as the sole workers' state in the 1920s gradually destroyed the basis for independent alternative Marxisms elsewhere. Under Stalin Marxism and the Soviet brand of communism became virtually identical and Marxism lost its critical and open character, and became a narrow set of dogmas whose chief purpose was to serve the national interests of the Russian state. Great Russian chauvinism was reborn under the active tutelage of Joseph Stalin.

Stalinism destroyed Lenin's Bolshevik party in the purges, and it came close to destroying Marxism as a system of ideas, so gravely did it pervert the meaning of ideas that were central to Marxism — the dialectical method, the dictatorship of the proletariat, proletarian internationalism, historical materialism, and so ruthlessly did it attempt to suppress all independent Marxist theory and practice throughout the world. With the discrediting of Stalinism in the 1950s, however, and the emergence of new socialist states and socialist movements entirely independent of Moscow, there has been a renaissance of Marxism in the West.

Leninist principles and the Bolshevik tradition were kept alive right through the era of Stalinist repression by Trotsky and the new parties he helped inspire, grouped in a Fourth International, although few of them were able to secure a large popular base and to wrest control of labour movements away from Stalinists or social democrats. Nevertheless Trotsky's writings and in particular his penetrating and pioneering analysis of the character of the Stalinist regime permitted the survival of a radical internationalist Marxism in the West.

Trotsky himself rejected the notions that the Soviet Union was state capitalist or that it represented an entirely new class mode of production. He argued that it was a society in transition which could either move forward to socialism or back to capitalism. Although a counter-revolution had taken place the central 'conquests of October', the taking of socialised property into public ownership, were still secure. Russia remained a workers' state though one with bureaucratic distortions and a political revolution was necessary to displace the Stalinist bureaucracy, and destroy the centralised, repressive institutions of Stalinist rule, so making the working class the ruling class once more. Otherwise he expected the bureaucracy gradually to return the economy to capitalism.

The main movement in the renewal of Marxism in the West has been away from any perspective that was centred around the imminence of revolution and the discussion of the best tactics to be adopted by the party of the proletariat. Instead Marxist thought has lost a great deal of its former optimism. The terrible lessons of the Russian experience, the eventual recognition that the great hopes raised by the Bolshevik revolution and the first workers' state were betrayed and shattered by Stalinism, were accompanied by widespread pessimism about the possibility of an early transition to socialism in the West, following a succession of major setbacks, especially the victory of Nazism over the German working class.

The proletarian revolution, Lenin constantly emphasised, was not something that Bolshevik parties could create. They could only prepare to lead it when it occurred. The basic predicament which Marxists have had to come to terms with is that only in the years immediately following the First World War has the proletariat revolution seemed imminent in Europe, and at no time has it seemed so in the United States. In part this has been due to the great historical defeats which working class movements suffered in the 1920s and 1930s, particularly in those countries where fascist regimes were established; in part because of the 'exceptional' character of the United States; in part because of the opportunity which was provided by the enormous changes brought about by the Second World War for the consolidation and reinvigoration of capitalism on a world basis. The productive forces proved to have scope for expansion within capitalism that the First World War generation of Marxists had never dreamed possible, and stable democratic republics multiplied as never before. The idea that there were social and political barriers to further accumulation of capital which could not be overcome, and which were creating political and military tensions that could only issue in war, was a perspective that was widely abandoned in the 1950s and 1960s.

The result is that whilst Marxism is more alive today intellectually than it has been for a long time, and Marx's thought is better understood in its full scope and power than it ever was by the Marxists of the Second International, Marxism is also questioned much more in its basic assumptions than it has ever been before, and by Marxists. In political terms this has involved the development of new perspectives, many of which have drawn inspiration from the work

of the Italian communist leader, Antonio Gramsci, who was
imprisoned under Mussolini, and died shortly after his release
in 1937. Gramsci has become a major focus for all those
currents within modern Marxism seeking a political strategy
for winning power and establishing socialism in the social
formations of Western Europe.

Much of Gramsci's most influential work was concerned
with an analysis of the relationship between state and civil
society in the social formations of the West, and how this
relationship differed from that which had existed in the East,
in Tsarist Russia. He directed attention to the strong ideological legitimacy enjoyed by Western states, in contrast to the
East, which relied much more openly on force. Such ideological legitimacy meant that the bourgeoisie exercised *hegemony*
over the proletariat; to a considerable degree the proletariat
consented to bourgeois rule. Gramsci wanted to dispense
entirely with the economic fatalism of some theorists of the
Second International who assumed that the economic base of
capitalism would necessarily break down, and that then its
ideological superstructure would crumble and its ultimate
reliance on force would be exposed. He argued instead that
there was no reason to suppose that economic crises in themselves would bring revolution closer, if the bourgeoisie
through its control of the major directing organs of ideology
in civil society — the Churches, schools, and media — still
retained ideological legitimacy and its ability to convince
the mass of citizens that the bougeois order was still capable
of satisfying their interests and conforming to popular
conceptions of how a society ought to be run.

It followed that the cultural and ideological hegemony of
the bourgeoisie had first to be broken before a successful
proletarian seizure of power and construction of a socialist
order could take place. The proletariat had to organise its
own hegemony over all other groups opposed to capitalism,
forming them into a political bloc which would eventually be
capable of taking the offensive against capitalism. The
organisation of hegemony whether by bourgeoisie or proletariat fell to intellectuals, and Gramsci argued that intellectuals
were becoming increasingly important since it was they who
articulated the interests of different groups and were responsible for maintaining hegemony. The revolutionary party

needed its own stratum of intellectuals who would assist in the long struggle to create an ideological climate favourable to socialism.

Analysis of cultural and ideological domination in capitalist societies as the major factor preventing the proletarian revolution developing, was also the major theme of the Frankfurt school of Marxists in the 1920s and 1930s, and their analysis was broadened still further into a pessimistic account of the nature of modern societies after the Second World War, particularly in the work of Herbert Marcuse. In France also the two most influential schools of Marxism since the war — the existentialist Marxism of Jean-Paul Sartre and the structuralist Marxism of Althusser — have both pointedly reduced the importance of the analysis of capital accumulation which was the heart of Marx's own work.

Marcuse concluded in his most famous work, *One Dimensional Man*, which was written in the United States and strongly influenced by his experience there, that the industrial proletariat was now entirely integrated within capitalist society and no longer a plausible agent of revolutionary change. This had come about as a result of certain structural changes in advanced capitalist societies, in particular the extent of government intervention in the economy to prevent economic crises and manipulation of consciousness to engineer consent. Technology had created material resources which allowed the permanent neutralisation of challenges to the dominant order. All advanced industrial societies, Marcuse concluded, whatever the political facade of their regimes, were totalitarian in the sense that the range of possibilities and needs that were permitted to individuals were those defined not by the individuals themselves, either in the market or through democratic institutions, but by the technical imperatives of the capitalist industrial system. Technical rationality which the Western ideology had proclaimed as the means of achieving a deeper rationality, the liberation of human beings, had become a supreme end in itself, in the process destroying the possibility of realising the utopia all Western ideologists had been committed to in some form.

This was partly due to the phenomenal material success of capitalism during the long post-war boom, but it was also, at least in some cases, due to new questioning about the Marxist belief in material progress and in rationality itself. The advent of modern technologies, particularly nuclear technologies, has destroyed faith in automatic human progress through the increase of human knowledge. Western rationality, the great liberator from toil, superstition, and oppression, now appears to many Marxists to have engendered in its latest stage of development its own forms of superstition and oppression, and to be itself a barrier to a free and fully human society. The ideal of material abundance has become widely doubted as a possible or desirable goal for socialist societies, given the scale of the ecological problems that unrestrained economic growth has caused, and the apparent impossibility of creating a world society which enjoys current American standards of living.

What has enjoyed a considerable revival is Marx's long-run analysis of the trends of accumulation of capital on a world scale, the tendency of capitalism, on one side, to develop the forces of production up to the point of full automation of production and the expulsion of living labour from the production process altogether; but, on the other, to experience increasingly severe crises and obstacles to accumulation. The collapse of the capitalist boom in the 1970s, and the new world economic crisis that ensued, appeared to confirm the enormous insight of Marx's analysis. But the class structure and political structures in the West which have developed in the last hundred years are very different from anything Marx experienced, and numerous Marxists and non-Marxists have argued that even if the cultural and ideological emphasis of some Western Marxists was mistaken, there is no automatic reason why renewed world recession should bring proletarian revolution and the achievement of socialism any closer. Many Trotskyists still insist that capitalism can only be overthrown on a world scale and that for this to be possible it must first be overthrown in the metropolitan centres of the West. They argue that the strategy of national roads to socialism pursued by Marxists in major working class parties like the Italian Communists and the British Labour Party means the accommodation of these parties to their own nation-states and their own bourgeoisies. The alternative pursued by many Marxists has been to pin their hopes for world socialism on socialist revolutions and socialist experiments in the Third World. But these are beyond the scope of this book.

5 Conclusion

Like liberalism, Marxism has had difficulty in reconciling its moral aspirations for a free and fully human social order with the nature of advanced industrial capitalism. In particular it has had to adjust in this century to three major developments — the failure of revolution in the West, the appearance of a major new stage of capitalist development, and the organisation of the Soviet Union claiming to be the world's first workers' and socialist state.

Marxism's radicalism derived from its image of socialism as a transitional form of society which would create the conditions for communism. So under socialism there would still be a state and law separate from the people and there would still be unequal rewards for unequal work. Private ownership of the means of production, however, would be abolished. Under communism, the state, money, and commodity production would disappear, the individual and the community would be reconciled through the kind of democracy established, and the principle of distribution according to need would be enforced.

Sustaining this image of socialism and communism as a practical possibility in the light of twentieth century developments has not been easy. Like many contemporary liberal thinkers Marxists have found it easier to concentrate on the tendencies of capitalist development rather than on how it can be overthrown. Just as liberal theorists have distinguished between individualism and collectivism, the laissez-faire state and the interventionist state, industrial society and post-industrial society, so Marxists have distinguished between competitive and monopoly capitalism. The first is the era of relatively small-scale production, relatively limited use of technology, minimal state involvement in the detail of production, the development of a world economy through trade, regulation of the whole world economy through the market and the law of value. The second is the era of large-scale production, the concentration and centralisation of production in the hands of finance capital, the rational exploitation of technology to raise productivity, the increase in social responsibility, intervention and regulation of the national economy, the rise of imperialism and the forcible division of the world market by the leading capitalist powers.

Within the stage of monopoly capitalism a third stage is distinguished — the stage of state monopoly capitalism. In this stage the interpenetration of the state apparatus and corporate capital, and the internationalisation of capital, have reached the point at which maintaining the consensus and avoiding the crisis have become the prime task. At the same time the world division of labour has progressed to the point where the major agents of accumulation on a world scale have become the multinationals, organising production and trade across and despite state boundaries. The old pattern of imperialism has shifted, and new centres of accumulation and financial power have arisen.

Within this kind of framework modern Marxists have devoted much attention to the analysis of the modern state, rejecting many of the formulations contained in the writings of Marx and Engels and of later Marxists. The simple conception of the state as an instrument of the ruling class has been discarded. In its place two major alternatives have developed. One has emphasised the specific character of politics and ideology and the need to study them in their own right, not as reflections or derivations from the economic base. The focus here is upon how bourgeois rule is organised and consolidated through political parties and ideological apparatuses; how modern states have been able to displace economic crises from the economic to the political sphere. The other has emphasised how the state must be analysed as one of the forms necessary for the reproduction of capital. This means the nature of the state comes to be analysed in the same way as the commodity, money, and accumulation are studied in *Capital*, as necessary forms taken by capital at different stages of its circulation and reproduction. The state is grasped not as an instrument of a dominant class, but as an agency performing functions which have to be performed if capital accumulation is to take place and capital is to be reproduced. The state is charged with maintaining capitalism as a system of production and exchange, and not with promoting any particular capitalist interests.

Such conceptions have increased the range of Marxist analyses of the state, and they have assisted in understanding the character of the Soviet Union. The consequences of capitalism as a system of technical rationality, class struggle, and capital accumulation, continue to be unravelled by Marxists. But the possibility of transforming this system into socialism has not moved appreciably closer. Hardly any Marxists in the West now see the Soviet Union as a society in transition towards communism, or as a possible model for a movement to socialism in the West itself.

8

Conclusion

This book has attempted to outline some of the major
themes and ideas of modern Western social and political
thought. The discussion has had to be highly selective and
offers no more than a rapid survey of the scope and form of
Western ideas. I have argued that modern Western thought is
best approached not as the latest emanation from some
ancient spirit of Western civilisation, but as a system of ideas
which at critical points denies and overturns the ideas and
values of the traditional, pre-capitalist culture of the West. Its
driving force has been persistent attempts accurately to
describe, theoretically to explain, and practically to assist or
resist the great transformation that has taken place in world
civilisation in the last two hundred years. Western states and
Western societies were the first where capitalism became
dominant for the first time and the conditions for the rise of
modern industry were created; where the processes of industrialisation and modernisation commenced, and where the
modern conception of the separation of *society* and *state* as
two distinct spheres first became developed. This is what
makes Western history and Western thought in the modern
era of special interest for world history and world thought.
Western states were the first to experience the transition and
Western thinkers were the first to seek to understand the
nature of the change that was taking place.

From such a standpoint what is striking about Western
thought is not the diversity of its methods or material, but
how many of its assumptions are held in common in its
various schools. The various branches of the Western ideology
and the various national schools of thought shared more with

one another than with the traditional systems of thought they displaced. This is principally because, as I have tried to show, so much of modern Western thought can be understood in relation to three major anchorage points: the modern state, civil society, and scientific rationalism. These three immensely complex developments in the organisation of Western societies shaped the response of intellectuals to the emergence of the new order and encouraged the growth of a broad movement of intellectual 'enlightenment', which did not cause but certainly assisted and helped to consolidate and justify the revolutions against political absolutism in Europe.

The critical shift that took place is still best described as the bourgeois revolution, although as I have argued, this is not to be identified, as in some Marxist interpretations, with a simple transfer of political power from a landed aristocracy to an industrial bourgeoisie. 'Bourgeois' had a crucial earlier meaning within the Western ideology. In liberal doctrine a 'bourgeois' meant a member of civil society, an individual citizen in his private capacity. The claim of liberalism was, and still is, not that the bourgeoisie conceived as a distinct sectional interest within civil society should rule, but that all should be bourgeois; everyone should have the same legal rights, duties, and privileges as everyone else. All should in certain respects be equal. Liberalism began, therefore, as a universal ideology, proclaiming universal rights, and it is the universalism of the Western ideology as a whole which is perhaps its most striking characteristic as a moral doctrine. It claimed to speak on behalf of all humanity and to justify social and political arrangements as rational depending on how far they accorded with basic natural rights or promoted happiness and justice. Such claims relied in part on traditional Christian and classical conceptions but they needed all the support which the new conceptions of the natural order and its relationship to the human realm could give. Certainly the concerted attempt to describe and explain reality rationally assisted the decisive break that was eventually made with all transcendental (including religious) and traditional conceptions of the world and marked out the terrain for the new ideological debates of modern times. It was a terrain founded upon both a moral and a rational discourse about human beings, their social relations and potentialities. The two did not always prove compatible.

The moral universalism and scientific rationalism of liberalism, however, although they cast the Western ideology into its enduring modern form, were double-edged weapons. The French Revolution showed that clearly enough. Liberalism was a universal ideology but its practical success depended on its serving particular social interests, and these interests naturally wished to set limits to the application of liberal doctrine, whenever the two conflicted. Most important was the question of property, the right to own it and accumulate it, to have it protected and to bequeath it. Social inequalities and social privileges, where these arose through the natural operation of individual self-interest in civil society, were not only tolerated but thought desirable by liberals. It was public legel inequalities that were detested.

This became one important area in modern political debate. The liberal ideal of a community of equal citizens and unequal property owners produced the socialist response which proclaimed that formal legal equality was a sham and that substantive equality, human emancipation, and social justice, demanded practical equality in the social sphere as well. The free and equal bourgeois society of liberalism was the foundation on which a new ruling class, the bourgeoisie, arose and was maintained, a class whose wealth and ownership of property were based directly on the poverty and exclusion from ownership of the majority of the population. For socialists real freedom and real equality, true universalism, required the overcoming of social as well as political and legal inequalities. The bourgeois revolution of liberalism was therefore denounced by socialists as only a partial and limited emancipation, which gave disproportionate benefits to one section of the new emancipated civil society. The term bourgeois acquired its modern pejorative overtones.

Liberalism and socialism are the fundamental components of the Western ideology. The great conservative Reaction of the nineteenth century arose in opposition to it, but was powerfully shaped by the new world it so abominated. It was forced to accept the mobilisation of the masses and the arrival of ideological debate, although it succeeded in adapting the initially revolutionary concept of nation for its own purposes. Many currents fed the great Reaction, including the romantic movement, as well as many anti-rational and anti-scientific currents in Western culture. They had important influence on the ideologies of the various nationalist and conservative movements that began to develop in the era of mass politics.

The real challenge to the Western ideology, however, came not from the Reaction, but from its growing inadequacy to cope with the way in which industrial societies themselves developed. The Western ideology derives from the period of transition but it became dominant and vastly extended in its range and applications in a quite new setting, the rise of world economy, world politics, and world industry. The politics of industrial societies have mostly been conducted in terms of the concepts and assumptions of systems of ideas that were first formulated when many of the characteristic features of industrial societies were not well understood or appreciated. The arrival of this new rational order has seen an enormous explosion in the numbers of intellectuals and in the range and importance of intellectual work, and a quite unprecedented growth of knowledge, information, and communication. Every sphere of social life has become more internally differentiated, more specialised, and more impersonal. This has assisted the rise of vast academic industries of enquiry, observation, and speculation about contemporary industrial societies, and separate disciplines have been established in field after field -- sociology, economics, political science, history, and numerous subdivisions of these -- which have produced a steady stream of description, analysis, and justification. But amidst the great flood of information and the increasingly important role played by intellectuals of different kinds in servicing and co-ordinating modern societies, new uncertainties and misgivings have constantly beset the leading doctrines of the Western ideology, even as their traditional opponents fade away.

The great political theorists, political economists, and natural philosophers of the transition period were succeeded by social theorists such as Durkheim and Weber. They extended the basic concepts of the Western ideology, and the analysis of civil society and the modern state in the altered context of a more developed industrial capitalist society, where such crucial modern trends as urbanisation, concentration and centralisation of capital, the separation of ownership and control, and the move towards mass democracy and mass culture were much further advanced. The concepts of bureaucracy, anomie, legitimacy, and the organic division of labour, continue the discussion of themes and problems which can be found in Hegel and Hobbes, particularly the relation of the modern state to civil society and the problem of social order.

Yet despite its great bulk what is most remarkable about modern Western thought is the extent to which it has stayed chained to its nineteenth century ideological formulations and how that has caused it to become increasingly pessimistic and uncertain because the ideology as a moral doctrine is more and more incapable of dealing with so many events and aspects of the modern world. Despite ideology being pronounced finished so often, the concepts and images it fashioned remain the universe of modern thought. Their continuing strength is in part because each major strand of the Western ideology offers a different way of theorising the central features of modern society.

In this book three major approaches to the analysis of modern industrial societies from within the Western ideology have been considered; the standpoint of the market, the standpoint of the state, and the standpoint of production and the labour process. To each there corresponds a different conception of democracy and a different conception of the relationship between the state and the economy, a different conception of the good society. These conceptions — the market order, social democracy, and socialism — are the three most powerful images of the good society which modern Western thought has produced. The central terms in Western political discourse, such as justice, rights, happiness, freedom, equality, order, rationality, and progress carry different meanings and a different content in the three approaches, but all three belong clearly to the same tradition. Each promises the reconciling of individual freedom, and therefore individual egoism and self-interest, with the maintaining of order and the promotion of the welfare of the whole society.

The theorists of the market order placed freedom before equality and democracy and saw the emancipation of the individual primarily in legal terms — the same legal rights for every individual. Formal equality and substantive inequality meant that the legitimacy of the market order would always be precarious, which is why so many liberals have been hostile to democracy, and have supported either a franchise restricted to the propertied or other devices designed at insulating government policy from too close accountability. The theorists of social democracy by contrast placed democracy and equality before freedom and emphasised that individual rights depended on prior membership of a community. The emancipation they proclaimed was political emancipation. The democracy comprising all citizens would exert such pressure on politicians and governments through elections and public opinion as to ensure collective measures to make the conditions of life more equal, to correct huge imbalances in the distribution of incomes, and to use public agencies to remedy shortcomings in the performance of markets. In this way the state would guarantee certain rights, opportunities, and services for all its members.

The socialist image of community in the new industrial society went beyond the community of individuals and of citizens and proclaimed the community of producers, as the only form in which the full emancipation of the individual could be accomplished. To legal and political emancipation socialists added social emancipation. They attacked the inequalities of civil society at their source by planning to abolish wage labour and the subordination of one class to another in the labour process. By placing the process of production itself under the direct control of the associated producers and creating a community in which social power was shared equally, the basis for an independent political power would also be destroyed. Socialists regarded the market order and social democracy to be founded upon a class mode of production, so they planned to abolish the bourgeois state as a sphere separate from civil society, because by maintaining the conditions for civil society to function it necessarily created and perpetuated the conditions for capitalism. The workers' state was projected as a state in which democracy would be 'participatory', rather than either parliamentary or bureaucratic; the central bureaucracy would be subordinate to the popular will expressed in councils and soviets, the standing army would be abolished, the people armed. The conflict between the particular will of the agents of the state and the general will of the people would be resolved by new institutional forms aimed at preventing the conflict from arising.

The socialist ideal has nowhere been realised in the West, and was only briefly attempted in Russia. The market order and social democracy have had a much more extended trial. Although the terms liberal and socialist have become hopelessly confused in political debate and practice (social democrats, for example, are sometimes called liberals and sometimes socialists), real divisions still persist, and there is still meaning in the contrast between *economic liberal* and *social democrat* which expresses the fundamental tension between liberty and democracy in modern liberalism. The first defines liberty primarily in economic and individualist terms, and therefore regards the state as no more than an external negative framework to promote individual interests. The second puts the primary emphasis on the collective life and basis of the community, and therefore treats freedom and individuality as resulting from the preoccupations of the state with its fundamental task — maintaining the equality of its citizens and preventing conflict.

Each of the three dominant approaches in modern Western thought has suffered in this century an internal crisis of confidence about its concepts, its values, its direction, though the disease has hardly been fatal, and in part it can be seen as a genuine crisis which has inspired at least partial recovery and new growth. The renewal of the critical vigour of Marxist thought in the last twenty years has been remarkable, and more recently liberalism also has shown signs of new development. Few liberals have, however, felt comfortable in the twentieth century, even if liberal tenets and liberal rhetoric have been more generally accepted than ever before. This stemmed from the realisation that what so threatened individualism and individuality were the very forces of democracy and rationalism that liberals once thought were its natural allies. What makes the deliberations of modern liberals so gloomy is the awareness that the very forces that liberated the individual now constrict and diminish him, that technical rationality involves bureaucratic and centralised organisation, and a style of life which tends to make human beings isolated and deprived, whatever its material level may be.

What liberals of all schools have had increasingly to recognise, therefore, is the inadequacy of describing and evaluating the complex interdependent societies of modern industrialism as though they were simply societies of self-sufficient individuals pursuing individual ends. As a consequence liberalism as a doctrine has experienced increasing tension between its principle of liberty and its commitment to democracy, and also between its principle of individuality and its commitment to rationalism. It has led to a partial surrender of liberalism's claim to be a universal moral doctrine. There has been an increasing retreat from the attempt to unite the injunction to individual fulfilment and the imperatives of a production process that is mechanised, bureaucratic, and impersonal, and on which arises a society of great complexity, great knowledge, and great wealth, but a society of strangers.

For a time social democracy appeared to have incorporated the advantages of liberalism whilst discarding its drawbacks and remedying the shortcomings of the market order. But social democratic regimes have experienced an increasing tension between equality and efficiency, between their need to maintain their legitimacy by pursuing equality and guaranteeing rights for all their members, and their need to keep the capitalist economy functioning efficiently. The limits of policies on welfare and economic intervention have all been dramatically exposed in recent years by world economic stagnation and low growth. Struggles over the size and the funding of government expenditure, which swelled disproportionately in more prosperous times, have come to the fore, as have struggles over certain kinds of rights, particularly certain trade union rights, and certain political liberties, which had been presumed secure. The social consensus which social democrats everywhere relied upon has become extremely fragile. The marrying of the collectivist impulses of democracy with the individualistic principle of the market economy has proved much more difficult than once it seemed, and only works well when the underlying rate of economic growth is strong and there is a material base to pay for social reforms.

Socialists in the West, however, are not in much of a position to benefit from the brooding pessimism of liberals or the discomfiture of social democrats. Marxism, it is true, has retained the moral universalism of the Western ideology. It still projects a future rational social order in which the interests and needs of all human beings will be secured. But Marxism has suffered its own great internal crisis, firstly in the experience of Stalinism and secondly because of the failure of the revolutionary potential of the industrial proletariat to materialise in the West itself. So remote did the prospect of the working class ever emerging as a conscious agent of revolution and liberation seem to many Marxists in the comfortable democratic republics of the West during the 1950s, that many, especially in the United States, abandoned it as a political concept altogether, and began to speculate on other agencies of social change that might still bring about some of the changes in the social order that generations of Western ideologists had worked for. Groups from the ghettos, the new 'class' of intellectuals, and Third World liberation movements have been favourite new social forces in recent years. To the extent that such analyses have gained ground within Marxism the emphasis of the whole doctrine has been shifted, usually accompanied by growing pessimism and resignation because the new groups could never play the role that the industrial proletariat plays in classical Marxism. This has been further reinforced by the growth of doubts about technology and about the commitment of Marxism to a society of material plenty as the necessary condition for socialism the only way of overcoming the constraints imposed by scarcity. Such a view implies an unlimited exploitation of natural resources. The naivety and one-sidedness of many early socialist views on nature and technology have been questioned as the full implications of the grossly unequal and imbalanced development of the world economy and distribution of resources resulting from two centuries of capitalist development is grasped. Pessimism has also arisen because of the practical problems of organising a socialist economy that is both more efficient than capitalism and that abolishes the kind of state with its repressive and centralised apparatus which maintains capitalist relations of production.

The imperialism of the West has been a decisive aspect of the history of modern times, not least in the realm of ideas. The Western ideology helped to overwhelm the cultures and civilisations of other parts of the world. Only Islam conducted any kind of successful resistance. But although the new world civilisation has been Western-dominated up to now, it is unlikely to remain so for ever. Already the Western ideology has undergone significant transformation in being adapted to Third World states and movements, and it is in any case Marxism that has enjoyed the greater success — the critique of the Western ideology has had more appeal than the core of the doctrine itself. Despite these qualifications no society or people has been able in the last two hundred years to maintain its independence from the world revolution initiated by the West. Western ideas and Western theories have become the property of the whole world just as Western technology has also, but the universal hopes and dreams of a new and higher social order have still to be fulfilled.

In his eleventh thesis on Feuerbach the young Marx wrote, 'Philosophers have only interpreted the world in various ways; the point is to change it'. This arresting formulation captures the impatient enthusiasm of the radicals to begin the construction of the new order that could carry through the tasks which the French Revolution had begun. Yet Marx was also well aware of the contradictory nature of progress. As he wrote in a passage about British rule in India:

> The bourgeois period of history has to create the material basis of the new world — on the one hand the universal intercourse founded upon the mutual dependency of mankind, and the means of that intercourse; on the other hand the development of the productive powers of man and the transformation of material production into a scientific domination of natural agencies. Bourgeois industry and commerce create these material conditions of a new world in the same way as geological revolutions have created the surface of the earth. When a great social revolution shall have mastered the results of the bourgeois epoch, the market of the world and the modern powers of production, and subjected them to the common control of the most advanced peoples, then only will human progress cease to resemble that hideous pagan idol, who would not drink the nectar but from the skulls of the slain.

This ambivalence towards the progress which capitalism has achieved becomes much stronger in the twentieth century. In one of his essays the German Marxist, Walter Benjamin, described the angel of history, his face turned towards the past as he contemplated the succession of disasters, failures, and atrocities that make up modern history:

> The angel would like to stay, awaken the dead, and make whole what has been smashed. But a storm is blowing from Paradise; it has got caught in his wings with such violence that the angel can no longer close them. The storm irresistibly propels him into the future to which his back is turned, while the pile of debris before him grows skyward. This storm is what we call progress.

In the twentieth century political developments have often posed a stark choice between socialism and barbarism and some societies have relapsed into barbarism. Barbarism is the antithesis of Enlightenment ideals and values because it represents the possibility that many of the gains of social and economic progress could be cancelled and reversed. The most striking examples of barbarism have been not the outbreaks of 'irrationalism', the re-emergence of old forms of mysticism and superstition, but the pursuit of irrational ends with rational means. The worst excesses of the twentieth century — the Nazi concentration camps, the Soviet labour camps, the development and deployment of modern weaponry in world wars and against movements of national liberation — are perfect examples of the rational choice and adaptation of means to achieve given ends, and could not have occurred had technical rationality not been consecrated as a supreme value of industrial society and its institutions organised accordingly. This is what makes Auschwitz and the Gulag and the techniques of twentieth-century warfare so modern, and why there is such unease and self-questioning today in all the main schools of Western thought.

The Western ideology was founded upon the idea that a rational social order could be constructed or evolved which by satisfying the interests of all its members would appear just and legitimate. The underlying human predicament has been perceived in modern Western thought to be how to reconcile the self-interest of individuals with the interests of the community and ultimately of the entire species, when the resources available to satisfy the wants and needs of individuals remain necessarily limited. This problem of how to maintain social order in the circumstances of the emergence of modern civil society and modern states was formulated with great clarity at the beginning of the modern era by Hobbes. His solution was uncompromising. Only fear of death was sufficiently strong to induce individuals to submit themselves to a sovereign authority. Only force could integrate human societies, keeping particular wills and particular interests in some kind of balance so that a reasonable degree of peace, security, and happiness might be enjoyed by all members of the Commonwealth.

Liberal doctrine since Hobbes has not emphasised the importance of force in holding human societies together. Instead it has stressed the idealism of the state, the way in which modern states have been organised so as to secure the active consent of their members. The state, this apparatus of force, comes to be understood as an apparatus which promotes order, happiness, reason, or justice, as in the idea of a market order in which all individuals are free within a legal framework to pursue whatever purposes they wish; or the idea of a social democracy in which broad equality of conditions and the rights of individuals and groups are guaranteed through public involvement. Both ideas were made much more plausible as justifications of social arrangements by the enormous increase in material resources which industrialism created.

Against these Marxism revived the ideas of Hobbes and Machiavelli that modern states were founded on and maintained by force, whatever the ideological disguise in which this was cloaked. Marxists denied that either a market order or a social democracy could in practice deliver what was promised and work to the advantage of all citizens, because both were founded on an organisation of the production process which constantly created conflict between the classes over how production was organised and how the product was distributed. Furthermore Marxists argued that the alleviation of scarcity which industrial capitalism had brought was only temporary and that as the economy became subject to increasingly severe economic crises so its ideological defences would be stripped away and the role of force in maintaining its class relations of production and distribution exposed.

Modern Marxists have had to recognise that matters are more complex since while no functioning capitalist society has approached the kind of moral ideal proclaimed in liberal ideology, the legitimacy of Western states has been remarkably unshaken either by economic crises or by the persistence of large structural inequalities in income and wealth.

Yet as many thinkers from all schools have noted, despite the impressive stability of Western states and the renewed vigour of capitalism in the first two post-war decades, the legitimacy of those states has gradually become more precarious as the reconciling of private wants and collective needs has become steadily more difficult. Western affluence encouraged a pronounced retreat of individuals into a private existence where what counted were individual consumption and family life at the expense either of the satisfactions to be obtained from meaningful work or from participation in the political community. The legitimacy of modern Western states has come to depend less on moral conceptions of either a market order or a social democracy, but on the provision of the material gratifications which individuals have come to expect as something to which they are entitled. But the gulf between the cultivation of individual life styles, which revolve around the pursuit of individual happiness and gratifications, and the political and economic orders, which revolve around the ideas of just order and technical rationality, has widened. The political order is now less and less perceived as a morally superior association which can easily bind its members for collective purposes, and the economic order is increasingly failing to provide the stream of material benefits on which the smooth workings of the other two realms depend.

In this renewed crisis of liberal thought and liberal practice socialism appears less of an alternative than it once did. Its own ideal and vision have been clouded and weakened by the way in which industrial societies have developed, and by the ways in which many of the socialist experiments which have taken place have been conducted. It no longer has the same

moral or intellectual power that it once had to convince
sufficient numbers that its practical solutions to the problems
of industrial societies are workable, or would result in a
realisation of a free, democratic, and peaceful social order,
and the reconciliation of the individual and community
which liberalism itself has failed to achieve. For the present
modern Western thought appears to have reached an impasse.
The practical and theoretical obstacles to further progress
along the traditional lines look formidable and no way
around them or over them is in sight. But as the various
threats to the continued survival of the human species mount,
so the need to find one does not diminish.

Guide to further reading

Modern Western social and political thought is a vast subject, and this book has done no more than outline some of its more important ideas and themes. There are many alternative approaches, and many aspects which have not been covered at all in these pages, or covered only very briefly. In this bibliography I have selected a number of books which explore in greater detail some of the themes I have raised.

A. General

Amongst general books which survey the whole of the Western tradition I would recommend R. Berki, *The History of Political Thought* (Dent, London, 1977), particularly useful for summaries of the thought of major thinkers; A. Macintyre, *A Short History of Ethics* (RKP, London, 1967), an incisive account of the social context of the tradition of moral philosophy in the West; and Sheldon Wolin, *Politics and Vision* (Allen & Unwin, London, 1961), a very rich and detailed survey of the whole sweep of Western political thought. For the development of sociological thought, two books by Robert Nisbet, *The Sociological Tradition* (Heinemann, London, 1967), and *The Social Philosophers* (Paladin, London, 1976) are stimulating and challenging; Raymond Aron, *Main Currents in Sociological Thought* (2 vols) (Penguin, Harmondsworth, 1968) surveys the development of sociological theory through an analysis of seven leading sociological thinkers; and G. Therborn, Science, *Class, and Society* (NLB, London, 1976) looks at the rise of modern social science and contrasts its standpoint with that of Marxism.

Two other invaluable general books are Raymond Williams, *Keywords* (Fontana, London, 1976), which analyses the different and changing historical meanings of key terms in Western political and social thought; and A. Arblaster and S. Lukes, *The Good Society* (Methuen, London, 1971), a very useful anthology of writing on the nature of the good society, selected from the whole of the Western tradition.

B. Western history

One of the best possible introductions, not only to Western history but to world history is the *Times Atlas of World History* (Times Books, London, 1978), edited by Geoffrey Barraclough. Its maps and historical summaries give an unrivalled overview of the world's political and economic development.

The study of Western history has changed considerably in the last thirty years. Some notable works of synthesis and interpretation include Geoffrey Barraclough, *An Introduction to Contemporary History* (Penguin, Harmondsworth, 1967); Barrington Moore Jnr, *The Social Origins of Dictatorship and Democracy* (Penguin, Harmondsworth, 1969); Perry Anderson, *Passages from Antiquity to Feudalism* (NLB, London, 1974) and *Lineages of the Absolutist State* (NLB, London, 1974); and Immanuel Wallerstein, *The Modern World System* (Academic Press, New York, 1974). Anderson and Wallerstein are particularly important for studying the period of transition from feudalism to capitalism. More specialised but invaluable for bringing together contributions to the continuing debate on this problem is R. Hilton (ed.), *The Transition from Feudalism to Capitalism* (NLB, London, 1976).

On the Enlightenment and the French Revolution, Norman Hampson's book *The Enlightenment* (Penguin, Harmondsworth, 1968) is very clear and comprehensive, whilst different accounts of the French Revolution can be found in R. Palmer, *The Age of the Democratic Revolution* (Princeton University Press, Princeton, 1959); A. Soboul, *The French Revolution* (NLB, London, 1974); and E. Hobsbawm, *The Age of Revolution* (Abacus, London, 1977). The last provides the most general and most illuminating survey.

For the rise of modern science there is much interesting material in L. Feuer, *The Scientific Intellectuals* (Basic Books,

New York, 1963), H. Butterfield, *The Origins of Modern Science* (Bell, London, 1957), J. D. Bernal, *Science in History* (Watts, London, 1954) and, R. G. Collingwood, *The Idea of Nature* (Oxford, 1965).

The Industrial Revolution and its political and social impact can be studied in K. Polanyi, *The Great Transformation* (Beacon Press, Boston, 1957) and P. Laslett, *The World We Have Lost* (Methuen, London, 1961). These approach the question from very different perspectives. Essential reading is E. P. Thompson, *The Making of the English Working Class* (Penguin, Harmondsworth, 1963). An important study of the concept of industrialism in Western thought is K. Kumar, *Prophecy and Progress* (Penguin, Harmondsworth, 1978), an excellent introduction to the different meanings attached to it. For the concepts of history and progress in Western thought see also R. G. Collingwood, *The Idea of History* (Oxford, 1946) and J. B. Bury, *The Idea of Progress* (Macmillan, London, 1920).

C. Liberalism

For general books on liberalism Guido de Ruggiero, *The History of European Liberalism* (OUP, London, 1927) is still hard to better for its detailed discussion of liberal ideas and the different national traditions of liberal thought. Harold Laski, *The Rise of European Liberalism* (Allen & Unwin, London, 1936) also provides a good historical survey. More recent studies include C. B. Macpherson, *The Life and Times of Liberal Democracy* (Oxford, 1977), which outlines three different models of democracy that liberals have presented; and David Manning, *Liberalism* (Dent, London, 1976), which presents liberal ideas from a philosophical standpoint. For the origins of the conception of the state and politics from which liberalism arose, there is the major study by Quentin Skinner, *The Foundations of Modern Political Thought* (Cambridge, 1978).

On specific authors, two very different interpretations of Locke are C. B. Macpherson, *The Political Theory of Possessive Individualism* (Oxford, 1962) and John Dunn, *The Political Thought of John Locke* (Cambridge, 1969). On Hobbes there is Macpherson again, and also H. Warrender, *The Political Philosophy of Hobbes* (Oxford, 1957) and

M. Goldsmith, *Hobbes' Science of Politics* (London, 1966).

Two very good recent books on Hegel's political and social thought are S. Avineri, *Hegel's Theory of the Modern State* (Cambridge, 1972), and R. Plant, *Hegel* (Allen & Unwin, London, 1973). For Rousseau, G. D. H. Cole's introduction to the Everyman Edition of the *Social Contract* and the *Discourses* (Dent, London, 1973) gives a clear summary; so does A. Cobban, *Rousseau and the Idea of the Modern State* (Allen & Unwin, London, 1974). For Paine, an excellent study of his thought and the context in which he wrote is E. Foner, *Tom Paine and Revolutionary America* (OUP, New York, 1976).

Bentham and the utilitarians are still well served by E. Halevy, *The Growth of Philosophic Radicalism* (Faber, London, 1928). See also S. R. Letwin, *The Pursuit of Certainty* (Cambridge, 1965). A very good study of the thought of John Stuart Mill is A. Ryan, *J. S. Mill* (RKP, London, 1974). See also the useful introduction by G. L. Williams to *Mill on Politics and Society* (Fontana, London, 1976).

One of the best brief surveys of liberalism which deserves a special mention is Steven Lukes, *Individualism* (Blackwell, Oxford, 1973) which analyses the wide range of meanings this central concept has had in different national intellectual traditions.

D. Marxism

The quality of academic writing on Marx has improved remarkably in the last twenty years. Important general works of interpretation include G. Lichtheim, *Marxism* (RKP, London, 1961), D. McLellan, *Karl Marx: His Life and Thought* (Macmillan, London, 1974), S. Avineri, *The Social and Political Thought of Karl Marx* (Cambridge, 1968), E. Mandel, *The Formation of the Economic Thought of Karl Marx* (NLB, London, 1971).

For the socialist movement as a whole there are two books by G. Lichtheim – *A Short History of Socialism* (Fontana, London, 1975) and *The Origins of Socialism* (Weidenfeld, London, 1969). There is also G. D. H. Cole's comprehensive *History of Socialist Thought* (in many volumes) (Macmillan, London, 1953). The history of anarchist ideas and anarchist movements is well surveyed in G. Woodcock, *Anarchism*

(Penguin, Harmondsworth, 1963).

For the Marxist tradition Lichtheim provides a general outline, so, in much greater detail, does L. Kolakowski in *Main Currents of Marxism* (three volumes) (Oxford, 1978). An important and challenging interpretation of the Marxist tradition is given by Perry Anderson in *Considerations on Western Marxism* (NLB, London, 1976). The most useful book of all for further study of the Marxist tradition is D. McLellan, *Marxism after Marx* (Macmillan, London, 1979). It provides comprehensive coverage and very useful bibliographies on all major Marxist schools since Marx's death.

Amongst the great wealth of secondary literature the following can be especially recommended: N. Geras, *The Legacy of Rosa Luxemburg* (NLB, London, 1976); S. Cohen, *Bukharin and the Bolshevik Revolution* (Wildwood House, London, 1974); C. Claudin, *The Communist Movement; From Comintern to Cominform* (Penguin, Harmondsworth, 1975). On Lenin two important books are N. Harding, *Lenin's Political Thought* (Macmillan, London, 1977), and M. Liebman, *Leninism under Lenin* (Merlin, London, 1980). On Trotsky, Isaac Deutscher's three volume biography, *The Prophet Armed, The Prophet Unarmed,* and *The Prophet Outcast* (Oxford, 1970) is indispensable. For Gramsci, Carl Boggs provides a useful brief introduction to his thought in *Gramsci's Marxism* (Pluto, London, 1976).

For general surveys of the Marxist theory of politics see Ralph Miliband, *Marxism and Politics* (Oxford, 1977), and R. Blackburn (ed.), *Revolution and Class Struggle* (Fontana, London, 1977), which reprints a number of important articles.

E. The theorists of industrial society

There are two outstanding books on Durkheim and Weber: Steven Lukes, *Emile Durkheim* (Allen Lane, London, 1973), and David Beetham, *Max Weber and the Theory of Modern Politics* (Allen & Unwin, London, 1974). Extremely valuable general surveys include A. Giddens, *Capitalism and Modern Social Theory* (Cambridge, 1971), which deals with Durkheim, Weber, and Marx, and R. Bendix, *Max Weber* (London, Methuen, 1966); and two books by T. Bottomore, *Political Sociology* (Hutchinson, London, 1979), and *Elites in Society*

(Penguin, Harmondsworth, 1965). For Keynes, see D. Moggridge, *Keynes* (Macmillan, London, 1976), and for Parsons, Alvin Gouldner, *The Coming Crisis of Western Sociology* Heinemann, London, 1971).

The history of the Reaction and European conservatism are well surveyed in N. O'Sullivan, *Conservatism* (Dent, London, 1976).

F. The impasse of the Western tradition

There is a wealth of writing on this from a wide variety of perspectives. See particularly: John Dunn, *Western Political Thought in the Face of the Future* (Cambridge, 1979); F. Hirsch, *The Social Limits to Growth* (RKP, London, 1977); D. Bell, *The Cultural Contradictions of Capitalism* (Heinemann, London, 1976); J. Habermas, *Legitimation Crisis* (Heinemann, London, 1976); R. Heilbroner, *An Inquiry into the Human Prospect* (Norton, New York, 1974); Tom Nairn, 'The Modern Janus' in *The Breakup of Britain* (NLB, London, 1977); Alvin Gouldner, *The Future of Intellectuals* (Macmillan, London, 1979); and L. Kolakowski (ed.), *The Socialist Idea* (Quartet, London, 1977).

G. Specially recommended for further reading are the following: R. Berki, *The History of Political Thought;* J. Dunn, *Western Political Thought in the Face of the Future*; A. Giddens, *Capitalism and Modern Social Theory*; E. Hobsbawm, *The Age of Revolution*; K. Kumar, *Prophecy and Progress*; G. Lichtheim, *A Short History of Socialism*; S. Lukes, *Individualism*; C. B. Macpherson, *The Life and Times of Liberal Democracy*; R. Miliband, *Marxism and Politics*; and R. Williams, *Keywords*.

Biographies

BACON, Francis (1561–1626)

English statesman and philosopher. He helped pioneer new inductive methods in scientific enquiry and collective scientific research. Main work: *The New Atlantis*.

BENTHAM, Jeremy (1748–1832)

English lawyer and political theorist. He became a leading advocate of parliamentary, administrative, and legal reform, and supported an economic policy of minimal government interference. He was the founder of the school of utilitarianism, which proposed that all government policies should be judged not for their conformity to abstract principles, but for their effects, specifically for their contribution to the greatest happiness of the greatest number. His works include *A Fragment on Government* (1776) and *An Introduction to the Principles of Morals and Legislation* (1823).

BERNSTEIN, Edward (1850–1932)

German socialist. He was a close associate of Engels, and after Engels' death became the leading advocate in the German Social Democratic Party (SPD) of the need to 'revise' Marxist doctrine to take account of a changed political and economic situation. His book *Evolutionary Socialism* (1899) became the centre of the revisionist controversy within the party, which at that time was the largest and most influential Marxist party in the world.

BODIN, Jean (1529–1596)

French jurist and administrator. He was employed in the service of the nobility and the Crown. Strongly influenced by the long-drawn-out wars of religion in France, he formulated one of the earliest theories of the secular character and the absolute sovereignty of the modern state. Main work: *The Six Books of the Commonwealth* (1576).

BONALD, Louis (1753–1840)

French philosopher and politician. A conservative who opposed all reform and became a leading intellectual figure in the Reaction.

BUKHARIN, Nikolai (1888–1938)

Russian Marxist theorist and political leader. He was one of the Bolshevik leaders and principal theorists of the party. After being closely associated with the policy of war communism during the civil war (1918–1921), he subsequently supported the New Economic Policy and became the advocate of a policy of gradual industrialisation, based on co-operation with the peasantry. Stalin first allied with him to crush the Left opposition, led by Trotsky, then purged Bukharin and his supporters, after 1928. Bukharin was executed in 1938 and has not yet been rehabilitated. His principal writings were *The Economic Theory of the Leisure Class; The ABC of Communism* (with E. Preobrazhensky); *Historical Materialism; Imperialism and World Economy; Economics of the Transformation Period.*

BURCKHARDT, Jacob (1818–1897)

Swiss professor of history and history of art. He was a pupil of Ranke, the German historian, and became a leading nineteenth-century critic of the threat posed by modern culture to traditional Western culture. His writings include: *Civilisation of the Renaissance in Italy* (1860) and *Reflections on History* (1905).

BURKE, Edmund (1729–1797)

English politician and political theorist. He was born in Dublin, entered Parliament in 1766 as a member of the Whig faction which was controlled by the Duke of Rockingham. He became a leading spokesman for the interests of the Whigs and the aristocracy. He strongly condemned British politics towards the colonies in America, but subsequently he was one of the first to attack the Revolution in France. This led him to break with those of his political allies who at first welcomed the Revolution. Burke's polemics against the French Revolution and his defence of English institutions made him the forerunner of a long line of conservative criticism and resistance to the trends which the Revolution unleashed. His most famous book was *Reflections on the Revolution in France* (1790).

CALVIN, John (1509–1564)

One of the leaders of the Protestant Reformation. He put forward the doctrine of predestination which stated that the destiny of each individual soul was already decided and could not be altered by acts of human will. His major work was *Institutes of the Christian Religion* (1536).

COLERIDGE, Samuel Taylor (1772–1834)

English poet and political theorist. He was one of the leaders of the romantic movement in England, and was a strong influence on John Stuart Mill because of the reasons for his opposition to utilitarianism and political economy. His political works include *Constitution of Church and State* (1830).

COMTE, Auguste (1798–1857)

French sociologist. He worked for a time as secretary to Saint-Simon, and developed the latter's ideas into a system of 'positive philosophy' or positivism as it became known. He coined the term sociology, and advocated the control of society by a new elite of scientists. He strongly influenced Emile Durkheim, and through him modern Western social thought.

COPERNICUS, Nicolaus (1473—1543)

Polish astronomer. He propounded the theory that the earth moved round the sun and was not at the centre of the universe. He was denounced by both Protestants and Catholics.

DARWIN, Charles (1809—1882)

English naturalist and geologist. As a result of observations during a three year voyage on HMS *Beagle* and subsequent life-long researches he was the first to formulate the theory of evolution in scientific terms. His greatest work, and the one which caused most controversy, was *On the Origin of Species* (1859). This destroyed the last pillar of the traditional Christian conception of the universe and man's place within it, and had considerable impact on social and political thought through the uncritical employment of Darwinian concepts such as the 'survival of the fittest' and 'natural selection'.

DESCARTES, René (1596—1650)

French philosopher. He pioneered new techniques of deductive reasoning and so helped found the tradition of analytic rationalism. His most famous work is the *Discourse on Method*.

DURKHEIM, Emile (1858—1917)

French sociologist. He was the first Frenchman to hold a chair of sociology (at Bordeaux in 1887). He subsequently became Professor at the Sorbonne in Paris (1902). He was politically active in the Dreyfus affair against the forces of the French Establishment — army, Church, and aristocracy — and he became one of the leading liberal critics of the way in which Dreyfus was treated. He was active again politically during the First World War, but his major impact came through his writings, which influenced the whole development of modern social science. He was opposed to individualism both as a political creed and as a method for social investigation, and his thought contributed to a general reassessment within the liberal tradition of collectivism and the role of the state. His four main books were *The Division of Labour in Society* (1893), *The Rules of Sociological Method* (1895), *Suicide* (1897), and *The Elementary Forms of the Religious Life* (1912).

ENGELS, Friedrich (1820–1895)

German socialist and political theorist. He was the life-long friend and collaborator of Karl Marx, whom he first met in 1843, as a result of Engels' book on *The Condition of the Working Class in England*. Together they wrote a number of works including *The German Ideology* (1846), and *The Communist Manifesto* (1848). They took an active part in the revolutionary movement in 1848. In the 1850s Engels sacrificed his own intellectual ambitions by working in his father's cotton firm in Manchester, so as to earn enough to support Marx and his family in London. He helped organise the First International in the 1860s. In the last decade of Marx's life, and still more after Marx's death in 1883, he became the major interpreter of Marx's ideas to a wider audience. He also edited volumes 2 and 3 of *Capital* from Marx's manuscripts. Important later works of Engels include *Anti-Dühring* (1878), *The Origin of the Family, Private Property, and the State* (1884), *Ludwig Feuerbach and the End of Classical German Philosophy* (1888).

GALILEO, Galilei (1564–1642)

Italian scientist. He was one of the greatest of the early scientists, and was persecuted by the Church for his acceptance of the Copernican hypothesis about the movement of the earth around the sun.

GRAMSCI, Antonio (1891–1937)

Italian communist and Marxist theorist. He was born in Sardinia in the backward, rural Italian 'South', and subsequently studied in Turin where he became active in revolutionary politics. He was a leader of the Turin Factory Council Movement, as the editor of *Ordine Nuovo*. On the founding of the PCI in 1921 Gramsci became one of its leaders and later, after Mussolini's seizure of power, he became general secretary of the party. He was imprisoned by the fascists in 1926, and it was in prison, although his health deteriorated, that he set down the writings for which he has become famous, *The Prison Notebooks*. He died, shortly after his release from prison, in 1937. His work, when it was widely disseminated after 1945, has had a major influence on modern Marxist thought, because in it he develops a new theory of the relationship between state and civil society in the West, and the conditions for a successful revolutionary strategy.

HAMILTON, Alexander (1757–1804)

American statesman and economist. He held office as secretary of the Treasury and was also one of the authors of the *Federalist Papers*, a conservative defence and interpretation of the constitution. He was a political opponent of Jefferson.

HAYEK, Friedrich von (1899–   )

Austrian political economist. He worked as an academic in Vienna (1921–31), London (1931–1950), Chicago (1950–62), and Freiburg (1962–69). His early work was in theoretical economics, but since the publication of *The Road to Serfdom* (1944), he has emerged as a major new exponent of the tradition of liberal constitutionalism and the idea of a market order. His major book is *The Constitution of Liberty* (1960).

HEGEL, Georg (1770–1831)

German philosopher. He held university posts at Jena, and later at Berlin. He strongly supported the French Revolution when he was young, and always remained committed to liberalism, although he increasingly became a defender of the existing Prussian state. His mature reflections on politics are contained in *The Philosophy of Right*, but his early writings, unpublished in his lifetime, are very important for the development of his thought. His philosophical system set out in the *Phenomenology of Spirit* and the *Science of Logic* was enormously influential in many different strands of Western thought, particularly because of the dialectical method that he developed in them.

HOBBES, Thomas (1588–1679)

English philosopher. He spent most of his life in the service of the Duke of Devonshire. He was strongly influenced by the English civil war and the overthrow of the monarchy in the 1640s. His most important book, which was widely condemned and even more widely read, was *Leviathan* (1651), notable for the uncompromising logic of its argument because it justified sovereignty in terms of the ability of a state to maintain order and security, rather than in terms of morality, tradition, or prescription.

HOBHOUSE, Leonard (1864–1929)

English sociologist. He taught at the London School of Economics, and was important in the development of the 'New Liberalism', which became an important component of British social democracy. His books include *Liberalism* (1911), *Democracy and Reaction* (1905), *Elements of Social Justice* (1922), and *Social Development* (1924).

HUME, David (1711–1776)

Scottish philosopher and historian. He was a leading figure in the Scottish Enlightenment, and a close friend of Adam Smith. He wrote widely on philosophy, history, and political economy. He is an important figure in the sceptical and empirical tradition of Anglo-Saxon thought, and was one of the first to insist on a rigorous separation between factual and moral statements. His works include *Treatise on Human Nature* (1739).

JEFFERSON, Thomas (1743–1826)

American statesman. He was the author of the Declaration of Independence and was one of the leaders and more radical theorists of the American Revolution, an associate for a period of Tom Paine. He was President between 1801 and 1808.

KANT, Immanuel (1724–1804)

German philosopher. He was the author of a philosophical system which rivals Hegel's in its scope and its attempt to seek the conditions for all knowledge. He sought to overcome

Hume's scepticism about what kinds of knowledge were possible. His moral theory, which was influenced by German Protestantism and by Rousseau, became very influential for the sharp distinction it drew between morality and interest. His major work was *The Critique of Pure Reason* (1781).

KAUTSKY, Karl (1854–1938)

German socialist. He was the leading theoretician in the German Social Democractic Party (SPD), and edited the party's newspaper, *die Neue Zeit*. He strongly opposed Bernstein during the revisionist controversy. Later he became a strong critic of the Bolshevik revolution, and sided with social democracy in the great schism between communism and social democracy which occurred in the 1920s. He was bitterly attacked by Lenin.

KEYNES, John Maynard (1883–1946)

English economist. He worked at Cambridge as an academic economist and also intermittently for the British Treasury. He became a leading critic of orthodox deflationary policies that were pursued between the two world wars, and devised practical measures to reduce unemployment which he subsequently justified theoretically in the *General Theory of Interest, Employment, and Money* (1936). His aim was to find a way of overcoming the capitalist slump without resorting to socialism. The middle way that he established became the intellectual basis for much social democratic thought, especially in Britain and the United States. Keynes advocated an extension of public responsibility to safeguard the liberal order and the liberal values he so prized. The class war, he said, will always find me on the side of the educated bourgeoisie.

LEIBNIZ, Gottfried (1646–1716)

German philosopher and mathematician. He was prominent amongst early scientists, and developed the calculus at the same time as Newton, and independently of him.

LENIN, (Vladimir Il'ich Ulyanov) (1870—1924)

Russian Marxist theorist and political leader. He became active in revolutionary politics at an early age. His brother was executed for his part in an attempted assassination of the Tsar. Lenin became leader of the Bolshevik faction after the split in the Russian Social Democratic Party in 1903. He established himself through his writings as the leading Marxist theorist and political strategist. Forced to spend much of his time in exile, he returned to Russia in 1917 following the February Revolution and the collapse of the monarchy. Once in Russia he became convinced of the need to organise for a seizure of power, and his prediction that the Bolsheviks could retain state power proved accurate. However his last years were spent in the shadow of the failure of the European revolution on which he had placed so many hopes, and of the encroachment of bureaucracy within the party. His major works include: *The Development of Capitalism in Russia* (1899), *What is to be Done?* (1902), *Imperialism* (1916), *State and Revolution* (1917), and *Left-Wing Communism: An Infantile Disorder* (1920).

LIST, Friedrich (1789—1846)

German economist. He spent fifteen years of his life (1825—40) in exile in America. He was influential in developing a system of national political economy which advocated protection, in opposition to the dominant liberal political economy and free trade policies of the British.

LOCKE, John (1632—1704)

English philosopher and political theorist. He was born in the west country and became a prominent spokesman for the Whig cause. He defended the overthrow of James II in 1688 and became one of the important early forerunners of liberalism. His writings were particularly influential in the American colonies. Apart from his political works he was the author of several important works on philosophy. His writings include *Two Treatises on Government* (1690), and *An Essay Concerning Human Understanding* (1690).

LUTHER, Martin (1483—1546)

The leader of the Protestant Reformation in Germany. He denounced the authority of the Pope, and also denounced the theories of Copernicus.

LUXEMBURG, Rosa (1870—1919)

German Marxist theorist and political leader. She was one of the radical leaders in the German Social Democratic Party. She opposed revisionism and broke with the party leadership when it supported the German war effort in 1914. She was sympathetic to the Bolsheviks, but critical of many aspects of the Russian Revolution. She was murdered by German army officers after an abortive uprising in 1919. Her books and pamphlets include *Reform or Revolution* (1899), *The Accumulation of Capital* (1913), *Leninism or Marxism?* (1918).

MACHIAVELLI, Niccolo (1469—1527)

Italian political theorist. He worked for most of his life in the service of the Florentine government. His most famous book, *The Prince*, became celebrated throughout Europe as an exposition of how a ruler without moral scruples might best achieve his ends. He is now viewed, however, as one of the first theorists who attempted to view the state in secular terms and to explore the interplay between consent and coercion in relations between rulers and ruled.

MAISTRE, Joseph de (1754—1821)

French philosopher and political theorist. He was an inveterate enemy of revolutionary ideas and of rationalism, and became a leading figure in the European Reaction.

MARCUSE, Herbert (1898—1979)

German philosopher and social theorist. A leading member of the Frankfurt school of German Marxists, he left Germany when the Nazis came to power and settled in the United States. He became famous firstly for his attempt to combine the insights of Marx and Freud in a theory of human liberation, and secondly for his analysis of modern America, which was extremely influential during the student upheavals in the 1960s. His main works are *Reason and Revolution* (1944), *Eros and Civilisation* (1956), and *One Dimensional Man* (1964).

MARX, Karl (1818–1883)

German socialist and political economist. He was born in Germany, but lived most of his adult life in England. He studied Hegelian philosophy in Berlin; became active as a political radical; and edited a radical newspaper in the Rhineland, for which he was expelled. He lived in Paris and Brussels at first, helping to organise, with Engels, the Communist League. Eventually he settled in England where he relied on financial support from Engels. In the 1850s Marx embarked on a gigantic scheme of study which produced his major works, although the total plan was never completed. In the 1860s he helped to organise the First International. His major writings, many of them not published in his lifetime were: *Economic and Philosophical Manuscripts* (1844); *German Ideology* (1846); *Poverty of Philosophy* (1847); *The Communist Manifesto* (1848); *The Eighteenth Brumaire* (1851); *Grundrisse* (1858); *Capital (three volumes, volume 1 published* 1867), *Therories of Surplus Value* (1862).

MICHELS, Robert (1876–1936)

German sociologist. A pupil of Max Weber, he argued that in every organisation, whatever its democratic pretensions, the iron law of oligarchy ensured that only a minority of leaders had control. He developed this thesis in his major work, *Political Parties* (1911) which was based on an analysis of the SPD.

MILL, James (1773–1836)

Scottish journalist and political theorist. A close associate of Jeremy Bentham and a leading exponent of the doctrines of utilitarianism and liberal political economy. His works include *An Essay on Government* (1828).

MILL, John Stuart (1806–1873)

English social and political theorist. He received a strict utilitarian upbringing from his father, James Mill, against which he rebelled when he was a young man. Subsequently he attempted to broaden the utilitarian tradition by introducing ideas from other schools of thought. He was strongly influenced both by the English romantic movement, and by Alexis de Tocqueville. He worked most of his life as an official for the East India Company, and was for a time a Member of Parliament. Together with his wife Harriet he set out his views on almost every social, political, and philosophical question. He wrote major works on philosophy and political economy but is best known for his political essays, particularly *On Liberty* (1859), *Considerations on Representative Government* (1861), *Utilitarianism* (1863).

MONTESQUIEU, Charles de Secondat, Baron de la Brède et
de Montesquieu (1689–1755)

French political theorist. He was a leading figure in the French Enlightenment. A great admirer of English political institutions, his major work was *The Spirit of the Laws* (1748).

NEWTON, Isaac (1646–1727)

English mathematician and scientist. He was famous for his formulation of the law of gravity and the invention of calculus, more generally for the elaboration of a theoretical framework in the *Principia* (1687) which held sway until Einstein's theory of relativity.

OSTROGORSKI, Moisei (1854–1919)

Russian political scientist. Like Michels he helped to pioneer the analysis of the inevitability of oligarchy in large-scale organisation. His major work was *Democracy and the Organisation of Political Parties* (1902), based on a study of the new mass parties in Britain.

PAINE, Thomas (1737–1809)

English radical. He worked as an independent artisan, and was involved in radical politics in England before emigrating to the United States where he became a leading exponent of the cause of the colonists in his pamphlet *Common Sense* (1776). He wrote his most famous work, *The Rights of Man*, as a reply to Burke's attack on the French Revolution. He spent some time in France during the Revolution and was briefly imprisoned. His other major work was *The Age of Reason*, an attack on Christianity. His epitaph was a line he wrote to George Washington, 'A share in two revolutions is living to some purpose.'

PARETO, Vilfredo (1848–1923)

Italian sociologist and economist. He was Professor at Lausanne from 1893, and became one of the pioneers of elite theory and equilibrium analysis. He was strongly opposed to socialism and accepted public honours from Mussolini.

PARSONS, Talcott (1902–1978)

American sociologist. He was noted for his attempted synthesis of the work of the classical sociologists in a single universal theory of social action. He pioneered structural functionalism which insisted on looking at societies and social processes primarily in terms of value orientations and value consensus. His books include *The Structure of Social Action* (1937) and *The Social System* (1951).

PROUDHON, Pierre (1809–1865)

French socialist and anarchist. His ideal was a community of independent artisans. He did not want to abolish property but to distribute it more equally so that everyone had some. His writings were extensive and covered most subjects. Among them is the essay *What is Property?* (1840). A later work, *The Philosophy of Poverty*, was strongly attacked by Marx in his *Poverty of Philosophy*.

RICARDO, David (1772–1823)

English political economist. He worked most of his life as a banker. In his writings, particularly *On the Principles of Political Economy and Taxation* (1817), he developed a systematic analytical framework for political economy. His approach, particularly his labour theory of value, greatly influenced certain socialists including Marx.

ROUSSEAU, Jean-Jacques (1712–1778)

French social and political theorist. He achieved early notoriety for his ferocious assault on many of the comfortable assumptions of Enlightenment thought. He was born in Geneva, but spent the greater part of his life in France. His political writings influenced the generation of radicals who took part in the French Revolution. They include *The Social Contract* (1762) and *The Discourses* (1750–55). He also had a lasting influence on theories of child development and education in his book *Emile* (1762).

SAINT-SIMON, Claude Henri de Rouvroy, Comte de Saint-Simon (1760–1825)

French social theorist. His conception of industrial society and his evaluation of the French Revolution through which he lived, proved enormously influential, especially within France, but also on social democratic and some socialist thought. His work became widely known through the work of his followers, particularly Auguste Comte.

SAVIGNY, Friedrich Carl von (1779–1861)
German legal thinker. A leading figure in the European Reaction.

SCHUMPETER, Joseph (1883–1950)
Austrian political economist, strongly influenced by Weber. He developed an important new conception of democracy which had great impact on American political science. His works include *Capitalism, Socialism and Democracy* (1949).

SMITH, Adam (1723–1790)
Scottish philosopher and political economist. He was a leading figure in the Scottish Enlightenment, and one of the first to treat political economy as a separate branch of enquiry, although his training was in moral philosophy. His most important book was *The Wealth of Nations* (1776). In his attempt to provide sound advice on policy for statesmen he pioneered analysis of the division of labour and the sphere of market exchange. His other works include *The Theory of Moral Sentiments* (1759).

SPENCER, Herbert (1820–1903)

English social theorist. He worked most of his life as an engineer. Drawing on theories of evolution in natural science he developed social theories which advocated unrestrained individualism in all spheres of social life. His books include *Social Statics* (1850), and *Man Versus the State* (1884).

SPINOZA, Benedictus de (1632–1677)

Dutch philosopher. An important figure in the scientific revolution and the new philosophy. His works include *Tractatus politicus*.

TOCQUEVILLE, Alexis de (1805–1859)

French social and political theorist. A French aristocrat, he tried in his writings to find some middle ground between Reaction and Revolution. During a trip to America he produced a commentary on American institutions, *Democracy in America* (1835). This book had a strong influence on John Stuart Mill and on later sociology. His second major work, *The Ancien Regime and the French Revolution*, was unfinished at the time of his death.

TÖNNIES, Ferdinand (1855–1936)

German sociologist. In his most famous book *Gemeinschaft und Gesellschaft* (1887), he analysed industrial society in terms of the contrast between these two terms.

TROTSKY, Lev Davidovich Bronstein (1879–1940)

Russian Marxist theorist and political leader. He took a leading part in the 1905 Revolution in St Petersburg and on the basis of this experience developed his theory of permanent revolution. Theoretical and personal disagreements with the Bolsheviks kept him outside their ranks until 1917, when he joined the Central Committee and organised the seizure of power in October. Subsequently his command of the Red Army was a vital factor in the victory of the Bolsheviks in the civil war. After Lenin's death he began to oppose Stalin's policy but was defeated and expelled in 1927. As an exile he wrote a great deal on the character of the Soviet regime as well as on the politics of other states. He organised the Fourth International, and was assassinated in Mexico on Stalin's orders in 1940. His extensive writings include *Results and Prospects, The History of the Russian Revolution, In Defence of Marxism*, and *The Revolution Betrayed* (1937).

WEBB, Sidney (1859–1947), Beatrice (1858–1943)

English political and social theorists. Founders of the Fabian Society in England and leading figures in the development of British social democracy. Sidney Webb helped draft the 1918 constitution of the British Labour Party and subsequently served as a Labour minister. Their works include *The History of Trade Unionism* and *Soviet Russia: A New Civilisation?*

WEBER, Max (1864–1920)

German sociologist. His academic career was frequently interrupted by illness. His scholarship and his devotion to his academic calling were intense and he produced a sociology of modern industrial society that was conceived on a massive scale and was intended in part as a counter to Marxism. He was strongly committed to liberal values and to the political interests of the bourgeoisie and the German nation-state. He became active in national liberal politics and seemed destined to play an important role in the politics of the Weimar Republic, when he died. His works include *Economy and Society, The Methodology of the Social Sciences, The Protestant Ethic and the Spirit of Capitalism.*

Glossary

The aim of this glossary is to provide brief, though not detailed or exhaustive, definitions of some of the main ideas discussed at much greater length in the text. In cases where a concept is very closely identified with one particular thinker this is indicated. Where there are important alternative meanings these are listed.

Absolutism. Political regimes in Europe in the early modern period characterised by centralisation of state authority and creation of modern state forms, but in which the interests of the landed aristocracy remained supreme.

Alienation. (1) The transfer of ownership. (2) The creation of an alien world not controlled by human beings but controlling them. Sale of labour power involved the alienation of the worker from the product of his labour, alienation from the act of labour itself, and alienation from the human species (Marx).

Anarchism. Libertarian and radical doctrine in early socialist movement. Emphasised natural human capacity for co-operation and altruism, the value of small-scale organisation, and the need to abolish the modern state.

Anomie. A condition of normlessness, resulting in the social isolation of individuals and the breakdown of those social rules keeping individual desires in check and in balance with the means for realising them (Durkheim).

Bureaucracy. (1) Government by central administration. (2) Co-ordination of large-scale public and private organisations through the specialisation of tasks, deployment of expertise, and a hierarchy of authority, so the institutionalising of technical rationality (Weber).

Capitalism. (1) The orientation of economic agents to economic activity governed by the principles of technical rationality (Weber). (2) A specific historical mode of production characterised by: (a) the production and circulation of commodities; (b) the buying and selling of labour power as a commodity by capital; (c) the extraction and realisation of surplus value; (d) the accumulation and reproduction of capital on an expanded scale (Marx).

Civil society. The sphere of private interests, associations, and material needs, independent of the state.

Collective conscience. The common values that shape individual experience and maintain social order and continuity (Durkheim).

Commodity. An article or service possessing both a use value (as a product of concrete useful labour) and an exchange value (embodying a certain quantity of socially necessary labour-time) (Marx).

Communism. The stage of historical development following socialism and characterised by the disappearance of the state as a power controlling society, the abolition of money and commodities, and distribution according to need (Marx).

Conservatism. Doctrine defending the institutions and values of the old order in Europe against the ideas and political movements of the Enlightenment and the French Revolution. Means of defence varied between diehard reaction and a strategy of concessions and adaptation.

Corporatism. (1) The suppression of independent trade unions by fascist regimes and forcible incorporation of the interests of labour into the interests of capital. (2) The tendency of social democratic regimes to regulate capitalist economies through tripartite representation and negotiation between government, industry, and trade unions, rather than parliaments and markets alone.

Cosmology. A theory of the universe.

Democracy. (1) Rule in the interests of the poor and the oppressed. (2) Universal suffrage, regular and free elections, civil and political liberties, education in citizenship. (3) A means of choosing between sets of leaders (Schumpeter). (4) Subordination of state agencies to organs of popular power.

Dictatorship of the proletariat. The class rule of the proletariat that follows the overthrow of the bourgeois state and the dictatorship of the bourgeoisie, and lays the foundations for socialism (Lenin).

Division of labour. (1) Specialisation of work between the sexes, town and country, and regions. (2) Specialisation of functions in the labour process in capitalism, particularly the separation of intellectual and manual labour.

Economy. (1) The needs and appropriations of the private household. (2) The social organisation of material production. (3) The system of market exchanges.

Elites. Minorities that (inevitably) control decision-making in large-scale organisations and complex societies (Pareto, Mosca).

Enlightenment. Eighteenth-century intellectual movement that emphasised the importance of reason in observing nature and ordering society.

Equality. (1) Equality before the law — implies inequality in everything else. (2) Equality of opportunity — implies positive discrimination to rescue the disadvantaged. (3) Equality of power — implies equal consideration of needs, therefore unequal distribution of resources.

Fascism. Movements of the Right whose ideology was nationalist and anti-communist, sometimes also racist and anti-capitalist, and which in practice destroyed representative institutions and political liberties, and forcibly crushed all independent organisations of the working class.

Freedom. (1) Freedom from interference and restraint. (2) Freedom as the enjoyment of certain opportunities and rights. (3) Freedom as the realisation of human capacities and individual autonomy.

Free trade. Doctrine advocating the removal of all barriers in the world economy to the movement of goods, capital, and labour.

Gemeinschaft. Small-scale, face-to-face community based on production for use and co-ordinated through family ties; contrasted with *Gesellschaft*, the large-scale, impersonal society, based on the production and circulation of commodities, and co-ordinated through the market and bureaucracy (Tönnies).

Hegemony. (1) Leadership exercised by the proletariat over other classes allied to it. (2) Leadership and influence exercised by the bourgeoisie over the proletariat, particularly through its control of education, the Churches, and the media, so gaining consent for its continued rule (Gramsci).

History. (1) The idea of an objective past. (2) The idea of an objective meaning in the past, of historical stages, of progress. (3) The idea of the past as a formless jumble of accidents, with no lessons and no practical authority in the present. (4) The idea of the historical relativity of all knowledge, of the uniqueness of every historical formation.

Ideology. (1) The science of ideas. (2) Ideas that express a false consciousness, concealing the real interests and needs of a social group or class. (3) Any systematic set of practical or theoretical ideas which articulate the interests of a group. (4) Sets of ideas which by mixing facts and values are irrational and unscientific (Parsons).

Imperialism. The stage of capitalist development characterised by the rise of finance capital and the military-bureaucratic state, by the division of the world between the leading capitalist powers to secure markets and raw materials and outlets for investment, and hence by increasing rivalry leading to war.

Individualism. (1) A negative, destructive, unregulated force of self-interest, undermining social order. (2) The principle of self-help, individual moral responsibility, equal individual rights, and the realisation of social welfare through the pursuit of private interests. (3) The idea of critical autonomy — the control exercised by individuals over their thoughts and actions. (4) The idea of individuality, of historical uniqueness, and the consequent limitations of technical rationality.

Industrial Revolution. The first industrial revolution was in Britain, beginning in the 1780s and based around cotton. Many historians now see its second phase in the 1830s and 1840s, based on iron and steel and engineering, as more significant. The term came to imply not just a change in economic organisation and techniques, but a transformation of social and political relations.

Labour. Human purposive activity, the process by which human beings interact with the natural world, help to shape it, and are in turn shaped by it.

Laissez-faire. Doctrine of minimal government intervention in the market transactions of civil society. The term disguises the extent to which governments were still expected to intervene to maintain the conditions for markets to function.

Liberalism. Doctrines of those who broadly supported the ideals and policies of the French Revolution, and which came to include equality before the law, representative government, economic individualism, and rationalism as a guide in politics and society.

Market order. The co-ordination of industrial societies through market exchange rather than administrative rationality.

Mercantilism. Economic policy of some absolutist states of state protection of domestic industry and commerce in the interests of national power and private wealth. Its existence is disputed by some historians.

Mode of production. The social organisation of labour, the combination of historically specific forces of production and relations of production. Examples include the slave mode, the feudal mode, and the capitalist mode (Marx).

Nationalism. Doctrine that every nation forms a natural political community and should have the right to self-determination and the control of its own affairs.

Permanent revolution. Theory that in economically backward countries the proletariat would not only have to take the lead in carrying through the bourgeois revolution but would have to proceed directly to the task of constructing socialism and extending the revolution beyond its borders if it was to survive (Trotsky).

Pluralism. Theory countering ideas of absolute sovereignty by viewing the state as one association amongst many, and arguing that power is dispersed among all the associations and interests of civil society, not concentrated in the state.

Protestant ethic. The orientation to work which enjoined unremitting effort and devotion, and abstention from leisure, luxury, and all immediate gratifications and diversions.

Rationality. (1) Purposive-rational action, involving the specification of goals and calculation of the most effective means of achieving them. (2) Activity governed by explicit rules and involving the use of specialised knowledge. (3) Commitment to certain ends — the idea of reason and the rational society; critical autonomy; the all-round development of the individual; the removal of obstacles to a just and harmonious social order.

Rechtstaat. The ideal of a state concerned only with the formulation and implementation of general rules, and refraining from interfering in the choices individuals make within those rules.

Reformation. The schism in the Roman Church, beginning in the sixteenth century, which led to the repudiation of papal authority in certain parts of Europe, notably Switzerland, northern Germany, Holland, Denmark, Sweden, England, and Scotland.

Renaissance. The intellectual movement in the fifteenth and sixteenth centuries, centred on Italy, which rediscovered and imitated classical ideas and models.

Revolution. (1) A cyclical change which reveals an underlying and unchanging pattern. (2) A fundamental change in the social and political order and in the relations and experiences of human beings.

Romantic movement. Cultural movement which questioned the narrow rationalism of the Enlightenment and proclaimed broader goals of human development and possibilities of human fulfilment.

Science. (1) Any systematic branch of knowledge. (2) Disciplines that approximate to the methods of the natural sciences, particularly in the use of mathematical models, the rules of experiment, and the testing of hypotheses.

Scientific revolution. Intellectual developments in the seventeenth century, including a widespread adoption of a new cosmology, the elaboration of new methods of enquiry, and the growth of a cosmopolitan scientific community.

Social contract. Doctrine concerning the origins of government. It implied (a) that human beings existed in the state of nature before they formed communities and set up states; (b) that governments should rest on the consent of the governed.

Social democracy. Working class parties, in which Marxism was often the most influential ideology. After the Russian Revolution and the split in the ranks of European social democracy, the term became reserved for those parties of the working class seeking reforms within the framework of a capitalist economy and representative state.

Socialism. Doctrine and political movement which became the main counter to liberalism in the nineteenth century whilst sharing many of its assumptions. Socialism diverged most fundamentally by treating capitalism as a new form of class society and the liberal representative state as the guarantor of the power and privileges of the bourgeoisie.

Sovereignty. (1) Absolute or legal sovereignty — the body given supreme authority in a state to make binding decisions on all citizens. (2) Actual or political sovereignty — the balance of power in a state which determines the content of the decisions that are made.

State. The idea of a public realm separate from the individuals who hold office in it, and separate from civil society. (1) As a civil association — the association that oversees the general arrangements of the whole community and maintains the conditions for individuals to pursue their own interests and activities. (2) As an ethical idea — the association whose membership transcends membership in the associations of civil society, and demands loyalty and commitment in the service of higher national ideals. (3) As an apparatus of domination — the agencies of administration, force, and law, which exist alongside but are separate from civil society, and whose purpose is to maintain in being the system of production and circulation, hence the rule of the class that dominates them.

State of nature. Based on the contrast between nature and society, and closely linked to the idea of a human *nature*. Implies a distinction between what is essential and permanent and what is illusory and transient.

Status. A form of stratification, separate from class, resting on considerations of prestige, life style, and group identity.

Superstructure. Political, legal, and ideological relations in a social formation. Contrasted with the 'base' — the social forces and social relations of production.

Totalitarianism. The total domination of civil society by the state, so that the distinction between public and private realms becomes meaningless.

Utility. The quality by which all actions, commodities and policies can be judged by calculating the amount of pain and pleasure they give to individuals. Utilitarianism is the doctrine that government policy should be determined by what gives the greatest happiness to the greatest number.

Whig. An outlook on politics shared by many in the shifting factions of the eighteenth-century English Parliament. It combined defence of the antiquated form of the constitution with a conception of limited government and the protection of a private sphere free from the interference of the crown.

Index